Juliana Horatia Gatty Ewing, W. L. Jones

We and the World

Juliana Horatia Gatty Ewing, W. L. Jones

We and the World

ISBN/EAN: 9783744724791

Printed in Europe, USA, Canada, Australia, Japan

Cover: Foto ©Thomas Meinert / pixelio.de

More available books at **www.hansebooks.com**

A Book for Boys.

BY

JULIANA HORATIA EWING,

AUTHOR OF "JAN OF THE WINDMILL," "SIX TO SIXTEEN," "A GREAT
EMERGENCY," "MRS. OVERTHEWAY'S REMEMBRANCES."

WITH ILLUSTRATIONS BY W. L. JONES.

BOSTON:
LITTLE, BROWN, AND COMPANY,
1899.

Dedicated

TO MY ELEVEN NEPHEWS,

WILLIAM, FRANCIS, STEPHEN, PHILIP, LEONARD,

GODFREY, AND DAVID SMITH;

REGINALD, NICHOLAS, AND IVOR GATTY;

AND ALEXANDER SCOTT GATTY.

J. H. E.

WE AND THE WORLD.

CHAPTER I.

*"*All these common features of English landscape evince a
calm and settled security, and hereditary transmission of home-
bred virtues and local attachments, that speak deeply and touch-
ingly for the moral character of the nation."*

Washington Irving's Sketch Book.

IT was a great saying of my poor mother's, especially if
my father had been out of spirits about the crops, or tne
rise in wages, or our prospects, and had thought better of
it again, and showed her the bright side of things, " Well,
my dear, I'm sure we've much to be thankful for."

Which they had, and especially, I often think, for the
fact that I was not the eldest son. I gave them more
trouble than I can think of with a comfortable conscience
as it was ; but they had Jem to tread in my father's
shoes, and he was a good son to them—GOD bless him
for it !

I can remember hearing my father say—"It's bad
enough to have Jack with his nose in a book, and his
head in the clouds, on a fine June day, with the hay all
out, and the glass falling : but if Jem had been a lad of
whims and fancies, I think it would have broken my poor
old heart."

I often wonder what made me bother my head with

B

books, and where the perverse spirit came from that possessed me, and tore me, and drove me forth into the world. It did not come from my parents. My mother's family were far from being literary or even enterprising, and my father's people were a race of small yeoman squires, whose talk was of dogs and horses and cattle and the price of hay. We were north-of-England people, but not of a commercial or adventurous class, though we were within easy reach of some of the great manufacturing centres. Quiet country folk we were; old fashioned, and boastful of our old-fashionedness, albeit it meant little more than that our manners and customs were a generation behindhand of the more cultivated folk, who live nearer to London. We were proud of our name too, which is written in the earliest registers and records of the parish, honourably connected with the land we lived on; but which may be searched for in vain in the lists of great or even learned Englishmen.

It never troubled dear old Jem that there had not been a man of mark among all the men who had handed on our name from generation to generation. He had no feverish ambitions, and as to books, I doubt if he ever opened a volume, if he could avoid it, after he wore out three horn-books and our mother's patience in learning his letters—not even the mottle-backed prayer-books which were handed round for family prayers, and out of which we said the psalms for the day, verse about with my father. I generally found the place, and Jem put his arm over my shoulder and read with me.

He was a yeoman born. I can just remember—when I was not three years old and he was barely four—the fright our mother got from his fearless familiarity with the beasts about the homestead. He and I were playing on the grass plat before the house when Dolly, an ill-tempered dun cow we knew well by sight and name, got into the garden and drew near us. As I sat on the grass

—my head at no higher level than the buttercups in the field beyond—Dolly loomed so large above me that I felt frightened and began to cry. But Jem, only conscious that she had no business there, picked up a stick nearly as big as himself, and trotted indignantly to drive her out. Our mother caught sight of him from an upper window, and knowing that the temper of the cow was not to be trusted, she called wildly to Jem, " Come in, dear, quick ! Come in ! Dolly's loose ! "

" I drive her out ! " was Master Jem's reply ; and with his little straw hat well on the back of his head, he waddled bravely up to the cow, flourishing his stick. The process interested me, and I dried my tears and encouraged my brother ; but Dolly looked sourly at him, and began to lower her horns.

" Shoo ! shoo !" shouted Jem, waving his arms in farm-ing-man fashion, and belabouring Dolly's neck with the stick. " Shoo ! shoo ! "

Dolly planted her forefeet, and dipped her head for a push, but catching another small whack on her face, and more authoritative " Shoos !" she changed her mind, and swinging heavily round, trotted off towards the field, followed by Jem, waving, shouting, and victorious. My mother got out in time to help him to fasten the gate, which he was much too small to do by himself, though, with true squirely instincts, he was trying to secure it.

But from our earliest days we both lived on intimate terms with all the live stock. " Laddie," an old black cart-horse, was one of our chief friends. Jem and I used to sit, one behind the other, on his broad back, when our little legs could barely straddle across, and to "grip " with our knees in orthodox fashion was a matter of principle, but impossible in practice. Laddie's pace was always discreet, however, and I do not think we should have found a saddle any improvement, even as to safety, upon his warm, satin-smooth back. We steered him more by

shouts and smacks than by the one short end of a dirty
rope which was our apology for reins ; that is, if we had
any hand in guiding his course.　I am now disposed to
think that Laddie guided himself

But our beast friends were many.　The yellow yard-dog
always slobbered joyfully at our approach ; partly moved,
I fancy, by love for us, and partly by the exciting hope of
being let off his chain.　When we went into the farmyard
the fowls came running to our feet for corn, the pigeons
fluttered down over out heads for peas, and the pigs
humped themselves against the wall of the stye as tightly
as they could lean, in hopes of having their backs
scratched.　The long sweet faces of the plough horses, as
they turned in the furrows, were as familiar to us as the
faces of any other labourers in our father's fields, and we
got fond of the lambs and ducks and chickens, and got
used to their being killed and eaten when our acquaintance
reached a certain date, like other farm-bred folk, which is
one amongst the many proofs of the adaptability of human
nature.

So far so good, on my part as well as Jem's.　That I
should like the animals " on the place "—the domesticated
animals, the workable animals, the eatable animals—this
was right and natural, and befitting my father's son.　But
my far greater fancy for wild, queer, useless, mischievous
and even disgusting creatures often got me into trouble.
Want of sympathy became absolute annoyance as I grew
older, and wandered farther, and adopted a perfect
menagerie of odd beasts in whom my friends could see no
good qualities : such as the snake I kept warm in my
trousers-pocket ; the stickleback that I am convinced I
tamed in his own waters ; the toad for whom I built a red
house of broken drainpipes at the back of the strawberry
bed, where I used to go and tickle his head on the sly ; and
the long-whiskered rat in the barn, who knew me well,
and whose death nearly broke my heart, though I had seen

generations of unoffending ducklings pass to the kitchen without a tear.

I think it must have been the beasts that made me take to reading : I was so fond of Buffon's 'Natural History,' of which there was an English abridgment in the dining-room bookshelves.

But my happiest reading days began after the book-seller's agent came round, and teased my father into taking in the ' Penny Cyclopædia ' ; and those numbers in which there was a beast, bird, fish, or reptile were the numbers for me !

I must, however, confess that if a love for reading had been the only way in which I had gone astray from the family habits and traditions, I don't think I should have had much to complain of in the way of blame.

My father " pish "ed and " pshaw "ed when he caught me " poking over " books, but my dear mother was inclined to regard me as a genius, whose learning might bring renown of a new kind into the family. In a quiet way of her own, as she went gently about household matters, or knitted my father's stockings, she was a great day-dreamer—one of the most unselfish kind, however ; a builder of air-castles, for those she loved to dwell in ; planned, fitted, and fur-nished according to the measure of her affections.

It was perhaps because my father always began by dis-paraging her suggestions that (by the balancing action of some instinctive sense of justice) he almost always ended by adopting them, whether they were wise or foolish. He came at last to listen very tolerantly when she dilated on my future greatness.

" And if he isn't quite so good a farmer as Jem, it's not as if he were the eldest, you know, my dear. I'm sure we've much to be thankful for that dear Jem takes after you as he does. But if Jack turns out a genius, which please God we may live to see and be proud of, he'll make plenty of money, and he must live with Jem when we're

gone, and let Jem manage it for him, for clever people are
never any good at taking care of what they get.   And when
their families get too big for the old house, love, Jack must
build, as he'll be well able to afford to do, and Jem must
let him have the land.   The Ladycroft would be as good
as anywhere, and a pretty name for the house.   It would
be a good thing to have some one at that end of the
property too, and then the boys would always be together."

Poor dear mother!   The kernel of her speech lay in
the end of it—"The boys would always be together."   I
am sure in her tender heart she blessed my bookish genius,
which was to make wealth as well as fame, and so keep
me "about the place," and the home birds for ever in the
nest.

I knew nothing of it then, of course ; but at this time
she used to turn my father's footsteps towards the Ladycroft every Sunday, between the services, and never
wearied of planning my house.

She was standing one day, her smooth brow knitted in
perplexity, before the big pink thorn, and had stood so
long absorbed in this brown study, that my father said,
with a sly smile—

"Well, love, and where are you now?"

"In the dairy, my dear," she answered quite gravely.
"The window is to the north of course, and I'm afraid the
thorn must come down."

My father laughed heartily.   He had some sense of
humour, but my mother had none.   She was one of the
sweetest-tempered women that ever lived, and never
dreamed that any one was laughing at her.   I have heard
my father say she lay awake that night, and when he
asked her why she could not sleep he found she was
fretting about the pink thorn.

"It looked so pretty to-day, my dear ; and thorns are
so bad to move!"

My father knew her too well to hope to console her by joking about it. He said gravely : "There's plenty of time yet, love. The boys are only just in trousers ; and we may think of some way to spare it before we come to bricks and mortar."

"I've thought of it every way, my dear, I'm afraid," said my mother with a sigh. But she had full confidence in my father—a trouble shared with him was half-cured, and she soon fell asleep.

She certainly had a vivid imagination, though it never was cultivated to literary ends. Perhaps, after all, I inherited that idle fancy, those unsatisfied yearnings of my restless heart, from her! Mental peculiarities are said to come from one's mother.

It was Jem who inherited her sweet temper.

Dear old Jem! He and I were the best of good friends always, and that sweet temper of his had no doubt much to do with it. He was very much led by me, though I was the younger, and whatever mischief we got into it was always my fault.

It was I who persuaded him to run away from school, under the, as it proved, insufficient disguise of walnut-juice on our faces and hands. It was I who began to dig the hole which was to take us through from the kitchen-garden to the other side of the world. (Jem helped me to fill it up again, when the gardener made a fuss about our having chosen the asparagus-bed as the point of departure, which we did because the earth was soft there.) In desert islands or castles, balloons or boats, my hand was first and foremost, and mischief or amusement of every kind, by earth, air, or water, was planned for us by me.

Now and then, however, Jem could crow over me. How he did deride me when I asked our mother the foolish question—"Have bees whiskers?"

The bee who betrayed me into this folly was a bumble of the utmost beauty. The bars of his coat "burned" as "brightly" as those of the tiger in Wombwell's menagerie, and his fur was softer than my mother's black velvet mantle. I knew, for I had kissed him lightly as he sat on the window-frame. I had seen him brushing first one side and then the other side of his head, with an action so exactly like that of my father brushing his whiskers on Sunday morning, that I thought the bee might be trimming his; not knowing that he was sweeping the flower-dust off his antennæ with his legs, and putting it into his waistcoat-pocket to make bee bread of.

It was the liberty I took in kissing him that made him not sit still any more, and hindered me from examining his checks for myself. He began to dance all over the window, humming his own tune, and before he got tired of dancing he found a chink open at the top sash, and sailed away like a spot of plush upon the air.

I had thus no opportunity of becoming intimate with him, but he was the cause of a more lasting friendship— my friendship with Isaac Irvine, the beekeeper. For when I asked that silly question, my mother said, "Not that I ever saw, love;" and my father said, "If he wants to know about bees, he should go to old Isaac. He'll tell him plenty of queer stories about them."

The first time I saw the beekeeper was in church, on Catechism Sunday, in circumstances which led to my disgracing myself in a manner that must have been very annoying to my mother, who had taken infinite pains in teaching us.

The provoking part of it was that I had not had a fear of breaking down. With poor Jem it was very different. He took twice as much pains as I did, but he could not get things into his head, and even if they did stick there he found it almost harder to say them properly. We began to learn the Catechism when we were three years old, and we went on till long after we were in trousers; and I am sure Jem never got the three words "and an

inheritor " tidily off the tip of his tongue within my remembrance. And I have seen both him and my mother
crying over them on a hot Sunday afternoon. He was
always in a fright when we had to say the Catechism in
church, and that day, I remember, he shook so that I
could hardly stand straight myself, and Bob Furniss, the
blacksmith's son, who stood on the other side of him,
whispered quite loud, " Eh ! see thee, how Master Jem
dodders ! " for which Jem gave him an eye as black as his
father's shop afterwards, for Jem could use his fists if he
could not learn by heart.

But at the time he could not even compose himself
enough to count down the line of boys and calculate what
question would come to him. I did, and when he found
he had only got the First Commandment, he was more at
ease, and though the second, which fell to me, is much
longer, I was not in the least afraid of forgetting it, for I
could have done the whole of my duty to my neighbour if
it had been necessary.

Jem got through very well, and I could hear my mother
blessing him over the top of the pew behind our backs ;
but just as he finished, no less than three bees, who had
been hovering over the heads of the workhouse boys
opposite, all settled down together on Isaac Irvine's bare
hand.

At the public catechising, which came once a year, and
after the second lesson at evening prayer, the grown-up
members of the congregation used to draw near to the end
of their pews to see and hear how we acquitted ourselves,
and, as it happened on this particular occasion, Master
Isaac was standing exactly opposite to me. As he leaned
forward, his hands crossed on the pew-top before him, I
had been a good deal fascinated by his face, which was a
very noble one in its rugged way, with snow-white hair
and intense, keenly observing eyes, and when I saw the
three bees settle on him without his seeming to notice it,

I cried, "They'll sting you!" before I thought of what · was doing; for I had been severely stung that week my self, and knew what it felt lik·, and how little good powder·blue does.

With attending to the bees I had not heard the parson say, "Second Commandment?" and as he was rather deaf he did not hear what I said. But of course he knew it was not long enough for the right answer, and he said, "Speak up, my boy," and Jem tried to start me by whispering, "Thou shalt not make to thyself"—but the three bees went on sitting on Master Isaac's hand, and though I began the Second Commandment, I could not take my eyes off them, and when Master Isaac saw this he smiled and nodded his white head, and said, "Never you mind me, sir. They won't sting the old beekeeper." This assertion so completely turned my head that every other idea went out of it, and after saying " or in the earth beneath " three times, and getting no further, the parson called out, "Third Commandment ? " and I was passed over—" out of respect to the family," as I was reminded for a twelvemonth afterwards—and Jem pinched my leg to comfort me, and my mother sank down on the seat, and did not take her face out of her pocket-handkerchief till the workhouse boys were saying "the sacraments."

My mother was our only teacher till Jem was nine and I was eight years old. We had a thin, soft-backed reading book, bound in black cloth, on the cover of which in gold letters was its name, 'Chick-seed without Chick-weed;' and in this book she wrote our names, and the date at the end of each lesson we conned fairly through. I had got into Part II., which was " in words of four letters," and had the chapter about the Ship in it, before Jem's name figured at the end of the chapter about the Dog in Part I.

My mother was very glad that this chapter seemed to please Jem, and that he learned to read it quickly, for, good-natured as he was, Jem was too fond of fighting and laying about him : and though it was only "in words of three letters," this brief chapter contained a terrible story and an excellent moral, which I remember well even now.

It was called " The Dog."

" Why do you cry? The Dog has bit my leg. Why did he do so? I had my bat and I hit him as he lay on the mat, so he ran at me and bit my leg. Ah, you may not use the bat if you hit the Dog. It is a hot day, and the Dog may go mad. One day a Dog bit a boy in the arm, and the boy had his arm cut off, for the Dog was mad. And did the boy die? Yes, he did die in a day or two. It is not fit to hit a Dog if he lie on the mat and is not a bad Dog. Do not hit a Dog, or a cat, or a boy."

Jem not only got through this lesson much better than usual, but he lingered at my mother's knees, to point with his own little stumpy forefinger to each recurrence of the words "hit a Dog," and read them all by himself.

"*Very* good boy," said Mother, who was much pleased. " And now read this last sentence once more, and very nicely."

" Do —not —hit — a— dog— or—a—cat—or—a—boy," read Jem in a high sing-song, and with a face of blank indifference, and then with a hasty dog's-ear he turned back to the previous page, and spelled out, " I had my bat and I hit him as he lay on the mat " so well, that my mother caught him to her bosom and covered him with kisses.

" He'll be as good a scholar as Jack yet ! " she exclaimed. " But don't forget, my darling, that my Jem must never 'hit a dog, or a cat, or a boy.' Now, love, you may put the book away."

Jem stuck out his lips and looked down, and hesitated. He seemed almost disposed to go on with his lessons. But he changed his mind, and shutting the book with a bang, he scampered off. As he passed the ottoman near the door, he saw Kitty, our old tortoise-shell puss, lying on it, and (moved perhaps by the occurrence of the word *cat* in the last sentence of the lesson) he gave her such a whack with the flat side of ' Chick-seed ' that she bounced up into the air like a sky-rocket, Jem crying out as he did so, " I had my bat, and I hit him as he lay on the mat."

It was seldom enough that Jem got anything by heart, but he had certainly learned this ; for when an hour later I went to look for him in the garden, I found him panting with the exertion of having laid my nice, thick, fresh green crop of mustard and cress flat with the back of the coal-shovel, which he could barely lift, but with which he was still battering my salad-bed, chanting triumphantly at every stroke, "I had my bat, and I hit him as he lay on the mat." He was quite out of breath, and I had not much difficulty in pummelling him as he deserved.

Which shows how true it is, as my dear mother said, that "you never know what to do for the best in bringing up boys."

Just about the time that we outgrew ' Chick-seed,' and that it was allowed on all hands that even for quiet country-folk with no learned notions it was high time we were sent to school, our parents were spared the trouble of looking out for a school for us by the fact that a school came to us instead, and nothing less than an " Academy " was opened within three-quarters of a mile of my father's gate.

Walnut-tree Farm was an old house that stood some little way from the road in our favourite lane—a lane full of wild roses and speedwell, with a tiny footpath of dis-jointed flags like an old pack-horse track. Grass and milfoil grew thickly between the stones, and the turf stretched halfway over the road from each side, for there was little traffic in the lane, beyond the yearly rumble of the harvesting waggons ; and few foot-passengers, except a labourer now and then, a pair or two of rustic lovers at sundown, a few knots of children in the blackberry season and the cows coming home to milking.

"HE GAVE HER SUCH A WHACK WITH THE FLAT SIDE
OF 'CHICK-SEED' THAT SHE BOUNCED UP INTO THE AIR
LIKE A SKY-ROCKET."

Jem and I played there a good deal, but then we lived close by.

We were very fond of the old place and there were two good reasons for the charm it had in our eyes. In the first place the old man who lived alone in it (for it had ceased to be the dwelling-house of a real farm) was an eccentric old miser, the chief object of whose existence seemed to be to thwart any attempt to pry into the daily details of it. What manner of stimulus this was to boyish curiosity needs no explanation, much as it needs excuse.

In the second place, Walnut-tree Farm was so utterly different from the house which was our home, that everything about it was attractive from mere unaccustomedness.

Our house had been rebuilt from the foundations by my father. It was square-built and very ugly, but it was in such excellent repair that one could never indulge a more lawless fancy towards any chink or cranny about it than a desire to "point" the same with a bit of mortar.

Why it was that my ancestor, who built the old house, and who was not a bit better educated or farther-travelled than my father, had built a pretty one, whilst my father built an ugly one, is one of the many things I do not know, and wish I did.

From the old sketches of it which my grandmother painted on the parlour handscreens, I think it must have been like a larger edition of the farm ; that is, with long mullioned windows, a broad and gracefully proportioned doorway with several shallow steps and quaintly-orna-mented lintel ; bits of fine work and ornamentation about the woodwork here and there, put in as if they had been done, not for the look of the thing, but for the love of it, and whitewash over the house-front, and over the apple-trees in the orchard.

That was what our ancestor's home was like ; and it was the sort of house that became Walnut-tree Academy, where Jem and I went to school.

CHAPTER II.

Sable :—" Ha, you ! A little more upon the dismal *(forming their countenances)* ; this fellow has a good mortal look, place him near the corpse ; that wainscot face must be o' top of the stairs ; that fellow's almost in a fright (that looks as if he were full of some strange misery) at the end of the hall. So— but I'll fix you all myself. Let's have no laughing now on any provocation.

The Funeral, STEELE.

AT one time I really hoped to make the acquaintance of the old miser of Walnut-tree Farm. It was when we saved the life of his cat.

He was very fond of that cat, I think, and it was, to say the least of it, as eccentric-looking as its master. One eye was yellow and the other was blue, which gave it a strange, uncanny expression, and its rust-coloured fur was not common either as to tint or markings.

How dear old Jem did belabour the boy we found torturing it ! He was much older and bigger than we were, but we were two to one, which we reckoned fair enough, considering his size, and that the cat had to be saved somehow. The poor thing's fore-paws were so much hurt that it could not walk, so we carried it to the farm, and I stood on the shallow doorsteps, and under the dial, on which was written—

" Tempora mutantur !"—

and the old miser came out, and we told him about the cat, and he took it and said we were good boys, and I hoped he would have asked us to go in, but he did not, though we lingered a little ; he only put his hand into his pocket, and very slowly brought out sixpence.

"No, thank you," said I rather indignantly. "We
don't want anything for saving the poor cat."

"I am very fond of it," he said apologetically, and
putting the sixpence carefully back; but I believe he
alluded to the cat.

I felt more and more strongly that he ought to invite
us into the parlour—if there was a parlour—and I took
advantage of a backward movement on his part to move
one shallow step nearer, and said, in an easy conversational
tone, "Your cat has very curious eyes."

He came out again, and his own eyes glared in the
evening light as he touched me with one of his fingers in a
way that made me shiver, and said, "If I had been an
old woman, and that cat had lived with me in the days
when this house was built, I should have been hanged, or
burned as a witch. Twelve men would have done it—twelve
reasonable and respectable men!" He paused, looking
over my head at the sky, and then added, "But in all good
conscience, mind, in all good conscience!"

And after another pause he touched me again (this time
my teeth chattered), and whispered loudly in my ear,
"Never serve on a jury!" After which he banged the
door in our faces, and Jem caught hold of my jacket and
cried, "Oh! he's quite mad, he'll murder us!" and we
took each other by the hand and ran home as fast as our
feet would carry us.

We never saw the old miser again, for he died some
months afterwards, and, strange to relate, Jem and I were
invited to the funeral.

It was a funeral not to be forgotten. The old man
had left the money for it, and a memorandum, with the
minutest directions, in the hands of his lawyer. If he had
wished to be more popular after his death than he had
been in his lifetime, he could not have hit upon any better
plan to conciliate in a lump the approbation of his
neighbours than that of providing for what undertakers

call " a first-class funeral." The good custom of honour-
ing the departed, and committing their bodies to the earth
with care and respect, was carried, in our old-fashioned
neighbourhood, to a point at which what began in reverence
ended in what was barely decent, and what was meant
to be most melancholy became absolutely comical.   But a
sense of the congruous and the incongruous was   not
cultivated amongst us, whereas solid value (in size, quantity
and expense) was perhaps overestimated.   So our furniture,
our festivities, and our funerals bore witness.

No one had ever seen the old miser's furniture, and **he**
gave no festivities ; but he made up for it in his funeral.

Children, like other uneducated classes, enjoy domestic
details, and going over the ins and outs of other people's
affairs behind their backs ; especially when the interest
is heightened by a touch of gloom, or perfected by the
addition of some personal importance in the matter. Jem
and I were always fond of funerals, but this funeral, and
the fuss that it made in the parish, we were never likely to
forget.

Even our own household was so demoralised by the grim
gossip of the occasion that Jem and I were accused of
being unable to amuse ourselves, and of listening to our
elders.   It was perhaps fortunate for us that a favourite
puppy died the day before the funeral, and gave us the
opportunity of burying him.

> " As if our whole vocation
> Were endless imitation——"

Jem and I had already laid our gardens waste, and built
a rude wall of broken bricks round them to make a churchyard ; and I can clearly remember that we had so far
profited by what we had overheard among our elders, that
I had caught up some phrases which I was rather proud
of displaying, and that I quite overawed Jem by the air
with which I spoke of " the melancholy occasion "—the

"wishes of deceased"—and the "feelings of survivors" when we buried the puppy.

It was understood that I could not attend the puppy's funeral in my proper person, because I wished to be the undertaker ; but the happy thought struck me of putting my wheelbarrow alongside of the brick wall with a note inside it to the effect that I had "sent my carriage as a mark of respect."

In one point we could not emulate the real funeral, that was carried out "regardless of expense." The old miser had left a long list of the names of the people who were to be invited to it and to its attendant feast, in which was not only my father's name, but Jem's and mine. Three yards was the correct length of the black silk scarves which it was the custom in the neighbourhood to send to dead people's friends ; but the old miser's funeral-scarves were a whole yard longer, and of such stiffly ribbed silk that Mr. Soot, the mourning draper, assured my mother that "it would stand of itself." The black gloves cost six shillings a pair, and the sponge-cakes, which used to be sent with the gloves and scarves, were on this occasion ornamented with weeping willows in white sugar.

Jem and I enjoyed the cake, but the pride we felt in our scarves and gloves was simply boundless. What pleased us particularly was that our funeral finery was not enclosed with my father's. Mr. Soot's man delivered three separate envelopes at the door, and they looked like letters from some bereaved giant. The envelopes were twenty inches by fourteen, and made of cartridge-paper ; the black border was two inches deep, and the black seals must have consumed a stick of sealing-wax among them. They contained the gloves and the scarves, which were lightly gathered together in the middle with knots of black gauze ribbon.

How exquisitely absurd Jem and I must have looked with four yards of stiff black silk attached to our little hats

C

I can imagine, if I cannot clearly remember. My dear mother dressed us and saw us off (for, with some curious relic of pre-civilised notions, women were not allowed to appear at funerals), and I do not think she perceived anything odd in our appearance. She was very gentle, and approved of everything that was considered right by the people she was used to, and she had only two anxieties about our scarves : first, that they should show the full four yards of respect to the memory of the deceased ; and secondly, that we should keep them out of the dust, so that they might " come in useful afterwards."

She fretted a little because she had not thought of changing our gloves for smaller sizes (they were eight and a quarter) ; but my father " pish "ed and " pshaw "ed, and said it was better than if they had been too small, and that we should be sure to be late if my mother went on fidgeting. So we pulled them on—with ease—and picked up the tails of our hatbands—with difficulty—and followed my father, our hearts beating with pride, and my mother and the maids watching us from the door. We arrived quite half an hour earlier than we need have done, but the Lane was already crowded with complimentary carriages, and curious bystanders, before whom we held our heads and hatbands up ; and the scent of the wild roses was lost for that day in an all-pervading atmosphere of black dye. We were very tired, I remember, by the time that our turn came to be put into a carriage by Mr. Soot, who murmured—" Pocket handkerchiefs, gentlemen "—and, following the example of a very pale-faced stranger who was with us, we drew out the clean handkerchiefs with which our mother had supplied us, and covered our faces with them.

At least Jem says he shut *his* eyes tight, and kept his face covered the whole way, but he always *was* so conscientious ! I held my handkerchief as well as I could with my gloves ; but I contrived to peep from

behind it, and to see the crowd that lined the road to
watch us as we wound slowly on.

If these outsiders, who only saw the procession and the
funeral, were moved almost to enthusiasm by the miser's
post-mortem liberality, it may be believed that the guests
who were bidden to the feast did not fail to obey the
ancient precept, and speak well of the dead. The tables
(they were rickety) literally groaned under the weight of
eatables and drinkables, and the dinner was so prolonged
that Jem and I got terribly tired, in spite of the fun of
watching the faces of the men we did not know, to see
which got the reddest.

My father wanted us to go home before the reading of
the will, which took place in the front parlour ; but the
lawyer said, " I think the young gentlemen should remain,"
for which we were very much obliged to him ; though the
pale-faced man said quite crossly—" Is there any special
reason for crowding the room with children, who are not
even relatives of the deceased ? " which made us feel so
much ashamed that I think we should have slipped out by
ourselves ; but the lawyer, who made no answer, pushed
us gently before him to the top of the room, which was
soon far too full to get out of by the door.

It was very damp and musty. In several places the
paper hung in great strips from the walls, and the oddest
part of all was that every article of furniture in the room,
and even the hearthrug, was covered with sheets of newspaper pinned over to preserve it. I sat in the corner of a
sofa, where I could read the trial of a man who murdered
somebody twenty-five years before, but I never got to the
end of it, for it went on behind a very fat man who sat
next to me, and he leaned back all the time and hid it.
Jem sat on a little footstool, and fell asleep with his head
on my knee, and did not wake till I nudged him, when
our names were read out in the will. Even then he only
half awoke, and the fat man drove his elbow into me and

hurt me dreadfully for whispering in Jem's ear that the old miser had left us ten pounds apiece, for having saved the life of his cat.

I do not think any of the strangers (they were distant connections of the old man ; he had no near relations) had liked our being there ; and the lawyer, who was very kind, had had to tell them several times over that we really had been invited to the funeral. After our legacies were known about they were so cross that we managed to scramble through the window, and wandered round the garden. As we sat under the trees we could hear high words within, and by-and-by all the men came out and talked in angry groups about the will. For when all was said and done, it appeared that the old miser had not left a penny to any one of the funeral party but Jem and me, and that he had left Walnut-tree Farm to a certain Mrs. Wood, of whom nobody knew anything.

" The wording is so peculiar," the fat man said to the pale-faced man and a third who had come out with them, " 'left to her as a sign of sympathy, if not an act of reparation.' He must have known whether he owed her any reparation or not, if he were in his senses."

" Exactly. IF he were in his senses," said the third man.

" Where's the money?—that's what I say," said the pale-faced man.

" Exactly, sir. That's what *I* say, too," said the fat man

" There are only two fields, besides the house," said the third. " He must have had money, and the lawyer knows of no investments of any kind, he says."

" Perhaps he has left it to his cat," he added, looking very nastily at Jem and me.

" It's oddly put, too," murmured the pale-faced relation. " The two fields, the house and furniture, and everything of every sort therein contained." And the lawyer coming up at that moment, he went slowly back into the house, looking about him as he went, as if he had lost something.

As the lawyer approached, the fat man got very red in the face.

" He was as mad as a hatter, sir," he said, " and we shall dispute the will."

" I think you will be wrong," said the lawyer blandly. " He was eccentric, my dear sir, very eccentric ; but eccentricity is not insanity, and you will find that the will will stand."

Jem and I were sitting on an old garden-seat, but the men had talked without paying any attention to us. At this moment Jem, who had left me a minute or two before, came running back and said : " Jack ! Do come and look in at the parlour-window. That man with the white face is peeping everywhere, and under all the newspapers, and he's made himself so dusty ! It's such fun ! "

Too happy at the prospect of anything in the shape of fun, I followed Jem on tiptoe, and when we stood by the open window with our hands over our mouths to keep us from laughing, the pale-faced man was just struggling with the inside lids of an old japanned tea-caddy.

He did not see us, he was too busy, and he did not hear us, for he was talking to himself, and we heard him say, " Everything of every sort therein contained."

I suppose the lawyer was right, and that the fat man was convinced of it, for neither he nor any one else disputed the old miser's will. Jem and I each opened an account in the Savings Bank, and Mrs. Wood came into possession of the place.

Public opinion went up and down a good deal about the old miser still. When it leaked out that he had worded the invitation to his funeral to the effect that being quite unable to tolerate the follies of his fellow-creatures, and the antics and absurdities which were necessary to entertain them, he had much pleasure in welcoming his neighbours to a feast, at which he could not reasonably be expected to preside—everybody who heard it agreed that he must have been mad.

But it was a long sentence to remember, and not a very easy one to understand, and those who saw the plumes and the procession, and those who had a talk with the undertaker, and those who got a yard more than usual of such very good black silk, and those who were able to remember what they had had for dinner, were all charitably inclined to believe that the old man's heart had not been far from being in the right place, at whatever angle his head had been set on.

And then by degrees curiosity moved to Mrs. Wood. Who was she? What was she like? What was she to the miser? Would she live at the farm?

To some of these questions the carrier, who was the first to see her, replied. She was "a quiet, genteel-looking sort of a grey-haired widow lady, who looked as if she'd seen a deal of trouble, and was badly off."

The neighbourhood was not unkindly, and many folk were ready to be civil to the widow if she came to live there.

"But she never will," everybody said. "She must let it. Perhaps the new doctor might think of it at a low rent, he'd be glad of the field for his horse. What could she do with an old place like that, and not a penny to keep it up with?"

What she did do was to have a school there, and that was how Walnut-tree Farm became Walnut-tree Academy.

CHAPTER III.

"What are little boys made of, made of?
What are little boys made of?"
Nursery Rhyme.

WHEN the school was opened, Jem and I were sent there at once. Everybody said it was "time we were sent somewhere," and that "we were getting too wild for home."

I got so tired of hearing this at last, that one day I was goaded to reply that " home was getting too tame for me." And Jem, who always backed me up, said, " And me too." For which piece of swagger we forfeited our suppers ; but when we went to bed we found pieces of cake under our pillows, for my mother could not bear us to be short of food, however badly we behaved.

I do not know whether the trousers had anything to do with it, but about the time that Jem and I were put into trousers we lived in a chronic state of behaving badly. What makes me feel particularly ashamed in thinking of it is, that I know it was not that we came under the pressure of any overwhelming temptations to misbehave and yielded through weakness, but that, according to an expressive nursery formula, we were " seeing how naughty we could be." I think we were genuinely anxious to see this undesirable climax ; in some measure as a matter of experiment, to which all boys are prone, and in which dangerous experiments, and experiments likely to be followed by explosion, are naturally preferred. Partly too from an irresistible impulse to "raise a row," and take one's luck of the results. This craving to disturb the calm current of events, and the good conduct and composure of one's neighbours as a matter of diversion, must be incomprehensible by phlegmatic people, who never feel it, whilst some Irishmen, I fancy, never quite conquer it, perhaps because they never quite cease to be boys. In any degree I do not for an instant excnse it, and in excess it must be simply intolerable by better-regulated minds.

But really boys who are pickles should be put into jars with sound stoppers, like other pickles, and I wonder that mothers and cooks do not get pots like those that held the forty thieves, and do it.

I fancy it was because we happened to be in this rough, defiant, mischievous mood, just about the time that Mrs. Wood opened her school, that we did not

particularly like our schoolmistress.   If I had been fifteen
years older, I should soon have got beyond the first
impression created by her severe dress, close widow's cap
and straight grey hair, and have discovered that the outline
of her face was absolutely beautiful, and I might possibly
have detected, what most people failed to detect, that an
odd unpleasing effect, caused by the contrast between her
general style, and an occasional lightness and rapidity
and grace of movement in her slender figure, came from
the fact that she was much younger than she looked
and affected to be.   The impression I did receive of her
appearance I communicated to my mother in far from
respectful pantomime.

"Well, love, and what do you think of Mrs. Wood?"
said she.

" I think," chanted I, in that high brassy pitch of voice
which Jem and I had adopted for this bravado period of
our existence—" I think she's like our old white hen that
turned up its eyes and died of the pip. Lack-a-daisy-dee !
Lack-a-daisy-dee ! "

And I twisted my body about, and strolled up and
down the room with a supposed travestie of Mrs. Wood's
movements.

"So she **is**," said faithful Jem.   " Lack-a-daisy-dee !
Lack-a-daisy-dee ! " and he wriggled about after me, and
knocked over the Berlin wool-basket.

" Oh dear, oh dear ! " said our poor mother.

Jem righted the basket, and I took a run and a flying
leap over it, and having cleared it successfully, took
another, and yet another, each one soothing my feelings
to the extent by which it shocked my mother's.   At the
third bound, Jem, not to be behindhand, uttered a piercing
yell from behind the sofa.

" Good gracious, what's the matter ? " cried my mother.

" It's the war-whoop of the Objibeway Indians," I
promptly explained, and having emitted another, to which

I flattered myself Jem's had been as nothing for hideous-
ness, we departed in file to raise a row in the kitchen.

Summer passed into autumn. Jem and I really liked
going to school, but it was against our principles at that
time to allow that we liked anything that we ought to like.

Some sincere but mistaken efforts to improve our
principles were made, I remember, by a middle-aged single
lady, who had known my mother in her girlhood, and
who was visiting her at this unlucky stage of our career.
Having failed to cope with us directly, she adopted the
plan of talking improvingly to our mother and at us, and
very severe some of her remarks were, and I don't believe
that Mother liked them any better than we did.

The severest she ever made were I think heightened in
their severity by the idea that we were paying unusual
attention, as we sat on the floor a little behind her one
day. We were paying a great deal of attention, but it
was not so much to Miss Martin as to a stock of woodlice
which I had collected, and which I was arranging on the
carpet that Jem might see how they roll themselves into
smooth tight balls when you tease them. But at last she
talked so that we could not help attending. I dared not
say anything to her, but her own tactics were available.
I put the woodlice back in my pocket, and stretching my
arms yawningly above my head, I said to Jem, "How
dull it is ! I wish I were a bandit."

Jem generally outdid me if possible, from sheer willingness and loyalty of spirit.

"*I* should like to be a burglar," said he.

And then we both left the room very quietly and
politely. But when we got outside I said, "I hate that
woman."

"So do I," said Jem ; "she regularly hectors over mother
—I hate her worst for that."

"So do I. Jem, doesn't she take pills ?"

"I don't know—why ?"

"I believe she does ; I'm certain I saw a box on her dressing-table. Jem, run like a good chap and see, and if there is one, empty out the pills and bring me the pill-box."

Jem obeyed, and I sat down on the stairs and began to get the woodlice out again. There were twelve nice little black balls in my hand when Jem came back with the pill-box.

"Hooray!" I cried ; "but knock out all the powder, it might smother them. Now, give it to me."

Jem danced with delight when I put the woodlice in and put on the lid.

"I hope she'll shake the box before she opens it," I said as we replaced it on the dressing-table.

"I hope she will, or they won't be tight. Oh, Jack ! Jack ! *How many do you suppose she takes at a time?*"

We never knew, and what is more, we never knew what became of the woodlice, for, for some reason, she kept our counsel as well as her own about the pill-box.

One thing that helped to reconcile us to spending a good share of our summer days in Walnut-tree Academy was that the schoolmistress made us very comfortable. Boys at our age are not very sensitive about matters of taste and colour and so forth, but even we discovered that Mrs. Wood had that knack of adapting rooms to their inhabitants, and making them pleasant to the eye, which seems to be a trick at the end of some people's fingers, and quite unlearnable by others. When she had made the old miser's rooms to her mind, we might have understood, if we had speculated about it, how it was that she had not profited by my mother's sound advice to send all his "rubbishy odds and ends" (the irregularity and ricketiness and dustiness of which made my mother shudder) to be "sold at the nearest auction-rooms, and buy some good solid furniture of the cabinet-maker who furnished for everybody in the neighbourhood, which would be the cheapest in the long-run, besides making the rooms look

"THERE WERE TWELVE NICE LITTLE BLACK BALLS IN
MY HAND WHEN JEM CAME BACK WITH THE PILL BOX."

like other people's at last." That she evaded similar re-
commendations of paperhangers and upholsterers, and of
wall-papers and carpets, and curtains with patterns that
would "stand," and wear best, and show dirt least, was a
trifle in the eyes of all good housekeepers, when our farm-
ing-man's daughter brought the amazing news with her to
Sunday tea, that "the missus" had had in old Sally, and
had torn the paper off the parlour, and had made Sally
"limewash the walls, for all the world as if it was a cellar."
Moreover, she had "gone over" the lower part herself,
and was now painting on the top of that. There was
nothing for it, after this news, but to sigh and conclude
that there was something about the old place which made
everybody a little queer who came to live in it.

But when Jem and I saw the parlour (which was now
the school-room), we decided that it "looked very nice,"
and was "uncommonly comfortable." The change was
certainly amazing, and made the funeral day seem longer
ago than it really was. The walls were not literally lime-
washed ; but (which is the same thing, except for a little
glue !) they were distempered, a soft pale pea-green.
About a yard deep above the wainscot this was covered
with a dark sombre green tint, and along the upper edge
of this, as a border all round the room, the schoolmistress
had painted a trailing wreath of white periwinkle. The
border was painted with the same materials as the walls,
and with very rapid touches. The white flowers were
skilfully relieved by the dark ground, and the varied tints
of the leaves, from the deep evergreen of the old ones to
the pale yellow of the young shoots, had demanded no new
colours, and were wonderfully life-like and pretty. There
was another border, right round the top of the room ; but
that was painted on paper and fastened on. It was a
Bible text—" Keep Innocency, and take heed to the thing
that is right, for that shall bring a man Peace at the last."
And Mrs. Wood had done the text also.

There were no curtains to the broad, mullioned window, which was kept wide open at every lattice ; and one long shoot of ivy that had pushed in farther than the rest had been seized, and pinned to the wall inside, where its growth was a subject of study and calculation, during the many moments when we were " trying to see " how little we could learn of our lessons. The black board stood on a polished easel ; but the low seats and desks were of plain pine like the floor, and they were scrupulously scrubbed. The cool tint of the walls was somewhat cheered by coloured maps and prints, and the schoolmistress's chair (an old carved oak one that had been much revived by beeswax and turpentine since the miser's days) stood on the left-hand side of the window—under " Keep Innocency," and looking towards " Peace at the last." I know, for when we were all writing or something of that sort, so that she could sit still, she used to sit with her hands folded and look up at it, which was what made Jem and me think of the old white hen that turned up its eyes ; and made Horace Simpson say that he believed she had done one of the letters wrong, and could not help looking at it to see if it showed. And by the schoolmistress's chair was the lame boy's sofa. It was the very old sofa covered with newspapers on which I had read about the murder, when the lawyer was reading the will. But she had taken off the paper, and covered it with turkey red, and red cushions, and a quilt of brown holland and red bordering, to hide his crumpled legs, so that he looked quite comfortable.

I remember so well the first day that he came. His father was a parson on the moors, and this boy had always wanted to go to school in spite of his infirmity, and at last his father brought him in a light cart down from the moors, to look at it ; and when he got him out of the cart, he carried him in. He was a big man, I remember, with grey hair and bent shoulders, and a very old coat, for it split a little at one of the seams as he was carrying him in, and we laughed.

When they got into the room, he put the boy down, keeping his arm round him, and wiped his face and said— " How deliciously cool ! "—and the boy stared all round with his great eyes, and then he lifted them to his father's face and said—" I'll come here. I do like it. But not to-day, my back is so bad."

And what makes me know that Horace was wrong, and that Mrs. Wood had made no mistake about the letters of the text, is that " Cripple Charlie "—as we called him —could see it so well with lying down. And he told me one day that when his back was very bad, and he got the fidgets and could not keep still, he used to fix his eyes on " Peace," which had gold round the letters, and shone, and that if he could keep steadily to it, for a good bit, he always fell asleep at the last. But he was very fanciful, poor chap !

I do not think it was because Jem and I had any real wish to become burglars that we made a raid on the walnuts that autumn. I do not even think that we cared very much about the walnuts themselves.

But when it is understood that the raid was to be a raid by night, or rather in those very early hours of the morning which real burglars are said almost to prefer ; that it was necessary to provide ourselves with thick sticks ; that we should have to force the hedge and climb the trees ; that the said trees grew directly under the owner's bedroom window, which made the chances of detection hazardously great ; and that walnut juice (as I have mentioned before) is of a peculiarly unaccommodating nature, since it will neither disguise you at the time nor wash off afterwards— it will be obvious that the dangers and delights of the ad- venture were sufficient to blunt, for the moment, our sense of the fact that we were deliberately going a-thieving.

" Shall we wear black masks?" said Jem.

On the whole I said " No," for I did not know where we should get them, nor, if we did, how we should keep them on.

" If she has a blunderbuss, and fires," said I, " you must duck your head, remember ; but if she springs the rattle we must cut and run."

" Will her blunderbuss be loaded, do you think ? " asked Jem. " Mother says the one in *their* room isn't ; she told me so on Saturday. But she says we're never to touch it, all the same, for you never can be sure about things of that sort going off. Do you think Mrs. Wood's will be loaded ? "

" It may be," said I, " and of course she might load it if she thought she heard robbers."

" I heard father say that if you shoot a burglar outside it's murder," said Jem, who seemed rather troubled by the thought of the blunderbuss ; " but if you shoot him inside it's self-defence."

" Well, you may spring a rattle outside, anyway," said I, " and if hers makes as much noise as ours, it'll be heard all the way here. So mind, if she begins, you must jump down and cut home like mad."

Armed with these instructions and our thick sticks, Jem and I crept out of the house before the sun was up or a bird awake. The air seemed cold after our warm beds, and the dew was so drenching in the hedge bottoms, and on the wayside weeds of our favourite lane, that we were soaked to the knees before we began to force the hedge. I did not think that grass and wild flowers could have held so much wet. By the time that we had crossed the orchard, and I was preparing to grip the grandly scored trunk of the nearest walnut-tree with my chilly legs, the heavy peeling, the hard cracking, and the tedious picking of a green walnut was as little pleasurable a notion as I had in my brain.

All the same, I said (as firmly as my chattering teeth

would allow) that I was very glad we had come when we did, for that there certainly were fewer walnuts on the tree than there had been the day before.

" She's been at them," said I, almost indignantly.

" Pickling," responded Jem with gloomy conciseness ; and spurred by this discovery to fresh enthusiasm for our exploit, we promptly planned operations.

" I'll go up the tree," said I, " and beat, and you can pick them as they fall."

Jem was, I fear, only too well accustomed to my arrogating the first place in our joint undertakings, and after giving me " a leg up " to an available bit of foothold, and handing up my stick, he waited patiently below to gather what I beat down.

The walnuts were few and far between, to say nothing of leaves between, which in walnut-trees are large. The morning twilight was dim, my hands were cold and feebler than my resolution. I had battered down a lot of leaves and twigs, and two or three walnuts ; the sun had got up at last, but rather slowly, as if he found the morning chillier than he expected, and a few rays were darting here and there across the lane, when Jem gave a warning " Hush ! " and I left off rustling in time to hear Mrs. Wood's bedroom lattice opened, and to catch sight of something pushed out into the morning mists.

" Who's there ? " said the schoolmistress.

Neither Jem nor I took upon us to inform her, and we were both seized with anxiety to know what was at the window. He was too low down and I too much buried in foliage to see clearly. Was it the rattle ? I took a hasty step downwards at the thought. Or was it the blunderbuss? In my sudden move I slipped on the dew-damped branch, and cracked a rotten one with my elbow, which made an appalling crash in the early stillness, and sent a walnut—pop ! on to Jem's hat, who had already ducked to avoid the fire of the blunderbuss. and now fell on his face under the fullest conviction that he had been shot.

"Who's there?" said the schoolmistress, and (my tumble having brought me into a more exposed position) she added, "Is that you, Jack and Jem?"

"It's me," said I, ungrammatically but stoutly, hoping that Jem at any rate would slip off.

But he had recovered himself and his loyalty, and unhesitatingly announced, "No, it's me," and was picking the bits of grass off his cheeks and knees when I got down beside him.

"I'm sorry you came to take my walnuts like this," said the voice from above. She had a particularly clear one, and we could hear it quite well. "I got a basketful on purpose for you yesterday afternoon. If I let it down by a string, do you think you can take it?"

Happily she did not wait for a reply, as we could not have got a word out between us; but by-and-by the basketful of walnuts was pushed through the lattice and began to descend. It came slowly and unsteadily, and we had abundant leisure to watch it, and also, as we looked up, to discover what it was that had so puzzled me in Mrs. Wood's appearance—that when I first discovered that it was a head and not a blunderbuss at the window I had not recognised it for hers.

She was without her widow's cap, which revealed the fact that her hair, though the two narrow, smooth bands of it which appeared every day beyond her cap were unmistakably grey, was different in some essential respects from (say) Mrs. Jones's, our grey-haired washer-woman. The more you saw of Mrs. Jones's head, the less hair you perceived her to have, and the whiter that little appeared. Indeed, the knob into which it was twisted at the back was much of the colour as well as of the size of a tangled reel of dirty white cotton. But Mrs. Wood's hair was far more abundant than our mother's, and it was darker underneath

than on the top—a fact which was more obvious when the
knot into which it was gathered in her neck was no longer
hidden. Deep brown streaks were mingled with the grey
in the twists of this, and I could see them quite well, for
the outline of her head was dark against the whitewashed
mullion of the window, and framed by ivy-leaves. As she
leaned out to lower the basket we could see her better and
better, and, as it touched the ground, the jerk pulled her
forward, and the knot of her hair uncoiled and rolled
heavily over the window-sill.

By this time the rays of the sun were level with the
windows, and shone full upon Mrs. Wood's face. I was
very much absorbed in looking at her, but I could not
forget our peculiar position, and I had an important
question to put, which I did without more ado.

" Please, madam, shall you tell Father ? "

" We only want to know," added Jem.

She hesitated a minute, and then smiled. " No ; I don't
think you'll do it again; " after which she disappeared.

"She's certainly no sneak," said I, with an effort to be
magnanimous, for I would much rather she had sprung
the rattle or fired the blunderbuss.

"And I say," said Jem, "isn't she pretty without her
cap ? "

We looked ruefully at the walnuts. We had lost all
appetite for them, and they seemed disgustingly damp,
with their green coats reeking with black bruises. But we
could not have left the basket behind, so we put our sticks
through the handles, and carried it like the Sunday
picture of the spies carrying the grapes of Eshcol.

And Jem and I have often since agreed that we never
in all our lives felt so mean as on that occasion, and we
sincerely hope that we never may.

Indeed it is only in some books and some sermons
that people are divided into " the wicked " and " the good,"
and that " the wicked " have no consciences at all. Jem

D

and I had wilfully gone thieving, but we were far from being utterly hardened, and the schoolmistress's generosity weighed heavily upon ours. Repentance and the desire to make atonement seem to go pretty naturally together, and in my case they led to the following dialogue with Jem, on the subject of two exquisite little bantam hens and a cock, which were our joint property, and which were known in the farmyard as "the Major and his wives."

These titles (which vexed my dear mother from the first) had suggested themselves to us on this wise. There was a certain little gentleman who came to our church, a brewer by profession, and a major in the militia by choice, who was so small and strutted so much that to the insolent observation of boyhood he was "exactly like" our new bantam cock. Young people are very apt to overhear what is not intended for their knowledge, and somehow or other we heard that he was "courting" (as his third wife) a lady of our parish. His former wives were buried in our churchyard. Over the first he had raised an obelisk of marble, so costly and affectionate, that it had won the hearts of his neighbours in general, and of his second wife in particular. When she died the gossips wondered whether the Major would add her name to that of her predecessor, or "go to the expense" of a new monument. He erected a second obelisk, and it was taller than the first (height had a curious fascination for him), and the inscription was more touching than the other. This time the material was Aberdeen granite, and as that is most difficult to cut, hard to polish, and heavy to transport, the expense was enormous. These two monstrosities of mortuary pomp were the pride of the parish, and they were familiarly known to us children (and to many other people) as "the Major's wives."

When we called the cock "the Major," we naturally called the hens "the Major's wives."

"My dears, I don't like that name at all," said my

mother. " I never like jokes about people who are dead.
And for that matter, it really sounds as if they were both
alive, which is worse."

It was during our naughty period, and I strutted on my
heels till I must have looked very like the little brewer
himself, and said, " And why shouldn't they both be
alive? Fancy the Major with two wives, one on each
arm, and both as tall as the monuments! What fun!"

As I said the words " one on each arm," I put up first
one and then the other of my own, and having got a
satisfactory impetus during the rest of my sentence, I
crossed the parlour as a catherine-wheel under my
mother's nose. It was a new accomplishment, of which
I was very proud, and poor Jem somewhat envious. He
was clumsy and could not manage it.

" Oh!" ejaculated my mother, " Jack, I must speak
to your father about those dangerous tricks of yours.
And it quite shocks me to hear you talk in that light way
about wicked things."

Jem was to my rescue in a moment, driving his hands
into the pockets of his blouse, and turning them up to see
how soon he might hope that his fingers would burst
through the lining.

" Jacob had two wives," he said ; and he chanted on,
quoting imperfectly from Dr. Watts's 'Scripture Catechism.' " And Jacob was a good man, therefore his
brother hated him."

" No, no, Jem," said I, " that was Abel. Jacob was
Isaac's younger son, and——"

" Hush! Hush! Hush!" said my mother. " You're
not to do Sunday lessons on weekdays. What terrible
boys you are!" And, avoiding to fight about Jacob's
wives with Jem, who was pertinacious and said very
odd things, my mother did what women often do and
are often wise in doing—she laid down her weapons and
began to beseech.

D 3

"My darlings, call your nice little hens some other names. Poor old mother doesn't like those."

I was melted in an instant, and began to cast about in my head for new titles. But Jem was softly obstinate, and he had inherited some of my mother's wheedling ways. He took his hands from his pockets, flung his arms recklessly round her clean collar, and began stroking (or *pooring*, as we called it) her head with his grubby paws. And as he *poored* he coaxed—"Dear nice old mammy! It's only us. What can it matter? Do let us call our bantams what we like."

And my mother gave in before I had time to.

The dialogue I held with Jem about the bantams after the walnut raid was as follows :—

" Jem, you're awfully fond of the ' Major and his wives,' I suppose ? "

"Ye-es," said Jem, "*I am.* But I don't mind, Jack, if you want them for your very own. I'll give up my share," —and he sighed.

" I never saw such a good chap as you are, Jem. But it's not that. I thought we might give them to Mrs. Wood. It was so beastly about those disgusting walnuts."

" I can't touch walnut pickle now," said Jem feelingly.

" It'd be a very handsome present," said I.

" They took a prize at the Agricultural," said Jem.

" I know she likes eggs. She beats 'em into a froth and feeds Charlie with 'em," said I.

" I think I could eat walnut pickle again if I knew she had the bantams," sighed Jem, who was really devoted to the little cock-major and the auburn-feathered hens.

"We'll take 'em this afternoon," I said.

We did so—in a basket, Eshcol-grape-wise, like the walnuts. When we told Mother, she made no objection. She would have given her own head off her shoulders if, by ill-luck, any passer-by had thought of asking for it. Besides, it solved the difficulty of the objectionable names.

Mrs. Wood was very loth to take our bantams, but of course Jem and I were not going to recall a gift, so she took them at last, and I think she was very much pleased with them.

She had got her cap on again, tied under her chin, and nothing to be seen of her hair but the very grey piece in front. It made her look so different that I could not keep my eyes off her whilst she was talking, though I knew quite well how rude it is to stare. And my head got so full of it that I said at last, in spite of myself, " Please, madam, why is it that part of your hair is grey and part of it dark?"

Her face got rather red, she did not answer for a minute, and Jem, to my great relief, changed the subject, by saying, "We were very much obliged to you for not telling Father about the walnuts."

Mrs. Wood leaned back against the high carving of her old chair and smiled, and said very slowly, "Would he have been very angry?"

"He'd have flogged us, I expect," said I.

"And I expect," continued Jem, "that he'd have said to us what he said to Bob Furniss when he took the filberts : 'If you begin by stealing nuts, you'll end by being transported.' Do you think Jack and I shall end by being transported?" added Jem, who had a merciless talent for applying general principles to individual cases.

Mrs. Wood made no reply, neither did she move, but her eyelids fell, and then her eyes looked far worse than if they had been shut, for there was a little bit open, with nothing but white to be seen. She was still rather red, and she did not visibly breathe. I have no idea for how many seconds I had gazed stupidly at her, when Jem gasped, " Is she dead?"

Then I became terror-struck, and crying, " Let's find Mary Anne!" fled into the kitchen, closely followed by Jem.

" She's took with them fits occasional," said Mary Anne, and depositing a dripping tin she ran to the parlour. We followed in time to see her stooping over the chair and speaking very loudly in the schoolmistress's ear—

" I'll lay ye down, ma'am, shall I ? "

But still the widow was silent, on which Mary Anne took her up iu her brawny arms, and laid her on " Cripple Charlie's " sofa, and covered her with the quilt.

We settled the Major and his wives into their new abode, and then hurried home to my mother, who put on her bonnet, and took a bottle of something, and went off to the farm.

She did not come back till tea-time, and then she was full of poor Mrs. Wood. " Most curious attacks," she explained to my father ; " she can neither move nor speak, and yet she hears everything, though she doesn't always remember afterwards. She said she thought it was 'trouble,' poor soul ! "

" What brought this one on ? " said my father.

" I can't make out," said my mother. " I hope you boys did nothing to frighten her, eh ? Are you sure you didn't do one of those dreadful wheels, Jack ? "

This I indignantly denied, and Jem supported me.

My mother's sympathy had been so deeply enlisted, and her report was so detailed, that Jem and I became bored at last, besides resenting the notion that we had been to blame. I gave one look into the strawberry jam pot, and finding it empty, said my grace and added, " Women are a poor lot, always turning up their eyes and having fits about nothing. I know one thing, nobody'll ever catch *me* being bothered with a wife."

"Nor me neither," said Jem.

CHAPTER IV.

"The bee, a more adventurous colonist than man."
W. C. Bryant.

"Some silent laws our hearts will make,
Which they shall long obey ;
We for the year to come may take
Our temper from to-day."
Wordsworth.

"YOU know what an Apiary is, Isaac, of course ? "

I was sitting in the bee-master's cottage, opposite to him, in an arm-chair, which was the counterpart of his own, both of them having circular backs, diamond-shaped seats, and chintz cushions with frills. It was the summer following that in which Jem and I had tried to see how badly we could behave ; this uncivilised phase had abated : Jem used to ride about a great deal with my father, and I had become intimate with Isaac Irvine.

"You know what an Apiary is, Isaac ? " said I.

" A what, sir ? "

" An A-P-I-A-R-Y."

" To be sure, sir, to be sure," said Isaac. " An *appyary* " (so he was pleased to pronounce it), " I should be familiar with the name, sir, from my bee-book, but I never calls my own stock anything but the beehives. *Beehives* is a good straightforward sort of a name, sir, and it serves my turn."

" Ah, but you see we haven't come to the B's yet," said I, alluding to what I was thinking of.

" Does your father think of keeping 'em, sir ? " said Isaac, alluding to what he was thinking of.

" Oh, he means to have them bound, I believe," was my reply.

The bee-master now betrayed his bewilderment, and we had a hearty laugh when we discovered that he had been talking about bees whilst I had been talking about the weekly numbers of the ' Penny Cyclopædia,' which had not as yet reached the letter B, but in which I had found an article on Master Isaac's craft, under the word Apiary, which had greatly interested me, and ought, I thought, to be interesting to the bee-keeper. Still thinking of this I said—

"Do you ever take your bees away from home, Isaac?"

"They're on the moors now, sir," said Isaac.

"*Are* they?" I exclaimed. "Then you're like the Egyptians, and like the French, and the Piedmontese; only you didn't take them in a barge."

"Why, no, sir. The canal don't go nigh-hand of the moors at all."

"The Egyptians," said I, leaning back into the capacious arms of my chair, and epitomising what I had read, "who live in Lower Egypt put all their beehives into boats and take them on the river to Upper Egypt. Right up at that end of the Nile the flowers come out earliest, and the bees get all the good out of them there, and then the boats are moved lower down to where the same kind of flowers are only just beginning to blossom, and the bees get all the good out of them there, and so on, and on, and on, till they've travelled right through Egypt, with all the hives piled up, and come back in the boats to where they started from."

"And every hive a mighty different weight to what it was when they did start, I'll warrant," said Master Isaac enthusiastically. "Did you find all that in those penny numbers, Master Jack?"

"Yes, and oh, lots more, Isaac! About lots of things and lots of countries."

"Scholarship's a fine thing," said the bee-master, " and seeing foreign parts is a fine thing, and many's the time

I've wished for both. I suppose that's the same Egypt that's in the Bible, sir ? "

" Yes," said I, " and the same river Nile that Moses was put on in the ark of bulrushes."

" There's no countries I'd like to see better than them Bible countries," said Master Isaac, " and I've wished it more ever since that gentleman was here that gave that lecture in the school, with the Holy Land magic-lantern. He'd been there himself, and he explained all the slides. They were grand, some of 'em, when you got 'em straight and steady for a bit. They're an awkward thing to manage, is slides, sir, and the schoolmaster he wasn't much good at 'em, he said, and that young scoundrel Bob Furniss and another lad got in a hole below the platform and pulled the sheet. But when you did get 'em, right side up, and the light as it should be, they *were* grand ! There was one they called the Wailing Place of the Jews, with every stone standing out as fair as the flags on this floor. John Binder, the mason, was at my elbow when that came on, and he clapped his hands, and says he, ' Well, yon beats all ! ' But the one for my choice, sir, was the Garden of Gethsemane by moonlight. I'd only gone to the penny places, for I'm a good size and can look over most folks' heads, but I thought I must see that a bit nearer, cost what it might. So I found a shilling, and I says to the young fellow at the door (it was the pupil-teacher), ' I must go a bit nearer to yon.' And he says, ' You're not going into the reserved seats, Isaac ? ' So I says, ' Don't put yourself about, my lad, I shan't interfere with the quality ; but if half a day's wage'll bring me nearer to the Garden of Gethsemane, I'm bound to go.' And I went. I didn't intrude myself on nobody, though one gentleman was for making room for me at once, and twice over he offered me a seat beside him. But I knew my manners, and I said, ' Thank you, sir, I can see as I stand.' And I did see right well, and kicked Bob Furniss too, which was good for all parties. But I'd like to see the very places themselves, Master Jack."

"So should I," said I ; "but I should like to go farther, all round the world, I think. Do you know, Isaac, you wouldn't believe what curious beasts there are in other countries, and what wonderful people and places! Why, we've only got to ATH—No. 135—now ; it leaves off at *Athanagilde*, a captain of the Spanish Goths—he's nobody, but there are *such* apes in that number! The Mono—there's a picture of him, just like a man with a tail and horrid feet, who used to sit with the negro women when they were at work, and play with bits of paper ; and a Quata, who used to be sent to the tavern for wine, and when the children pelted him he put down the wine and threw stones at them. And there are pictures in all the numbers, of birds and ant-eaters and antelopes, and I don't know what. The Mono and the Quata live in the West Indies, I think. You see, I think the A's are rather good numbers ; very likely, for there's America, and Asia, and Africa, and Arabia, and Abyssinia, and there'll be Australia before we come to the B's. Oh, Isaac! I do wish I could go round the world ! "

I sighed, and the bee-master sighed also, with a profundity that made his chair creak, well-seasoned as it was. Then he said, " But I'll say this, Master Jack, next to going to such places the reading about 'em must come. A penny a week's a penny a week to a poor man, but I reckon I shall have to make shift to take in those numbers myself."

Isaac did not take them in, however, for I used to take ours down to his cottage, and read them aloud to him instead. He liked this much better than if he had had to read to himself—he said he could understand reading better when he heard it than when he saw it. For my own part I enjoyed it very much, and I fancy I read rather well, it

being a point on which Mrs. Wood expended much trouble
with us.

"Listen, Isaac," said I on my next visit; "this is what
I meant about the barge "—and resting the Penny Number
on the arm of my chair, I read aloud to the attentive bee-
master—"'Goldsmith describes from his own observation
a kind of floating apiary in some parts of France and
Piedmont. They have on board of one barge, he says,
threescore or a hundred beehives——'"

"That's an appy-ary if ye like, sir!" ejaculated Master
Isaac, interrupting his pipe and me to make way for the
observation.

"Somebody saw 'a convoy of *four thousand* hives——'
on the Nile," said I.

The bee-master gave a resigned sigh. "Go on, Master
Jack," said he.

"'—well defended from the inclemency of an accidental
storm,'" I proceeded; "'and with these the owner float
quietly down the stream; one beehive yields the proprietor
a considerable income. Why, he adds, a method similar
to this has never been adopted in England, where we
have more gentle rivers and more flowery banks than in
any other part of the world, I know not; certainly it
might be turned to advantage, and yield the possessor a
secure, though perhaps a moderate, income.'"

I was very fond of the canal which ran near us (and
was, for that matter, a parish boundary): and the barges,
with their cargoes, were always interesting to me; but a
bargeful of bees seemed something quite out of the
common. I thought I should rather like to float down a
gentle river between flowery banks, surrounded by beehives on which I could rely to furnish me with a secure
though moderate income; and I said so.

"So should I, sir," said the bee-master. "And I
should uncommon like to ha' seen the one beehive that
brought in a considerable income. Honey must have

been very dear in those parts, Master Jack.   However, it's
in the book, so I suppose it's right enough."

I made no defence of the veracity of the ' Cyclopædia,'
for I was thinking of something else, of which, after a few
moments, I spoke.

"Isaac, you don't stay with your bees on the moors.
Do you ever go to see them ? "

"To be sure I do, Master Jack, nigh every Sunday
through the season.   I start after I get back from morning
church, and I come home in the dark, or by moonlight.
My missus goes to church in the afternoons, and for that
bit she locks up the house."

"Oh, I wish you'd take me next time ! " said I.

"To be sure I will, and too glad, sir, if you're allowed
to go."

That *was* the difficulty, and I knew it.   No one who
has not lived in a household of old-fashioned middle-class
country folk of our type has any notion how difficult it is
for anybody to do anything unusual therein.   In such a
well-fitted but unelastic establishment the dinner-hour,
the carriage horses, hot water, bedtime, candles, the post,
the wash-day, and an extra blanket, from being the
ministers of one's comfort, become the stern arbiters of
one's fate.   Spring cleaning—which is something like
what it would be to build, paint, and furnish a house,
and to " do it at home "—takes place as naturally as the
season it celebrates ; but if you want the front door kept
open after the usual hour for drawing the bolts and
hanging the robbers' bell, it's odds if the master of the
house has not an apoplectic fit, and if servants of twelve
and fourteen years' standing do not give warning.

And what is difficult on weekdays is on Sundays next
door to impossible, for obvious reasons.

But one's parents, though they have their little ways
like other people, are, as a rule—oh, my heart ! made
sadder and wiser by the world's rough experiences, bear

witness !—very indulgent ; and after a good many ups
and downs, and some compromising and coaxing, I got
my way.

On one point my mother was firm, and I feared this
would be an insuperable difficulty. I must go twice to
church, as our Sunday custom was—a custom which she
saw no good reason for me to break. It is easy to smile
at her punctiliousness on this score ; but after all these
years, and on the whole, I think she was right. An unexpected compromise came to my rescue, however : Isaac
Irvine's bees were in the parish of Cripple Charlie's
father, within a stone's throw (by the bee-master's strong
arm) of the church itself, which was a small minster
among the moors. Here I promised faithfully to attend
evening prayer, for which we should be in time ; and I
started, by Isaac Irvine's side, on my first real "expedition" on the first Sunday in August, with my mother's
blessing and a threepenny-bit with a hole in it, "in case
of a collection."

We dined before we started, I with the rest, and Isaac
in our kitchen ; but I had no great appetite—I was too
much excited—and I willingly accepted some large sandwiches made with thick slices of home-made bread and
liberal layers of home-made potted meat, "in case I
should feel hungry" before I got there.

It pains me to think how distressed my mother was
because I insisted on carrying the sandwiches in a red
and orange spotted handkerchief, which I had purchased
with my own pocket-money, and to which I was deeply
attached, partly from the bombastic nature of the pattern,
and partly because it was big enough for any grown-up
man. "It made me look like a tramping sailor," she said.
I did not tell her that this was precisely the effect at
which I aimed, though it was the case ; but I coaxed her
into permitting it, and I abstained from passing a certain
knowing little ash stick through the knot, and hoisting **the**

bundle over my left shoulder, till I was well out of the grounds.

My efforts to spare her feelings on this point, however, proved vain. She ran to the landing-window to watch me out of sight, and had a full view of my figure as I swaggered with a business-like gait by Isaac's side up the first long hill, having set my hat on the back of my head with an affectation of profuse heat, my right hand in the bee-master's coat-pocket for support, and my left holding the stick and bundle at an angle as showy and sailor-like as I could assume.

" And they'll just meet the Ebenezer folk coming out of chapel, ma'am ! " said our housemaid over my mother's shoulder, by way of consolation.

Our journey was up-hill, for which I was quite prepared. The blue and purple outline of the moors formed the horizon line visible from our gardens, whose mistiness or clearness was prophetic of the coming weather, and over which the wind was supposed to blow with uncommon " healthfulness." I had been there once to blow away the whooping-cough, and I could remember that the sandy road wound up and up, but I did not appreciate till that Sunday how tiring a steady ascent of nearly five miles may be.

We were within sight of the church and within hearing of the bells, when we reached a wayside trough, whose brimming measure was for ever overflowed by as bright a rill as ever trickled down a hill-side.

" It's only the first peal," said Master Isaac, seating himself on the sandy bank, and wiping his brows.

My well-accustomed ears confirmed his statement. The bells moved too slowly for either the second or the third peal, and we had twenty minutes at our disposal.

It was then that I knew (for the first but not the last time) what refreshment for the weary a spotted handker-chief may hold. The bee-master and I divided the sand-

should have been generous, and faces that should have
been noble, and aims that should have been high, are
blurred and blunted by the real weight of real everyday care.

There are yet others ; in which the spirit is too strong
for mortal accidents to pull it down—minds that the
narrowest career cannot vulgarise—faces to which care
but adds a look of pathos—souls which keep their aims
and faiths apart from the fluctuations of " the things that
are seen." The personal influence of natures of this type
is generally very large, and it was very large in the case
of Cripple Charlie's father, and made him a sort of
Prophet, Priest, and King over a rough and scattered
population, with whom the shy, scholarly poor gentleman
had not otherwise much in common.

It was his personal influence, I am sure, which made
the congregation so devout ! There is one rule which, I
believe, applies to all congregations, of every denomination,
and any kind of ritual, and that is, that the enthusiasm of
the congregation is in direct proportion to the enthusiasm
of the minister ; not merely to his personal worth, nor even
to his popularity, for people who rather dislike a clergy-
man, and disapprove of his service, will say a louder Amen
at his giving of thanks if his own feelings have a touch of
fire, than they would to that of a more perfunctory parson
whom they liked better. As is the heartiness of the priest,
so is the heartiness of the people—with such strictness that
one is disposed almost to credit some of it to actual mag-
netism. *Response* is no empty word in public worship.

It was no empty word on this occasion. From the
ancient clerk (who kept a life-interest in what were now
the duties of a choir) to some gaping farm-lads at my back,
everybody said and sang to the utmost of his ability. I
may add that Isaac and I involuntarily displayed a zeal
which was in excess of our Sunday customs ; and if my
tongue moved glibly enough with the choir, the bee-master
found many an elderly parishioner besides himself and the

clerk who "took" both prayer and praise at such independent paces as suited their individual scholarship, spectacles, and notions of reverence.

It crowned my satisfaction when I found that there was to be a collection. The hymn to which the churchwardens moved about, gathering the pence, whose numbers and noisiness seemed in keeping with the rest of the service, was a well-known one to us all. It was the favourite evening hymn of the district. I knew every syllable of it, for Jem and I always sang hymns (and invariably this one) with my dear mother, on Sunday evening after supper. When we were good, we liked it, and, picking one favourite after another, we often sang nearly through the hymn-book. When we were naughty, we displayed a good deal of skill in making derisive faces behind my mother's back, as she sat at the piano, without betraying ourselves, and in getting our tongues out and in again during the natural pauses and convolutions of the tune. But these occasional fits of boyish profanity did not hinder me from having an equally boyish fund of reverence and enthusiasm at the bottom of my heart, and it was with proud and pleasurable emotions that I heard the old clerk give forth the familiar first lines—

> "Soon shall the evening star with silver ray
> Shed its mild lustre o'er this sacred day,"

and got my threepenny-bit ready between my finger and thumb.

Away went the organ, which was played by the vicar's eldest daughter—away went the vicar's second daughter, who "led the singing" from the vicarage pew with a voice like a bird—away went the choir, which, in spite of surplices, could not be cured of waiting half a beat for her— and away went the congregation—young men and maidens, old men and children—in one broad tide of somewhat irregular harmony. Isaac did not know the words as well

E

as I did, so I lent him my hymn-book ; one result of which
was, that the print being small, and the sense of a hymn
being in his view a far more important matter than the
sound of it, he preached rather than sang—in an unequal
cadence which was perturbing to my more musical ear—
the familiar lines—

> " Still let each awful truth our thoughts engage,
> That shines revealed on inspiration's page ;
> Nor those blest hours in vain amusement waste
> Which all who lavish shall lament at last."

During the next verse my devotions were a little distracted by the gradual approach of a churchwarden for
my threepenny-bit, which was hot with three verses of
expectant fingering.   Then, to my relief, he took it, and
the beemaster's contribution, and I felt calmer, and
listened to the little prelude which it was always the
custom for the organist to play before the final verse of a
hymn.   It was also the custom to sing the last verse as
loudly as possible, though this is by no means invariably
appropriate.   It fitted the present occasion fairly enough.
From where I stood I could see the bellows-blower (the
magnetic current of enthusiasm flowed even to the back
of the organ) nerve himself to prodigious pumping—
Charlie's sister drew out all the stops—the vicar passed
from the prayer-desk to the pulpit with the rapt look of a
man who walks in a prophetic dream—we pulled ourselves
together, Master Isaac brought the hymn-book close to his
glasses, and when the tantalising prelude was past we
burst forth with a volume which merged all discrepancies.
As far as I am able to judge of my own performance, I
fear I *bawled* (I'm sure the boy behind me did)—

> " Father of Heaven ! in Whom our hopes confide,
> Whose power defends us, and Whose precepts guide,
> In life our Guardian, and in death our Friend,
> Glory supreme be Thine till time shall end ! "

The sermon was short, and when the service was over
Master Isaac and I spent a delightful afternoon with his
bees among the heather. The "evening star" had come
out when we had some tea in the village inn, and we
walked home by moonlight. There was neither wind nor
sun, but the air was almost oppressively pure. The moonshine had taken the colour out of the sandy road and the
heather, and had painted black shadows by every boulder,
and most things looked asleep except the rill that went on
running. Only we and the rabbits, and the night moths
and the beetles, seemed to be stirring. An occasional bat
appeared and vanished like a spectral illusion, and I saw
one owl flap across the moor with level wings against the
moon.

"Oh, I *have* enjoyed it !" was all I could say when I
parted from the beemaster.

"And so have I, Master Jack," was his reply, and he
hesitated as if he had something more to say, and then he
said it. " I never enjoyed it as much, and you can thank
your mother, sir, with old Isaac's duty, for sending us to
church. I'm sure I don't know why I never went before
when I was up yonder, for I always took notice of the bells.
I reckon I thought I hadn't time, but you can say, with
my respects, sir, that please GOD I shan't miss again."

I believe he never did ; and " Cripple Charlie's " father
came to look on him as half a parishioner.

I was glad I had not shirked Evening Prayer myself,
though (my sex and age considered) it was not to be
expected that I should comfort my mother's heart by
confessing as much. Let me confess it now, and confess
also that if it was the first time, it was not the last that I
have had cause to realise—oh women, for our sakes
remember it !—into what light and gentle hands GOD lays
the reins that guide men's better selves.

The most remarkable event of the day happened at the

end of it. Whilst Isaac was feeling the weight of one of
his hives, and just after I lost chase of a very peculiar-
looking beetle, from his squeezing himself away from me
under a boulder, I had caught sight of a bit of white
heather, and then bethought me of gathering a nosegay
(to include this rarity) of moor flowers and grasses for Mrs.
Wood. So when we reached the lane on our way home,
I bade Isaac good-night, and said I would just run in
by the back way into the farm (we never called it the
Academy) and leave the flowers, that the schoolmistress
might put them in water. Mary Ann was in the kitchen.

"Where's Mrs. Wood?" said I, when she had got over
that silly squeak women always give when you come
suddenly on them.

"Dear, dear, Master Jack! what a turn you did give
me! I thought it was the tramp."

"What tramp?" said I.

"Why, a great lanky man that came skulking here a
bit since, and asked for the missus. She was down the
garden, and I've half a notion he went after her. I wish
you'd go and look for her, Master Jack, and fetch her in.
It's as damp as dear knows what, and she takes no more
care of herself than a baby. And I'd be glad to know that
man was off the place. There's wall-fruit and lots of
things about, a low fellow like that might pick up."

My ears felt a little hot at this allusion to low fellows
and garden thieving, and I hurried off to do Mary Ann's
bidding without further parley. There was a cloud over
the moon as I ran down the back garden, but when I was
nearly at the end the moon burst forth again, so that I
could see. And this was what I saw :—

First, a white thing lying on the ground, and it was the
widow's cap, and then Mrs. Wood herself, with a gaunt
lanky-looking man, such as Mary Ann had described.
Her head came nearly to his shoulder, as I was well able
to judge, for he was holding it in his hands and had laid

his own upon it, as if it were a natural resting-place. And his hair coming against the darker part of hers, I could see that his was grey all over. Up to this point I had been too much stupefied to move, and I had just become conscious that I ought to go, when the white cap lying in the moonlight seemed to catch his eye as it had caught mine ; and he set his heel on it with a vehemence that made me anxious to be off. I could not resist one look back as I left the garden, if only to make sure that I had not been dreaming. No, they were there still, and he was lifting the coil of her hair, which I suppose had come down when the cap was pulled off, and it took the full stretch of his arm to do so, before it fell heavily from his fingers.

When I presented myself to my mother with the bunch of flowers still in my hand, she said, " Did my Jack get these for mother ? "

I shook my head. " No, mother. For Mrs. Wood."

" You might have called at the farm as you passed," said she.

" I did ! " said I.

" Couldn't you see Mrs. Wood, love ? "

" Yes, I saw her, but she'd got the tramp with her."

" What tramp ? " asked my mother in a horror-struck voice, which seemed quite natural to me, for I had been brought up to rank tramps in the same " dangerous class " with mad dogs, stray bulls, drunken men, and other things which it is undesirable to meet.

" The great lanky one," I explained, quoting from Mary Ann.

" What was he doing with Mrs. Wood ? " asked my mother anxiously.

I had not yet recovered from my own bewilderment, and was reckless of the shock inflicted by my reply.

" *Pooring* her head, and kissing it."

CHAPTER V.

"To each his sufferings ; all are men
Condemned alike to groan.
The tender for another's pain——"

Gray.

NOT even the miser's funeral had produced in the neighbourhood anything like the excitement which followed
that Sunday evening. At first my mother—her mind
filled by the simplest form of the problem, namely, that
Mrs. Wood was in the hands of a tramp—wished my
father to take the blunderbuss in his hand and step down
to the farm. He had "pish"ed and "psha"ed about the
blunderbuss, and was beginning to say more, when I was
dismissed to bed, where I wandered back over the moors
in uneasy dreams, and woke with the horror of a tramp's
hand upon my shoulder. After suffering the terrors of
night for some time, and finding myself no braver with
my head under the bedclothes than above them, I began
conscientiously to try my mother's family recipe for "bad
dreams and being afraid in the dark." This was to "say
over" the Benedicite correctly, which (if by a rare chance
one were still awake at the end) was to be followed by a
succession of the hymns one knew by heart. It required
an effort to *begin*, and to *really try*, but the children of
such mothers as ours are taught to make efforts, and once
fairly started, and holding on as a duty, it certainly did
tend to divert the mind from burglars and ghosts, to get
the beasts, creeping things, and fowls of the air into their
right places in the chorus of benedictions. That Jem
never could discriminate between the "Dews and Frosts"

'WHEN I DID OPEN MY EYES, JEM WAS SITTING AT THE
END OF MY BED, DYING TO TELL ME THE NEWS."

and " Frost and Cold " verses needs no telling. I have
often finished and still been frightened and had to fall
back upon the hymns, but this night I began to dream
pleasanter dreams of Charlie's father and the bee
master before I got to the holy and humble men of
heart.

I slept long then, and Mother would not let me be
awakened. When I did open my eyes Jem was sitting a
the end of my bed, dying to tell me the news.

" Jack ! you have waked, haven't you ? I see your eyes.
Don't shut 'em again. What *do* you think ? *Mrs. Wood's
husband has come home !* "

I never knew the ins and outs of the story very exactly.
At the time that what did become generally known was
fresh in people's minds Jem and I were not by way of being
admitted to " grown-up " conversations ; and though Mrs.
Wood's husband and I became intimate friends, I neither
wished nor dared to ask him more about his past than he
chose to tell, for I knew enough to know that it must be
almost intolerable pain to recall it.

What we had all heard of the story was this. Mr.
Wood had been a head clerk in a house of business. A
great forgery was committed against his employers, and
he was accused. He was tried, condemned, and sentenced
to fourteen years' penal servitude, which, in those days,
meant transportation abroad. For some little time the
jury had not been unanimous. One man doubted the
prisoner's guilt—the man we afterwards knew as the old
miser of Walnut-tree Farm. But he was overpersuaded
at last, and Mr. Wood was convicted and sentenced. He
had spent ten years of his penal servitude in Bermuda
when a man lying in Maidstone Jail under sentence of
death for murder, confessed (amongst other crimes of
which he disburdened his conscience), that it was he,
and not the man who had been condemned, who had
committed the forgery. Investigation confirmed the

truth of this statement, and Mr. Wood was " pardoned " and brought home.

He had just come. He was the tramp.

In this life the old miser never knew that his first judgment had been the just one, but the doubt which seems always to have haunted him—whether he had not helped to condemn the innocent—was the reason of his bequest to the convict's wife, and explained much of the mysterious wording of the will.

It was a tragic tale, and gave a terrible interest to the gaunt, white-haired, shattered-looking man who was the hero of it. It had one point of special awe for me, and I used to watch him in church and think of it, till I am ashamed to say that I forgot even when to stand up and sit down. He had served ten years of his sentence. Ten years! Ten times three hundred and sixty-five days! All the days of the years of my life. The weight of that undeserved punishment had fallen on him the year that I was born, and all that long, long time of home with Mother and Father and Jem—all the haymaking summers and snowballing winters—whilst Jem and I had never been away from home, and had had so much fun, and nothing very horrid that I could call to mind except the mumps—he had been an exile working in chains. I remember rousing up with a start from the realisation of this one Sunday to find myself still standing in the middle of the Litany. My mother was behaving too well herself to find me out, and though Jem was giggling he dared not move, because he was kneeling next my father, whose back was turned to me. I knelt down, and started to hear the parson say—" show Thy pity upon all prisoners and captives ! " And then I knew what it is to wish when it is too late. For I did so wish I had really prayed for prisoners and captives every Sunday, because then I should have prayed for that poor man nearly all the long time he had been so miserable ; for we began to go to church very early, and one learns to pray easier and sooner than one learns anything else.

All this had happened in the holidays, but when they were over school opened as before, and with additional scholars ; for sympathy was wide and warm with the schoolmistress. Strangely enough, both partners in the firm which had prosecuted Mr. Wood were dead. Their successors offered him employment, but he could not face the old associations. I believe he found it so hard to face any one that this was the reason of his staying at home for a time and helping in the school. I don't think we boys made him uncomfortable as grown-up strangers seemed to do, and he was particularly fond of " Cripple Charlie."

This brought me into contact with him, for Charlie and I were great friends. He was as well pleased to be read to out of the penny numbers as the beemaster, and he was interested in things of which Isaac Irvine was completely ignorant.

Our school was a day-school, but Charlie had been received by Mrs. Wood as a boarder. His poor back could not have borne to be jolted to and from the moors every day. So he lived at Walnut-tree Farm, and now and then his father would come down in a light cart lent by one of the parishioners, and take Charlie home from Saturday to Monday, and then bring him back again.

The sisters came to see him too, by turns, sometimes walking and sometimes riding a rough-coated pony, who was well-content to be tied to a gate, and eat some of the grass that overgrew the lane. And often Charlie came to *us*, especially in haytime, for haycocks seem very comfortable (for people whose backs hurt) to lean against ; and we could cover his legs with hay too, as he liked them to be hidden. There is no need to say how tender my mother was to him, and my father used to look at him half puzzledly and half pitifully, and always spoke to him in quite a different tone of voice to the one he used with other boys.

Jem gave Charlie the best puppy out of the curly brown spaniel lot ; but he didn't really like being with him, though he was sorry for him, and he could not bear seeing his poor legs.

"They make me feel horrid," Jem said. "And even when they're covered up, I know they're there."

"You're a chip of the old block, Jem," said my father. "I'd give a guinea to a hospital any day sooner than see a patient. I'm as sorry as can be for the poor lad, but he turns me queer, though I feel ashamed of it. I like things *sound.* Your mother's different ; she likes 'em better for being sick and sorry, and I suppose Jack takes after her."

My father was wrong about me. Pity for Charlie was not half of the tie between us. When he was talking, or listening to the penny numbers, I never thought about his legs or his back, and I don't now understand how anybody could.

He read and remembered far more than I did, and he was even wilder about strange countries. He had as adventurous a spirit as any lad in the school, cramped up as it was in that misshapen body. I knew he'd have liked to go round the world as well as I, and he often laughed and said—"What's more, Jack, if I'd the money I would. People are very kind to poor wretches like me all over the world. I should never want a helping hand, and the only difference between us would be, that I should be carried on board-ship by some kindhearted blue-jacket, and you'd have to scramble for yourself."

He was very anxious to know Isaac Irvine, and when I brought the beemaster to see him, they seemed to hold friendly converse with their looks even before either of them spoke. It was a bad day with Charlie, but he set his lips against the pain and raised himself on one arm to stare out of his big brown eyes at the old man, who met them with as steady a gaze out of his. Then Charlie lowered himself again, and said in a tone of voice by which I knew he was pleased, " I'm so glad you've come to see me, old Isaac. It's very kind of you. Jack says you know a lot about live things, and that you like the numbers we like in the ' Penny Cyclopædia.' I wanted to see you, for I think you and I are much in the same boat ; you're old, and I'm crippled, and we're both too poor to travel. But Jack's to go, and when he's gone, you and I'll follow him on the map."

" GOD willing, sir," said the beemaster ; and when he said that, I knew how sorry he felt for poor Charlie, for when he was moved he always said very short things, and generally something religious.

And for all Charlie's whims and fancies, and in all his pain and fretfulness, and through fits of silence and sensitiveness, he had never a better friend than Isaac Irvine. Indeed the beemaster was one of those men (to be found in all ranks), whose delicate tenderness might not be guessed from the size and roughness of the outer man.

Our neighbours were all very kind to Mr. Wood in their own way, but they were a little impatient of his slowness to be sociable, and had, I think, a sort of feeling that the ex-convict ought not only to enjoy evening parties more than other people, but to be just a little more grateful for being invited.

However, one must have a strong and sensitive imagination to cultivate wide sympathies when one lives a quiet, methodical life in the place where one's father and grandfather lived out quiet methodical lives before one ; and I do not think we were an imaginative race.

The schoolmaster (as we used to call him) had seen and suffered so much more of life than we, that I do not think he resented the clumsiness of our sympathy ; but now I

look back I fancy that he must have felt as if he wanted
years of peace and quiet in which to try and forget the
years of suffering. Old Isaac said one day, " I reckon the
master feels as if he wanted to sit down and say to
hisself over and over again, ' I'm a free man, I'm a free
man, I'm a free man,' till he can fair trust himself to
believe it."

Isaac was probably right, and perhaps evening parties,
though they are meant for treats, are not the best places
to sit down and feel free in, particularly when there are a
lot of strange people who have heard a dreadful story
about you, and want to see what you look like after it.

During the summer holidays Jem and I were out the
whole day long. When we came in I was ready for the
Penny Numbers, but Jem always fell asleep, even if he did
not go to bed at once. My father did just the same. I
think their feeling about houses was of a perfectly
primitive kind. They looked upon them as comfortable
shelter for sleeping and eating, but not at all as places in
which to pursue any occupation. Life, for them, was lived
out-of-doors.

I know now, how dull this must have made the evenings
for my mother, and that it was very selfish of me to wait
till my father was asleep (for fear he should say "no"),
and then to ask her leave to take the Penny Numbers
down to the farm and sit with Cripple Charlie.

Now and then she would go too, and chat with Mrs.
Wood, whilst the schoolmaster and I were turning the
terrestrial globe by Charlie's sofa ; but as a rule Charlie
and I were alone, and the Woods went round the homestead together, and came home, hand in hand, through
the garden, and we laughed to think how we had taken
him for a tramp.

And sometimes on a summer's evening, when we talked
and read aloud to each other across a quaint oak table that
had been the miser's, of far-away lands and strange birds

of gorgeous plumage, the schoolmaster sat silent in the arm-chair by the open lattice, resting his white head against the mullion that the ivy was creeping up, and listened to the blackbirds and thrushes as their songs dropped by odd notes into silence, and gazed at the near fields and trees, and the little homestead with its hayricks on the hill, when the grass was apple-green in the gold mist of sunset : and went on gazing when that had faded into fog, and the hedgerow elms were black against the sky, as if the eye could not be filled with seeing, nor the ear with hearing !

CHAPTER VI.

*"*Who, doomed to go in company with Pain,
Turns his necessity to glorious gain."

Wordsworth.

" JACK," said Charlie, " listen ! "

He was reading bits out of the numbers to me, whilst I was rigging a miniature yacht to sail on the dam ; and Mrs. Wood's husband was making a plan of something at another table, and occasionally giving me advice about my masts and sails. " It's about the South American forests," said Charlie. "' There every tree has a character of its own ; each has its peculiar foliage, and probably also a tint unlike that of the trees which surround it. Gigantic vegetables of the most different families intermix their branches ; five-leaved bignonias grow by the side of bonduc-trees ; cassias shed their yellow blossoms upon the rich fronds of arborescent ferns ; myrtles and eugenias, with their thousand arms contrast with the elegant simplicity of palms ; and among the airy foliage of the mimosa, the ceropia elevates its giant leaves and heavy

candelabra-shaped branches. Of some trees the trunk is
perfectly smooth, of others it is defended by enormous
spines, and the whole are often apparently sustained by
the slanting stems of a huge wild fig-tree. With us, the
oak, the chestnut, and the beech seem as if they bore no
flowers, so small are they and so little distinguishable
except by naturalists ; but in the forests of South America
it is often the most gigantic trees that produce the most
brilliant flowers ; cassias hang down their pendants of
golden blossoms, vochisias unfold their singular bunches ;
corollas, longer than those of our foxglove, sometimes
yellow or sometimes purple, load the arborescent bignonias ; while the chorisias are covered, as it were, with
lilies, only their colours are richer and more varied ;
grasses also appear in form of bamboos, as the most graceful of trees ; bauhinias, bignonias, and aroideous plants
cling round the trees like enormous cables ; orchideous
plants and bromelias overrun their limbs, or fasten themselves to them when prostrated by the storm, and make
even their dead remains become verdant with leaves and
flowers not their own.' ''

Though he could read very well, Charlie had, so far,
rather stumbled through the long names in this de-
scription, but he finished off with fluency, not to say
enthusiasm. " ' Such are the ancient forests, flourishing
in a damp and fertile soil, and clothed with perpetual
green.' ''

I was half-way through a profound sigh when I caught
the schoolmaster's eye, who had paused in his plan-
making and was listening with his head upon his
hand.

" What a groan ! " he exclaimed. " What's the
matter ? "

" It sounds so splendid ! " I answered, " and I'm so
afraid I shall never see it. I told Father last night I
should like to be a sailor, but he only said ' Stuff and

nonsense,' and that there was a better berth waiting for me in Uncle Henry's office than any of the Queen's ships would provide for me ; and Mother begged me never to talk of it any more, if I didn't want to break her heart "—and I sighed again.

The schoolmaster had a long smooth face, which looked longer from melancholy, and he turned it and his arms over the back of the chair, and looked at me with the watchful listening look his eyes always had ; but I am not sure if he was really paying much attention to me, for he talked (as he often did) as if he were talking to himself.

" I wanted to be a soldier," he said, " and my father wouldn't let me. I often used to wish I had run away and enlisted, when I was with Quartermaster McCulloch, of the Engineers (he'd risen from the ranks and was younger than me), in Bermuda."

" Bermuda ! That's not very far from South America, is it ? " said I, looking across to the big map of the world. " Is it very beautiful, too ? "

The schoolmaster's eyes contracted as if he were short-sighted, or looking at something inside his own head. But he smiled as he answered :—

" The poet says—

" ' A pleasing land of drowsy-head it is,
Of dreams that wave before the half-shut eye ;
And of gay castles in the clouds that pass,
For ever flushing round a summer sky.' "

" But are there any curious beasts and plants and that sort of thing ? " I asked.

" I believe there were no native animals originally," said the schoolmaster. " I mean inland ones. But the fowls of the air and the fishes of the sea are of all lovely forms and colours. And such corals and sponges, and sea-anemones, blooming like flowers in the transparent pools of the warm blue water that washes the coral reefs and fills the little creeks and bays ! "

I gasped—and he went on. " The commonest trees, I think, are palms and cedars. Lots of the old houses were built of cedar, and I've heard of old cedar furniture to be picked up here and there, as some people buy old oak out of English farmhouses. It is very durable and deliciously scented. People used to make cedar bonfires when the smallpox was about, to keep away infection. The gardens will grow anything, and plots of land are divided by oleander hedges of many colours."

" Oh—h ! " ejaculated I, in long-drawn notes of admiration. The schoolmaster's eyes twinkled.

" Not only," continued he, " do very gaudy lobsters and quaint cray-fish and crabs with lanky legs dispute your attention on the shore with the shell-fish of the loveliest hues ; there is no lack of remarkable creatures indoors. Monstrous spiders, whose bite is very unpleasant, drop from the roof ; tarantulas and scorpions get into your boots, and cockroaches, hideous to behold and disgusting to smell, invade every place from your bed to your store-cupboard. If you possess anything from food and clothing to books and boxes, the ants will find it and devour it, and if you possess a garden the mosquitoes will find you and devour you."

" Oh—h ! " I exclaimed once more, but this time in a different tone.

Mr. Wood laughed heartily. " Tropical loveliness has its drawbacks, Jack. Perhaps some day when your clothes are moulded, and your brain feels mouldy too with damp heat, and you can neither work in the sun nor be at peace in the shade, you may wish you were sitting on a stool in your uncle's office, undisturbed by venomous insects, and cool in a November fog."

I laughed too, but I shook my head.

"No. I shan't mind the insects if I can get there. Charlie, were those wonderful ants old Isaac said you'd been reading about, Bermuda ants?"

I did not catch Charlie's muttered reply, and when I looked round I saw that his face was buried in the red cushions, and that he was (what Jem used to call) "in one of his tempers."

I don't exactly know how it was. I don't think Charlie was jealous or really cross, but he used to take fits of fancying he was in the way, and out of it all (from being a cripple), if we seemed to be very busy without him, especially about such things as planning adventures. I knew what was the matter directly, but I'm afraid my consolation was rather clumsy.

" Don't be cross, Charlie," I said ; " I thought you were listening too, and if it's because you think you won't be able to go, I don't believe there's really a bit more chance of my going, though my legs *are* all right."

" Don't bother about me," said Charlie ; " but I wish you'd put these numbers down, they're in my way." And he turned pettishly over.

Before I could move, the schoolmaster had taken the papers, and was standing over Charlie's couch, with his right hand against the wall, at the level of his head, and his left arm hanging by his side ; and I suppose it was his attitude which made me notice, before he began to speak, what a splendid figure he had, and how strong he looked. He spoke in an odd, abrupt sort of voice, very different from the way he had been talking to me, but he looked down at Charlie so intensely, that I think he felt it through the cushions, and lifted his head.

" When your father has been bringing you down here, or at any time when you have been out amongst other people, have you ever overheard them saying, ' Poor chap ! it's a sad thing,' and things of that kind, as if they were sorry for you ? "

F

Cripple Charlie's face flushed scarlet, and my own cheeks burned, as I looked daggers at the schoolmaster, for what seemed a brutal insensibility to the lame boy's feelings. He did not condescend, however, to meet my eyes. His own were still fixed steadily on Charlie's and he went on.

"*I've heard it.* My ears are quick, and for many a Sunday after I came I caught the whispers behind me as I went up the aisle, 'Poor man!' 'Poor gentleman!' 'He looks bad, too!' One morning an old woman, in a big black bonnet, said, 'Poor soul!' so close to me, that I looked down, and met her withered eyes, full of tears—for me!—and I said, 'Thank you, mother,' and she fingered the sleeve of my coat with her trembling hand (the veins were standing out on it like ropes), and said, 'I've knowed trouble myself, my dear. The Lord bless yours to you!'"

"It must have been Betty Johnson," I interpolated; but the schoolmaster did not even look at me.

"You and I," he said, bending nearer to Cripple Charlie, "have had our share of this life's pain so dealt out to us that any one can see and pity us. My boy, take a fellow-sufferer's word for it, it is wise and good not to shrink from the seeing and pitying. The weight of the cross spreads itself and becomes lighter if one learns to suffer with others as well as with oneself, to take pity and to give it. And as one learns to be pained with the pains of others, one learns to be happy in their happiness and comforted by their sympathy, and then no man's life can be quite empty of pleasure. I don't know if my troubles have been lighter or heavier ones than yours——"

The schoolmaster stopped short, and turned his head so that his face was almost hidden against his hand upon the wall. Charlie's big eyes were full of tears, and I am sure I distinctly felt my ears poke forwards on my head with anxious curiosity to catch what Mr. Wood would tell us about that dreadful time of which he had never spoken.

"When I was your age," he said bluntly, "I was unusually lithe and active and strong for mine. When I was half as old again, I was stronger than any man I knew, and had many a boyish triumph out of my strength, because I was slender and graceful, and this concealed my powers. I had all the energies and ambitions natural to unusual vigour and manly skill. I wanted to be a soldier, but it was not to be, and I spent my youth at a desk in a house of business. I adapted myself, but none the less I chafed whenever I heard of manly exploits, and of the delights and dangers that came of seeing the world. I used to think I could bear anything to cross the seas and see foreign climes. I did cross the Atlantic at last— a convict in a convict ship (GOD help any man who knows what that is!), and I spent the ten best years of my manhood at the hulks working in chains. You've never lost freedom, my lad, so you have never felt what it is not to be able to believe you've got it back. You don't know what it is to turn nervous at the responsibility of being your own master for a whole day, or to wake in a dainty room, with the birds singing at the open window, and to shut your eyes quickly and pray to go on dreaming a bit, because you feel sure you're really in your hammock in the hulks."

The schoolmaster lifted his other hand above his head, and pressed both on it, as if he were in pain. What Charlie was doing I don't know, but I felt so miserable I could not help crying, and had to hunt for my pocket-handkerchief under the table. It was full of acorns, and by the time I had emptied it and dried my eyes, Mr. Wood was lifting Charlie in his arms, and arranging his cushions.

"Oh, thank you!" Charlie said, as he leant back; "how comfortable you have made me!"

"I have been sick-nurse, amongst other trades. For some months I was a hospital warder."

F 2

"Was that when——" Charlie began, and then he stopped short, and said, " Oh, I beg your pardon ! "

" Yes ; it was when I was a convict," said the school-master. " No offence, my boy. If I preach I must try to practise. Jack's eyes are dropping out of his head to hear more of Bermuda, and you and I will put our whims and moods on one side, and we'll all tell travellers' tales together."

Cripple Charlie kept on saying " Thank you," and I know he was very sorry not to be able to think of anything more to say, for he told me so. He wanted to have thanked him better because he knew that Mr. Wood had talked about his having been a convict, when he did not like to talk about it, just to show Charlie that he knew what pain, and not being able to do what you want, feel like, and that Charlie ought not to fancy he was neglected.

And that was the beginning of all the stories the schoolmaster used to tell us, and of the natural history lessons he gave us, and of his teaching me to stuff birds, and do all kinds of things.

We used to say to him, " You're better than the penny numbers, for you're quite as interesting, and we're sure you're true." And the odd thing was that he made Charlie much more contented, because he started him with so many collections, whilst he made me only more and more anxious to see the world.

CHAPTER VII.

THE lane was full of colour that autumn, the first autumn of the convict's return. The leaves turned early, and fell late, and made the hedges gayer than when the dog-roses were out; for not only were the leaves of all kinds brighter than many flowers, but the berries (from the holly and mountain-ash to the hips and haws) were so thick set, and so red and shining, that, as my dear mothei said, "they looked almost artificial."

I remember it well, because of two things. First, that Jem got five of the largest hips we had ever seen off a leafless dog-rose branch which stuck far out of the hedge, and picked the little green coronets off, so that they were smooth and glossy, and egg-shaped, and crimson on one side and yellow on the other ; and then he got an empty chaffinch's nest close by and put the five hips into it, and took it home, and persuaded Alice our new parlourmaid that it was a robin redbreast's nest with eggs in it. And she believed it, for she came from London and knew no better.

The second thing I remember that autumn by, is that everybody expected a hard winter because of the berries being so fine, and the hard winter never came, and the birds ate worms and grubs and left most of the hedge fruits where they were.

November was bright and mild, and the morning frosts

only made the berries all the glossier when the sun came out. We had one or two snow-storms in December, and then we all said, "Now it's coming !" but the snow melted away and left no bones behind. In January the snow lay longer, and left big bones on the moors, and Jem and I made a slide to school on the pack track, and towards the end of the month the milldam froze hard, and we had slides fifteen yards long, and skating ; and Winter seemed to have come back in good earnest to fetch his bones away.

Jem was great fun in frosty weather ; Charlie and I used to die of laughing at him. I think cold made him pugnacious ; he seemed always ready for a row, and was constantly in one. The January frost came in our Christmas holidays, so Jem had lots of time on his hands ; he spent almost all of it out of doors, and he devoted a good deal of it to fighting with the rough lads of the village. There was a standing subject of quarrel, which is a great thing for either tribes or individuals who have a turn that way. A pond at the corner of the lower paddock was fed by a stream which also fed the milldam ; and the milldam was close by, though, as it happened, not on my father's property. Old custom made the milldam the winter resort of all the village sliders and skaters, and my father displayed a good deal of toleration when those who could not find room for a new slide, or wished to practise their "outer edge" in a quiet spot, came climbing over the wall (there was no real thoroughfare) and invaded our pond.

Perhaps it is because gratitude is a fatiguing virtue, or perhaps it is because self-esteem has no practical limits, that favours are seldom regarded as such for long. They are either depreciated, or claimed as rights ; very often both. And what is common in all classes is almost universal amongst the uneducated. You have only to make a system of giving your cast-off clothes to some shivering family, and you will not have to wait long for an eloquent essay on their shabbiness, or for an outburst of sincere indignation if you venture to reserve a warm jacket for a needy relative. Prescriptive rights, in short, grow faster than pumpkins, which is amongst the many warnings life affords us to be just as well as generous. Thence it had come about that the young roughs of the village regarded our pond to all winter intents and purposes as theirs, and my father as only so far and so objectionably concerned in the matter that he gave John Binder a yearly job in patching up the wall which it took them three months' trouble to kick a breach in.

Our neighbours were what is called "very independent" folk. In the grown-up people this was modified by the fact that no one who has to earn his own livelihood can be quite independent of other people ; if he would live he must let live, and throw a little civility into the bargain. But boys of an age when their parents found meals and hobnailed boots for them whether they behaved well or ill, were able to display independence in its roughest form. And when the boys of our neighbourhood were rough, they were very rough indeed.

The village boys had their Christmas holidays about the same time that we had ours, which left them as much spare time for sliding and skating as we had, but they had their dinner at twelve o'clock, whilst we had ours at one, so that any young roughs who wished to damage our pond were just comfortably beginning their mischief as Jem and I were saying grace before meat, and the thought of it took away our appetites again and again.

That winter they were particularly aggravating. The December frost was a very imperfect one, and the mill-dam never bore properly, so the boys swarmed over our pond, which was shallow and safe. Very few of them could even hobble on skates, and those few carried the art no farther than by cutting up the slides. But thaw came on, so that there was no sliding, and then the young roughs amused themselves with stamping holes in the soft ice with their hobnailed heels. When word came to us that they were taking the stones off our wall and pitching them down on to the soft ice below, to act as skaters' stumblingblocks for the rest of that hard winter which we expected, Jem's indignation was not greater than mine. My father was not at home, and indeed, when we had complained before, he rather snubbed us, and said that we could not want the whole of the pond to ourselves, and that he had always lived quietly with his neighbours and we must learn to do the same, and so forth. No action at all calculated to assuage our thirst for revenge was likely to be taken by him, so Jem and I held a council by Charlie's sofa, and it was a council of war. At the end we all three solemnly shook hands, and Charlie was left to write and despatch brief notes of summons to our more distant schoolmates, whilst Jem and I tucked up our trousers, wound our comforters sternly round our throats, and went forth in different directions to gather the rest.

(Having lately been reading about the Highlanders, who used to send round a fiery cross when the clans were called to battle, I should have liked to do so in this instance ; but as some of the Academy boys were no greater readers than Jem, they might not have known what it meant, so we abandoned the notion.)

There was not an Academy boy worth speaking of who was in time for dinner the following day ; and several of them brought brothers, or cousins to the fray. By half-past twelve we had crept down the field that was on the other side of our wall, ar.d had hidden ourselves in various corners of a cattle-shed, where a big cart and some sail-cloth and a turnip heap provided us with ambush. By-and-by certain familiar whoops and hullohs announced that the enemy was coming. One or two bigger boys

made for the dam (which I confess was a relief to us),
but our own particular foes advanced with a rush upon the
wall.

"They hevn't coomed yet, hev they?" we heard the
sexton's son say, as he peeped over at our pond.

"Noa," was the reply. "It's not gone one yet."

"It's gone one by t' church. I yeard it as we was
coming up t' lane."

"T' church clock's always hafe-an-hour fasst, thee
knows."

"It isn't!"

"It is."

"T' church clock's t' one to go by, anyhow," the sexton's
son maintained.

His friend guffawed aloud.

"And it's a reight un to go by too, my sakes! when
thee feyther shifts t' time back'ards and for'ards every
Sunday morning to suit hissen."

"To suit hissen! To suit t' ringers, ye mean!" said
the sexton's son.

"What's thou to do wi' t' ringers?" was the reply,
enforced apparently by a punch in the back, and the two
lads came cuffing and struggling up the field, much to my
alarm, but fortunately they were too busy to notice us.

Meanwhile, the rest had not been idle at the wall. Jem
had climbed on the cart, and peeping through a brick hole
he could see that they had with some difficulty disengaged
a very heavy stone. As we were turning our heads to
watch the two lads fighting near our hiding-place, we
heard the stone strike with a heavy thud upon the rotten
ice below, and it was echoed by a groan of satisfaction
from above.

("Ready!" I whispered.)

"Yon'll break somebody's nose when it's frosted in,"
cried Bob Furniss, in a tone of sincere gratification.

"Eh, Tim Binder! there'll be a rare job for thee feyther

next spring, fettling up this wall, by t' time we've done wi' it."

" Let me come," we heard Tim say.   " Thou can't handle a stone.   Let me come.   Th' ice is as soft as loppered milk, and i' ten minutes I'll fill yon bit they're so chuff of skating on, as thick wi' stones as a quarry."

(" Now ! " I said.)

Our foes considerably outnumbered us, but I think they were at a disadvantage.   They had worked off a good deal of their steam, and ours was at explosion point.   We took them by surprise and in the rear.   They had had some hard exercise, and we were panting to begin.   As a matter of fact those who could get away ran away.   We caught all we could, and punched and pummelled and rolled them in the snow to our hearts' content.

Jem never was much of a talker, and I never knew him speak when he was fighting ; but three several times on this occasion, I heard him say very stiffly and distinctly (he was on the top of Tim Binder), " I'll fettle thee ! I'll fettle thee ! I'll fettle thee ! "

The battle was over, the victory was ours, but the campaign was not ended, and thenceforward the disadvantages would be for us.   Even real warfare is complicated when men fight with men less civilized than themselves ; and we had learnt before now that when we snowballed each other or snowballed the rougher " lot " of village boys, we did so under different conditions.   *We* had our own code of honour and fairness, but Bob Furniss was not above putting a stone into a snowball if he owed a grudge.

So when we heard a rumour that the bigger " roughs " were going to join the younger ones, and lie in wait to " pay us off " the first day we came down to the ice, I cannot say we felt comfortable, though we resolved to be courageous.   Meanwhile, the thaw continued, which suspended operations, and gave time, which is good for healing ; and Christmas came, and we and our foes met and mingled in the mummeries of the season, and wished each other Happy New Years, and said nothing about the pond.

How my father came to hear of the matter we did not know at the time, but one morning he summoned Jem and me, and bade us tell him all about it. I was always rather afraid of my father, and I should have made out a very stammering story, but Jem flushed up like a turkey-cock, and gave our version of the business very straightforwardly. The other side of the tale my father had evidently heard, and we fancied he must have heard also of the intended attack on us, for it never took place, and we knew of interviews which he had with John Binder and others of our neighbours ; and when the frost came in January, we found that the stones had been taken out of the pond, and my father gave us a sharp lecture against being quarrelsome and giving ourselves airs, and it ended with—" The pond is mine. I wish you to remember it because it makes it your duty to be hospitable and civil to the boys I allow to go on it. And I have very decidedly warned them and their parents to remember it, because if my permission for fair amusement is abused to damage and trespass, I shall withdraw the favour and prosecute intruders. But the day I shut up my pond from my neighbours, I shall forbid you and Jack to go on it again unless the fault is more entirely on one side than it's likely to be when boys squabble."

My father waved our dismissal, but I hesitated.

" The boys won't think we told tales to you to get out of another fight ? " I gasped.

" Everybody knows perfectly well how I heard. It came to the sexton's ears, and he very properly informed me."

I felt relieved, and the first day we had on the ice went off very fairly. The boys were sheepish at first and slow to come on, and when they had assembled in force they were inclined to be bullying. But Jem and I kept our tempers, and by-and-by my father came down to see us, and headed a long slide in which we and our foes were combined. As he left he pinched Jem's frosty ear, and said, "Let me hear if there's any real malice, but don't double your fists at every trifle. Slide and let slide ! slide and let slide ! " And he took a pinch of snuff and departed.

And Jem was wonderfully peaceable for the rest of the day. A word from my father went a long way with him. They were very fond of each other.

I had no love of fighting for fighting's sake, and I had other interests besides sliding and skating ; so I was well satisfied that we got through the January frost without further breaches of the peace. Towards the end of the month we all went a good deal upon the milldam, and Mr. Wood (assisted by me as far as watching, handing tools and asking questions went) made a rough sledge, in which he pushed Charlie before him as he skated ; and I believe the village boys, as well as his own schoolfellows, were glad that Cripple Charlie had a share in the winter fun, for wherever Mr. Wood drove him, both sliders and skaters made way.

And even on the pond there were no more real battles that winter. Only now and then some mischievous urchin tripped up our brand new skates, and begged our pardon as he left us on our backs. And more than once, when "the island " in the middle of the pond was a very fairyland of hoarfrosted twigs and snow-plumed larches, I have seen its white loveliness rudely shaken, and skating round to discover the cause, have beheld Jem, with cheeks redder than his scarlet comforter, return an " accidental " shove with interest ; or, posed like a ruffled robin red-breast, to defend a newly-made slide against intruders.

CHAPTER VIII.

" He it was who sent the snowflakes
Sifting, hissing through the forest ;
Froze the ponds, the lakes, the rivers,
*   *   *   *   *   *
Shinbegis, the diver, feared not."
The Song of Hiawatha.

THE first day of February was mild, and foggy, and
cloudy, and in the night I woke feeling very hot, and
threw off my quilt, and heard the dripping of soft rain in
the dark outside, and thought, " There goes our skating."
Towards morning, however, I woke again, and had to pull
the quilt back into its place, and when I started after
breakfast to see what the dam looked like, there was a
sharpish frost, which, coming after a day of thaw, had
given the ice such a fine smooth surface as we had not
had for long.

I felt quite sorry for Jem, because he was going in the
dogcart with my father to see a horse, and as I hadn't
got him to skate with, I went down to the farm after
breakfast, to see what Charlie and the Woods were going
to do.   Charlie was not well, but Mr. Wood said he
would come to the dam with me after dinner, as he had
to go to the next village on business, and the dam lay in
his way.

" Keep to the pond this morning, Jack," he added, to
my astonishment.   " Remember it thawed all yesterday ;
and if the wheel was freed and has been turning, it has
run water off from under the ice, and all may not be sound
that's smooth."

The pond was softer than it looked, but the milldam

was most tempting. A sheet of "glare ice," as Americans say, smooth and clear as a newly-washed window-pane. I did not go on it, but I brought Mr. Wood to it in the afternoon, in the full hope that he would give me leave.

We found several young men on the bank, some fastening their skates and some trying the ice with their heels, and as we stood there the numbers increased, and most of them went on without hesitation; and when they rushed in groups together, I noticed that the ice slightly swayed.

" The ice bends a good deal," said Mr. Wood to a man standing next to us.

" They say it's not so like to break when it bends," was the reply ; and the man moved on.

A good many of the elder men from the village had come up, and a group, including John Binder, now stood alongside of us.

" There's a good sup of water atop of it," said the mason ; and I noticed then that the ice seemed to look wetter, like newly-washed glass still, but like glass that wants wiping dry.

" I'm afraid the ice is not safe," said the schoolmaster.

" It's a tidy thickness, sir," said John Binder, and a heavy man, with his hands in his pockets and his back turned to us, stepped down and gave two or three jumps, and then got up again, and, with his back still turned towards us, said—

" It's reight enough."

" It's right enough for one man, but not for a crowd, I'm afraid. Was the waterwheel freed last night, do you know ? "

" It was loosed last night, but it's froz again," said a bystander.

" It's not freezing now," said the schoolmaster, " and you may see how much larger that weak place where the stream is has got since yesterday. However," he added, good-humouredly, " I suppose you think you know your own milldam and its ways better than I can ? "

" Well," said the heavy man, still with his back to us, " I reckon we've slid on this dam a many winters afore *you* come. No offence, I hope ? "

" By no means," said the schoolmaster ; " but if you old hands do begin to feel doubtful as the afternoon goes on, call off those lads at the other end in good time. And if you could warn them not to go in rushes together—but perhaps they would not listen to you," he added with a spice of malice.

" I don't suppose they would, sir," said John Binder, candidly. " They're very venturesome, is lads."

" I reckon they'll suit themselves," said the heavy man, and he jumped on to the ice, and went off, still with his back to us.

" If I hadn't lived so many years out of England and out of the world," said the schoolmaster, turning to me with a half vexed laugh, " I don't suppose I should discredit myself to no purpose by telling fools they are in danger. Jack ! will you promise me not to go on the dam this afternoon ?"

" It is dangerous, is it ?" I asked reluctantly ; for I wanted sorely to join the rest.

" That's a matter of opinion, it seems. But I have a wish that you should not go on till I come back. I'll be as quick as I can. Promise me."

" I promise," said I.

" Will you walk with me ?" he asked. But I refused. I thought I would rather watch the others ; and accordingly, after I had followed the schoolmaster with my eyes as he strode off at a pace that promised soon to bring him back, I put my hands into my pockets and joined the groups of watchers on the bank. I suppose if I had thought about it, I might have observed that though I was dawdling about, my nose and ears and fingers were not nipped.

Mr. Wood was right,—it had not been freezing for hours past.

The first thing I looked for was the heavy man. He was so clumsy looking that I quite expected him to fall when he walked off on to ice only fit for skaters. But as I looked closer I saw that the wet on the top was beginning to have a curdled look, and that the glassiness of the milldam was much diminished. The heavy man's heavy boots got good foothold, and several of his friends, seeing this, went after him. And my promise weighed sorely on me.

The next thing that drew my attention was a lad of about seventeen, who was skating really well. Indeed, everybody was looking at him, for he was the only one of the villagers who could perform in any but the clumsiest fashion, and, with an active interest that hovered between jeering and applause, his neighbours followed him up and down the dam. As I might not go on, I wandered up and down the bank too, and occasionally joined in a murmured cheer when he deftly evaded some intentional blunderer, or cut a figure at the request of his particular friends. I got tired at last, and went down to the pond, where I ploughed about for a time on my skates in solitude, for the pond was empty. Then I ran up to the house to see if Jem had come back, but he had not, and I returned to the dam to wait for the schoolmaster.

The crowd was larger than before, for everybody's work-hours were over ; and the skater was still displaying himself. He was doing very difficult figures now, and I ran round to where the bank was covered with people watching him. In the minute that followed I remember three things with curious distinctness. First, that I saw Mr. Wood coming back, only one field off, and beckoned to him to be quick, because the lad was beginning to cut a double three backwards, and I wanted the schoolmaster to see it. Secondly, that the sight of him seemed suddenly to bring to my mind that we were all on the far side of the dam, the side he thought dangerous. And thirdly, that, quickly as my eyes passed from Mr. Wood to the skater, I caught sight of a bloated-looking young man, whom we all knew as a sort of typical " bad lot," standing with another man who was a great better, and from a movement between them, it just flashed through my head that they were betting as to whether the lad would cut the double three backwards or not.

He cut one—two—and then he turned too quickly and his skate caught in the softening ice, and when he came headlong, his head struck, and where it struck it went through. It looked so horrible that it was a relief to see him begin to struggle ; but the weakened ice broke around him with every effort, and he went down.

For many a year afterwards I used to dream of his face as he sank, and of the way the ice heaved like the breast of some living thing, and fell back, and of the heavy waves that rippled over it out of that awful hole. But great as was the shock, it was small to the storm of shame and agony that came over me when I realized that every com-rade who had been around the lad had saved himself by a rush to the bank, where we huddled together, a gaping crowd of foolhardy cowards, without skill to do anything or heart to dare anything to save him.

At the time it maddened me so, that I felt that if I could not help the lad I would rather be drowned in the hole with him, and I began to scramble in a foolish way down the bank, but John Binder caught me by the arm and pulled me back, and said (I suppose to soothe me),

" Yon's the schoolmaster, sir ;" and then I saw Mr. Wood fling himself over the hedge by the alder thicket (he was rather good at high jumps), and come flying along the bank towards us, when he said—

" What's the matter ? "

G

I threw my arms round him and sobbed, "He was cutting a double three backwards, and he went in."

Mr. Wood unclasped my arms and turned to the rest. "What have you done with him?" he said. "Did he hurt himself?"

If the crowd was cowardly and helpless, it was not indifferent; and I shall never forget the haggard faces that turned by one impulse, where a dozen grimy hands pointed—to the hole.

"He's drowned dead." "He's under t' ice." "He went right down," several men hastened to reply, but most of them only enforced the mute explanation of their pointed finger, with "He's yonder."

For yet an instant I don't think Mr. Wood believed it, and then he seized the man next to him (without looking, for he was blind with rage) and said—

"He's yonder, *and you're here?*"

As it happened, it was the man who had talked with his back to us. He was very big and very heavy, but he reeled when Mr. Wood shook him, like a feather caught by a storm.

"You were foolhardy enough an hour ago," said the schoolmaster. "Won't one of you venture on to your own dam to help a drowning man?"

"There's none on us can swim, sir," said John Binder "It's a bad job"—and he gave a sob that made me begin to cry again, and several other people too—"but where'd be t' use of drowning five or six more atop of him?"

"Can any of you run if you can't swim?" said the schoolmaster. "Get a stout rope—as fast as you can, and send somebody for the doctor and a bottle of brandy, and a blanket or two to carry him home in. Jack! Hold these."

I took his watch and his purse, and he went down the bank and walked on to the ice; but after a time his feet went through as the skater's head had gone.

"It ain't a bit of use. There's naught to be done," said the bystanders : for, except those who had run to do Mr. Wood's bidding, we were all watching and all huddled closer to the edge than ever. The schoolmaster went down on his hands and knees, on which a big lad, with his hands in his trouser pockets, guffawed.

"What's he up to now?" he asked.

"Thee may haud thee tongue if thee can do naught," said a mill-girl who had come up. "I reckon he knows what he's efter better nor thee." She had pushed to the front, and was crouched upon the edge, and seemed very much excited. "GOD bless him for trying to save t' best lad in t' village i' any fashion, say I ! There's them that's nearer kin to him and not so kind."

Perhaps the strict justice of this taunt prevented a reply (for there lurks some fairness in the roughest of us), or perhaps the crowd, being chiefly men, knew from experience that there are occasions when it is best to let a woman say her say.

"Ye see he's trying to spread hisself out," John Binder explained in pacific tones. "I reckon he thinks it'll bear him if he shifts half of his weight on to his hands."

The girl got nearer to the mason, and looked up at him with her eyes full of tears.

"Thank ye, John," she said. "D'ye think he'll get him out?"

"Maybe, he will, my lass. He's a man that knows what he's doing. I'll say so much for him."

"Nay!" added the mason sorrowfully. "Th' ice 'll never hold him—his hand's in—and there goes his knee. Maester ! maester !" he shouted, "Come off ! come off !" and many a voice besides mine echoed him, "Come off ! come off ! "

The girl got John Binder by the arm, and said hoarsely, "Fetch him off ! He's a reight good 'un—over good to be drownded, if—if it's of no use." And she sat down on the bank, and pulled her millshawl over her head, and cried as I had never seen anyone cry before.

I was so busy watching her that I did not see that Mr. Wood had got back to the bank. Several hands were held out to help him up, but he shook his head and said— " Got a knife? "

Two or three jack knives were out in an instant. He pointed to the alder thicket. " I want two poles," he said, " sixteen feet long, if you can, and as thick as my wrist at the bottom."

" All right, sir."

He sat down on the bank, and I rushed up and took one of his cold wet hands in both mine, and said, " Please please, don't go on any more."

" He must be dead ever so long ago," I added, repeating what I had heard.

" He hasn't been in the water ten minutes," said the schoolmaster, laughing. " Jack! Jack! you're not half ready for travelling yet. You must learn not to lose your head and your heart and your wits and your sense of time in this fashion, if you mean to be any good at a pinch to yourself or your neighbours. Has the rope come? "

" No, sir."

" Those poles? " said the schoolmaster, getting up.

" They're here! " I shouted, as a young forest of poles came towards us, so willing had been the owners of the jack-knives. The thickest had been cut by the heavy man, and Mr. Wood took it first.

" Thank you, friend," he said. The man didn't speak, and he turned his back as usual, but he gave a sideways surly nod before he turned. The schoolmaster chose a second pole, and then pushed both before him right out on to the ice, in such a way that with the points touching each other they formed a sort of huge A, the thicker ends being the nearer to the bank.

" Now Jack," said he, " pay attention; and no more

blubbering, There's always plenty of time for giving way *afterwards.*"

As he spoke he scrambled on to the poles, and began to work himself and them over the ice, wriggling in a kind of snake fashion in the direction of the hole. We watched him breathlessly, but within ten yards of the hole he stopped. He evidently dared not go on ; and the same thought seized all of us—"Can he get back?" Spreading his legs and arms he now lay flat upon the poles, peering towards the pole as if to try if he could see anything of the drowning man. It was only for an instant, then he rolled over on to the rotten ice, smashed through, and sank more suddenly than the skater had done.

The mill-girl jumped up with a wild cry and rushed to the water, but John Binder pulled her back as he had pulled me. Martha, our housemaid, said afterwards (and was ready to take oath on the gilt-edged church service my mother gave her) that the girl was so violent that it took fourteen men to hold her ; but Martha wasn't there, and I only saw two, one at each arm, and when she fainted they laid her down and left her, and hurried back to see what was going on. For tenderness is an acquired grace in men, and it was not common in our neighbourhood.

What was going on was that John Binder had torn his hat from his head and was saying, " I don't know if there's aught we *can* do, but I can't go home myself and leave him yonder. I'm a married man with a family, but I don't vally *my* life if——"

But the rest of this speech was drowned in noise more eloquent than words, and then it broke into cries of " See thee !—It is—it's t' maester ! and he has— no !—yea !—he *has*—he's gotten him. Polly, lass ! he's fetched up thy Arthur by t' hair of his head."

It was strictly true. The schoolmaster told me afterwards how it was. When he found that the ice would bear no longer, he rolled into the water on purpose, but, to his horror, he felt himself seized by the drowning man, which pulled him suddenly down. The lad had risen once, it seems, though we had not seen him, and had got a breath of air at the hole, but the edge broke in his numbed fingers, and he sank again and drifted under the ice. When he rose the second time, by an odd chance it was just where Mr. Wood broke in, and his clutch of the schoolmaster nearly cost both their lives.

" If ever," said Mr. Wood, when he was talking about it afterwards, " if ever, Jack, when you're out in the world you get under water, and somebody tries to save you ; when he grips *you*, don't seize *him*, if you can muster self-control to avoid it. If you cling to him, you'll either drown both, or you'll force him to do as I did—throttle you, to keep you quiet."

" Did you ? " I gasped.

" Of course I did. I got him by the throat and dived with him—the only real risk I ran, as I did not know how deep the dam was."

" It's an old quarry," said I.

" I know now. We went down well, and I squeezed his throat as we went. As soon as he was still we naturally rose, and I turned on my back and got him by the head. I looked about for the hole, and saw it glimmering above me like a moon in a fog, and then up we came."

When they did come up, our joy was so great that for the moment we felt as if all was accomplished ; but far the hardest part really was to come. When the schoolmaster clutched the poles once more, and drove one under the lad's arms and under his own left arm, and so kept his burden afloat whilst he broke a swimming-path for himself with the other, our admiration of his cleverness gave place to the blessed thought that it might now be possible to help him. The sight of the poles seemed suddenly to suggest it, and in a moment every spare pole had been seized, and, headed by our heavy friend, eight or ten men plunged in, and, smashing the ice before them, waded out to meet the schoolmaster. On the bank we were dead silent ; in the water they neither stopped nor spoke till it was breast high round their leader.

I have often thought, and have always felt quite sure, that if the heavy man had gone on till the little grey waves and the bits of ice closed over him, not a soul of those who followed him would—nay, *could*—have turned back. Heroism, like cowardice, is contagious, and I do not think there was one of us by that time who would have feared to dare or grudged to die.

As it was, the heavy man stood still and shouted for the rope. It had come, and perhaps it was not the smallest effect of the day's teaching, that those on the bank payed it out at once to those in the water till it reached the leader, without waiting to ask why he wanted it. The grace of obedience is slow to be learnt by disputatious northmen, but we had had some hard teaching that afternoon.

When the heavy man got the rope he tied the middle part of it round himself, and, coiling the shorter end, he sent it, as if it had been a quoit, skimming over the ice towards the schoolmaster. As it unwound itself it slid along, and after a struggle Mr. Wood grasped it. I fancy he fastened it round the lad's body ; and got his own hands freer to break the ice before them. Then the heavy man turned, and the long end of the line, passing from hand to hand in the water, was seized upon the bank by every one who could get hold of it. I never was more squeezed and buffeted in my life ; but we fairly fought for the privilege of touching if it were but a strand of the rope that dragged them in.

And a flock of wild birds, resting on their journey at the other end of the milldam, rose in terror and pursued their seaward way ; so wild and so prolonged were the echoes of that strange, speechless cry in which collective man gives vent to overpowering emotion.

It is odd, when one comes to think of it, but I know it
is true, for two sensible words would have stuck in my own
throat and choked me, but I cheered till I could cheer no
longer.

CHAPTER IX.

" In doubtful matters Courage may do much :—In desperate,
—Patience."

Old Proverb.

THE young skater duly recovered, and thenceforward
Mr. Wood's popularity in the village was established,
and the following summer he started a swimming-class,
to which the young men flocked with more readiness
than they commonly showed for efforts made to improve
them.

For my own part I had so realised, to my shame, that
one may feel very adventurous and yet not know how to
venture or what to venture in the time of need, that my
whole heart was set upon getting the schoolmaster to
teach me to swim and to dive, with any other lessons in
preparedness of body and mind which I was old enough
to profit by.   And if the true tales of his own experiences
were more interesting than the Penny Numbers, it was
better still to feel that one was qualifying in one's own
proper person for a life of adventure.

During the winter Mr. Wood built a boat, which was
christened the *Adela*, after his wife.   It was an interesting
process to us all.   I hung about and did my best to be
helpful, and both Jem and I spoiled our every-day
trousers, and rubbed the boat's sides, the day she was
painted.   It was from the *Adela* that Jem and I
had our first swimming-lessons, Mr. Wood lowering us
with a rope under our arms, by which he gave us as

much support as was needed, whilst he taught us how to strike out.

We had swimming-races on the canal, and having learned to swim and dive without our clothes, we learnt to do so in them, and found it much more difficult for swimming and easier for diving. It was then that the trousers we had damaged when the *Adela* was built came in most usefully, and saved us from having to attempt the at least equally difficult task of persuading my mother to let us spoil good ones in an amusement which had the unpardonable quality of being " very odd."

Dear old Charlie had as much fun out of the boat as we had, though he could not learn to dive. He used to look as if every minute of a pull up the canal on a sunny evening gave him pleasure ; and the brown Irish spaniel Jem gave him used to swim after the boat and look up in Charlie's face as if it knew how he enjoyed it. And later on, Mr. Wood taught Bob Furniss to row and Charlie to steer ; so that Charlie could sometimes go out and feel quite free to stop the boat when and where he liked. That was after he started so many collections of insects and water-weeds, and shells, and things you can only see under a microscope. Bob and he used to take all kinds of pots and pans and nets and dippers with them, so that Charlie could fish up what he wanted, and keep things separate. He was obliged to keep the live things he got for his fresh-water aquarium in different jam-pots, because he could never be sure which would eat up which till he knew them better, and the water-scorpions and the dragon-fly larvæ ate everything. Bob Furniss did not mind pulling in among the reeds and waiting as long as you wanted. Mr. Wood sometimes wanted to get back to his work, but Bob never wanted to get back to his. And he was very good-natured about getting into the water and wading and grubbing for things ; indeed, I think he got to like it.

At first Mr. Wood had been rather afraid of trusting Charlie with him. He thought Bob might play tricks with the boat, even though he knew how to manage her, when there was only one helpless boy with him. But Mrs. Furniss said, " Nay! Our Bob's a bad 'un, but he's not one of that sort, he'll not plague them that's afflicted." And she was quite right; for though his father said he could be trusted with nothing else, we found he could be trusted with Cripple Charlie.

It was two days before the summer holidays came to an end that Charlie asked me to come down to the farm and help him to put away his fern collection and a lot of other things into the places that he had arranged for them in his room ; for now that the schoolroom was wanted again, he could not leave his papers and boxes about there. Charlie lived at the farm altogether now. He was better there than on the moors, so he boarded there and went home for visits.   The room Mrs. Wood had given him was the one where the old miser had slept. In a memorandum left with his will it appeared that he had expressed a wish that the furniture of that room should not be altered, which was how they knew it was his. So Mrs. Wood had kept the curious old oak bed (the back of which was fastened into the wall), and an old oak press, with a great number of drawers with brass handles to them, and all the queer furniture that she found there, just as it was.   Even the brass warming-pan was only rubbed and put back in its place, and the big bellows were duly hung up by the small fireplace. But everything was so polished up and cleaned, the walls repapered with a soft grey-green paper spangled with dogdaisies, and the room so brightened up with fresh blinds and bedclothes, and a bit of bright carpet, that it did not look in the least dismal, and Charlie was very proud and very fond of it.   It had two windows, one where the beehive was, and one very sunny one, where he had a balm of gilead that Isaac's wife gave him, and his old medicine-bottles full of cuttings on the upper ledge. The old women used to send him "slippings" off their fairy roses and myrtles and fuchsias, and they rooted very well in that window, there was so much sun.

Charlie had only just begun a fern collection, and I had saved my pocket-money (I did not want it for anything else) and had bought him several quires of cartridge-paper ; and Dr. Brown had given him a packet of medicine-labels to cut up into strips to fasten his specimens in with, and the collection looked very well and very scientific ; and all that remained was to find a good place to put it away in. The drawers of the press were of all shapes and sizes, but there were two longish very shallow ones that just matched each other, and when I pulled one of them out, and put the fern-papers in, they fitted exactly, and the drawer just held half the collection. I called Charlie to look, and he hobbled up on his crutches and was delighted, but he said he should like to put the others in himself, so I got him into a chair, and shut up the full drawer and pulled out the empty one, and went downstairs for the two mole-skins we were curing, and the glue-pot, and the toffy-tin, and some other things that had to be cleared out of the schoolroom now the holidays were over.

When I came back the fern-papers were still outside, and Charlie was looking flushed and cross.

" I don't know how you managed," he said, " but I can't get them in. This drawer must be shorter than the other ; it doesn't go nearly so far back."

" Oh yes, it does, Charlie ! " I insisted, for I felt as certain as people always do feel about little details of that kind. " The drawers are exactly alike ; you can't have got the fern-sheets quite flush with each other," and I began to arrange the trayful of things I had brought upstairs in the bottom of the cupboard.

" I *know* it's the drawer," I heard Charlie say. (" He's as obstinate as possible," thought I.)

Then I heard him banging at the wood with his fists
and his crutch. (" He *is* in a temper ! " was my mental
comment.) After this my attention was distracted for a
second or two by seeing what I thought was a bit of toffy
left in the tin, and biting it and finding it was a piece of
sheet-glue.   I had not spit out all the disgust of it, when
Charlie called me in low, awe-struck tones : " Jack ! come
here.   Quick ! "

I ran to him.   The drawer was open, but it seemed to
have another drawer inside it, a long narrow, shallow one.

"I hit the back, and this sprang out," said Charlie.
" It's a secret drawer—and look ! "

I did look.   The secret drawer was closely packed with
rolls of thin leaflets, which we were old enough to
recognise as bank-notes, and with little bags of wash-
leather ; and when Charlie opened the little bags they
were filled with gold.

There was a paper with the money, written by the old
miser, to say that it was a codicil to his will, and that
the money was all for Mrs. Wood.   Why he had not left
it to her in the will itself seemed very puzzling, but his
lawyer (whom the Woods consulted about it) said that he
always did things in a very eccentric way, but generally
for some sort of reason, even if it were rather a freaky one,
and that perhaps he thought that the relations would be
less spiteful at first if they did not know about the money,
and that Mrs. Wood would soon find it, if she used and
valued his old press.

I don't quite know whether there was any fuss with the
relations about this part of the bequest, but I suppose the
lawyer managed it all right, for the Woods got the money
and gave up the school.   But they kept the old house,
and bought some more land, and Walnut-tree Academy
became Walnut-tree Farm once more.   And Cripple
Charlie lived on with them, and he was so happy, it really
seemed as if my dear mother was right when she said to

my father, " I am so pleased, my dear, for that poor boy's sake, I can hardly help crying. He's got two homes and two fathers and mothers, where many a young man has none, as if to make good his affliction to him."

It puzzles me, even now, to think how my father could have sent Jem and me to Crayshaw's School. (Nobody ever called him Mr. Crayshaw except the parents of pupils who lived at a distance. In the neighbourhood he and his whole establishment were lumped under the one word *Crayshaw's*, and as a farmer hard by once said to me, " Crayshaw's is universally disrespected.")

I do not think it was merely because " Crayshaw's " was cheap that we were sent there, though my father had so few reasons to give for his choice that he quoted that among them. A man with whom he had had business dealings (which gave him much satisfaction for some years, and more dissatisfaction afterwards) did really, I think, persuade my father to send us to this school, one evening when they were dining together.

Few things are harder to guess at than the grounds on which an Englishman of my father's type " makes up his mind "; and yet the question is an important one, for an idea once lodged in his head, a conviction once as much his own as the family acres, and you will as soon part him from the one as from the other. I have known little matters of domestic improvements, in which my mother's comfort was concerned and her experience conclusive, for which he grudged a few shillings, and was absolutely impenetrable by her persuasions and representations. And I have known him waste pounds on things of the most curious variety, foisted on him by advertising agents without knowledge, trial, or rational ground of confidence. I suppose that persistency, a glibber tongue than he himself possessed, a mass of printed rubbish which always looks imposing to the unliterary, that primitive combination of authoritativeness and hospitality which makes

some men as ready to say Yes to a stranger as they are to
say No at home, and perhaps some lack of moral courage,
may account for it.   I can clearly remember how quaintly
sheepish my father used to look after committing some
such folly, and how, after the first irrepressible fall of
countenance, my mother would have defended him
against anybody else's opinion, let alone her own.   Young
as I was I could feel that, and had a pretty accurate
estimate of the value of the moral lecture on faith in one's
fellow-creatures, which was an unfailing outward sign of
my father's inward conviction that he had been taken in
by a rogue.   I knew too, well enough, that my mother's
hasty and earnest Amen to this discourse was an equally
reliable token of her knowledge that my father sorely
needed defending, and some instinct made me aware also
that my father knew that this was so.   That he knew that
it was that tender generosity towards one's beloved, in
which so many of her sex so far exceed ours, and not an
intellectual conviction of his wisdom, which made her
support what he had done, and that feeling this he felt
dissatisfied, and snapped at her accordingly.

The dislike my dear mother took to the notion of our
going to Crayshaw's only set seals to our fate, and the
manner of her protests was not more fortunate than the
matter.   She was timid and vacillating from wifely habit,
whilst motherly anxiety goaded her to be persistent and
almost irritable on the subject.   Habitually regarding her
own wishes and views as worthless, she quoted the Woods
at every turn of her arguments, which was a mistake, for
my father was sufficiently like the rest of his neighbours
not to cotton very warmly to people whose tastes,
experiences, and lines of thought were so much out of the
common as those of the ex-convict and his wife.   Moreover, he had made up his mind, and when one has done
that, he is proof against seventy men who can render a
reason.

To rumours which accused "Crayshaw's" of undue severity, of discomfort, of bad teaching and worse manners, my father opposed arguments which he allowed were "oldfashioned" and which were far-fetched from the days of our great-grandfather.

A strict schoolmaster was a good schoolmaster, and if more parents were as wise as Solomon on the subject of the rod, Old England would not be discredited by such a namby-pamby race as young men of the present day seemed by all accounts to be. It was high time the boys did rough it a bit; would my mother have them always tied to her apron-strings? Great Britain would soon be Little Britain if boys were to be brought up like young ladies. As to teaching, it was the fashion to make a fuss about it, and a pretty pass learning brought some folks to, to judge by the papers and all one heard. His own grandfather lived to ninety-seven, and died sitting in his chair, in a bottle-green coat and buff breeches. He wore a pigtail to the day of his death, and never would be contradicted by anybody. He had often told my father that at the school *he* went to, the master signed the receipts for his money with a cross, but the usher was a bit of a scholar, and the boys had cream to their porridge on Sundays. And the old gentleman managed his own affairs to ninety-seven, and threw the doctor's medicine-bottles out of the window then. He died without a doubt on his mind or a debt on his books, and my father (taking a pinch out of Great-Grandfather's snuff-box) hoped Jem and I might do as well.

In short we were sent to "Crayshaw's."

It was not a happy period of my life. It was not a good or wholesome period ; and I am not fond of recalling it. The time came when I shrank from telling Charlie everything, almost as if he had been a girl. His life was lived in such a different atmosphere, under such different conditions I could not trouble him, and I did not believe

he could make allowances for me. But on our first arrival
I wrote him a long letter (Jem never wrote letters), and the
other day he showed it to me. It was a first impression,
but a sufficiently vivid and truthful one, so I give it here.

CRAYSHAW'S (for that's what they call it here, and a
beastly hole it is).

Monday.

MY DEAR OLD CHARLIE,—We came earlier than was
settled, for father got impatient and there was nothing to
stop us, but I don't think old Crayshaw liked our coming
so soon. You never saw such a place, it's so dreary. A
boy showed us straight into the schoolroom. There are
three rows of double desks running down the room and
disgustingly dirty, I don't know what Mrs. Wood would
say, and old Crayshaw's desk is in front of the fire, so that
he can see all the boys sideways, and it just stops any heat
coming to them. And there he was, and I don't think
father liked the look of him particularly, you never saw
an uglier. Such a flaming face and red eyes like Bob
Furniss's ferret and great big whiskers ; but I'll make you
a picture of him, at least I'll make two pictures, for Lewis
Lorraine says he's got no beard on Sundays, and rather a
good one on Saturdays. Lorraine is a very rum fellow,
but I like him. It was he showed us in, and he did catch it
afterwards, but he only makes fun of it. Old Crayshaw's
desk had got a lot of canes on one side of it and a most
beastly dirty snuffy red and green handkerchief on the
other, and an ink-pot in the middle. He made up to father
like anything and told such thumpers. He said there were
six boys in one room, but really there's twelve. Jem and I
sleep together. There's nothing to wash in and no prayers.
If you say them you get boots at your head, and one hit
Jem behind the ear, so I pulled his sleeve and said, " Get
up, you can say them in bed." But you know Jem, and
he said, " Wait till I've done, *God bless father and*

mother," and when he had, he went in and fought, and I
backed him up, and then old Crayshaw found us, and oh,
how he did beat us !

—— *Wednesday.* Old Snuffy is a regular brute, and I
don't care if he finds this and sees what I say. But he
won't, for the milkman is taking it. He always does if
you can pay him. But I've put most of my money into
the bank. Three of the top boys have a bank, and we all
have to deposit, only I kept fourpence in one of my boots.
They give us bank-notes for a penny and a halfpenny ;
they make them themselves. The sweetshop takes them.
They only give you eleven penny notes for a shilling in
the bank, or else it would burst. At dinner we have a lot
of pudding to begin with, and it's very heavy. You can
hardly eat anything afterwards. The first day Lorraine
said quite out loud and very polite, " Did you say *duff
before meat*, young gentlemen ?" and I couldn't help
laughing, and old Snuffy beat his head horridly with his
dirty fists. But Lorraine minds nothing ; he says he
knows old Snuffy will kill him some day, but he says he
doesn't want to live, for his father and mother are dead ;
he only wants to catch old Snuffy in three more boobytraps before he dies. He's caught him in four already.
You see, when old Snuffy is cat-walking he wears goloshes
that he may sneak about better, and the way Lorraine
makes boobytraps is by balancing cans of water on the
door when it's ajar, so that he gets doused, and the can
falls on his head, and strings across the bottom of the
door, not far from the ground, so that he catches his
goloshes and comes down. The other fellows say that old
Crayshaw had a lot of money given him in trust for
Lorraine, and he's spent it all, and Lorraine has no one to
stick up for him, and that's why Crayshaw hates him.

—— *Saturday.* I could not catch the milkman, and
now I've got your letter, though Snuffy read it first. Jem
and I cry dreadful in bed. That's the comfort of being

H

together. I'll try and be as good as I can, but you don't
know what this place is. It's very different to the farm.
Do you remember the row about that book Horace
Simpson got? I wish you could see the books the boys
have here. At least I don't wish it, for I wish I didn't
look at them, the milkman brings them ; he always will if
you can pay him. When I saw old Snuffy find one in
Smith's desk, I expected he would half kill him, but he
didn't do much to him, he only took the book away ; and
Lorraine says he never does beat them much for that, because he doesn't want them to leave off buying them, because he wants them himself. Don't tell the Woods this.
Don't tell mother Jem and I cry, or else she'll be miserable.
I don't so much mind the beatings (Lorraine says you get
hard in time), nor the washing at the sink—nor the duff
puddings—but it is such a beastly hole, and he is such an
old brute, and I feel so dreadful I can't tell you. Give my
love to Mrs. Wood and to Mr. Wood, and to Carlo and to
Mary Anne, and to your dear dear self, and to Isaac when
you see him.

And I am your affectionate friend,

JACK.

P. S. Jem sends his best love, and he's got two black
eyes.

P. S. No. 2. You would be sorry for Lorraine if you
knew him. Sometimes I'm afraid he'll kill himself, for he
says there's really nothing in the Bible about suicide. So
I said—killing yourself is as bad as killing anybody else.
So he said—is stealing from yourself as bad as stealing
from anybody else? And we had a regular *argue*. Some
of the boys argle-bargle on Sundays, he says, but most of
them fight. When they differ, they put tin-tacks with
the heads downwards on each other's places on the forms
in school, and if they run into you and you scream, old
Snuffy beats you. The milkman brings them, by the half

ɔunce, with very sharp points, if you can pay him. Most of the boys are a horrid lot, and so dirty. Lorraine is as dirty as the rest, and I asked him why, and he said it was because he'd thrown up the sponge ; but he got rather red, and he's washed himself cleaner this morning. He says he has an uncle in India, and some time ago he wrote to him, and told him about Crayshaw's, and gave the milkman a diamond pin, that had been his father's, and Snuffy didn't know about, to post it with plenty of stamps, but he thinks he can't have put plenty on, for no answer ever came. I've told him I'll post another one for him in the holidays. Don't say anything about this back in your letters. He reads 'em all.

—— *Monday.* I've caught the milkman at last, he'll take it this evening. The lessons here are regular rubbish. I'm so glad I've a good knife, for if you have you can dig holes in your desk to put collections in. The boy next to me has earwigs, but you have to keep a look-out, or he puts them in your ears. I turned up a stone near the sink this morning, and got five woodlice for mine. It's considered a very good collection.

CHAPTER X.

"But none inquired how Peter used the rope,
Or what the bruise that made the stripling stoop ;
None could the ridges on his back behold,
None sought him shiv'ring in the winter's cold.
    *   *   *   *   *
The pitying women raised a clamour round."
              Crabbe, " *The Borough.*"

A GREAT many people say that all suffering is good for one, and I am sure pain does improve one very often, and

H 2

in many ways.   It teaches one sympathy, it softens and it
strengthens.   But I cannot help thinking that there are
some evil experiences which only harden and stain.   The
best I can say for what we endured at Crayshaw's is that
it *was* experience, and so I suppose could not fail to teach
one something, which, as Jem says, was "more than
Snuffy did."

The affection with which I have heard men speak of
their schooldays and schoolmasters makes me know that
Mr. Crayshaw was not a common type of pedagogue.   He
was not a common type of man, happily ; but I have met
other specimens in other parts of the world in which his
leading quality was as fully developed, though their lives
had nothing in common with his except the opportunities
of irresponsible power.

The old wounds are scars now, it is long past and over,
and I am grown up, and have roughed it in the world ;
but I say quite deliberately that I believe that Mr. Crayshaw was not merely a harsh man, uncultured and incon-
siderate, having need and greed of money, taking pupils
cheap, teaching them little or nothing, and keeping a kind
of rough order with too much flogging,—but that the
mischief of him was that he was possessed by a passion
(not the less fierce because it was unnatural) which grew
with indulgence and opportunity, as other passions grow,
and that this was a passion for cruelty.

One does not rough it long in this wicked world without
seeing more cruelty both towards human beings and
towards animals than one cares to think about ; but a
large proportion of common cruelty comes of ignorance,
bad tradition and uncultured sympathies.   Some painful
outbreaks of inhumanity, where one would least expect it,
are no doubt strictly to be accounted for by disease.   But
over and above these common and these exceptional
instances, one cannot escape the conviction that irresponsible power is opportunity in all hands and a direct

temptation in some to cruelty, and that it affords horrible development to those morbid cases in which cruelty becomes a passion.

That there should ever come a thirst for blood in men as well as tigers, is bad enough but conceivable when linked with deadly struggle, or at the wild dictates of revenge. But a lust for cruelty growing fiercer by secret and unchecked indulgence, a hideous pleasure in seeing and inflicting pain, seems so inhuman a passion that we shrink from acknowledging that this is ever so.

And if it belonged to the past alone, to barbarous despotisms or to savage life, one might wisely forget it ; for the dark pages of human history are unwholesome as well as unpleasant reading, unless the mind be very sane in a body very sound. But those in whose hands lie the destinies of the young and of the beasts who serve and love us, of the weak, the friendless, the sick and the insane, have not, alas ! this excuse for ignoring the black records of man's abuse of power !

The records of its abuse in the savage who loads women's slender shoulders with his burdens, leaves his sick to the wayside jackal, and knocks his aged father on the head when he is past work ; the brutality of slave-drivers, the iniquities of vice-maddened eastern despots ;— such things those who never have to deal with them may afford to forget.

But men who act for those who have no natural protectors, or have lost the power of protecting themselves, who legislate for those who have no voice in the making of laws, and for the brute creation, which we win to our love and domesticate for our convenience ; who apprentice pauper boys and girls, who meddle with the matters of weak women, sick persons, and young children, are bound to face a far sadder issue. That even in these days, when human love again and again proves itself not only stronger than death, but stronger than all the selfish hopes of life ;

when the everyday manners of everyday men are conces-
sions of courtesy to those who have not the strength to
claim it ; when children and pet animals are spoiled to
grotesqueness ; when the good deeds of priest and physi-
cian, nurse and teacher, surpass all earthly record of them
—man, as man, is no more to be trusted with unchecked
power than hitherto.

The secret histories of households, where power should
be safest in the hands of love ; of hospitals, of schools, of
orphanages, of poorhouses, of lunatic-asylums, of religious
communities founded for GOD'S worship and man's pity,
of institutions which assume the sacred title as well as the
responsibilities of Home—from the single guardian of
some rural idiot to the great society which bears the
blessed Name of Jesus—have not each and all their dark
stories, their hushed-up scandals, to prove how dire is the
need of public opinion without, and of righteous care
within, that what is well begun should be well continued ?

If anyone doubts this, let him pause on each instance,
one by one, and think of what he has seen, and heard, and
read, and known of ; and he will surely come to the conviction that human nature cannot, even in the very service
of charity, be safely trusted with the secret exercise of
irresponsible power, and that no light can be too fierce to
beat upon and purify every spot where the weak are
committed to the tender mercies of the consciences of the
strong.

Mr. Crayshaw's conscience was not a tender one, and
very little light came into his out-of-the-way establishment,
and no check whatever upon his cruelty. It had various
effects on the different boys. It killed one in my day, and
the doctor (who had been "in a difficulty" some years
back, over a matter through which Mr. Crayshaw helped
him with bail and testimony) certified to heart disease,
and we all had our pocket-handkerchiefs washed, and went
to the funeral. And Snuffy had cards printed with a

black edge, and several angels and a broken lily, and the
hymn—

"Death has been here and borne away
    A brother from our side ;
Just in the morning of his day,
    As young as we he died,"

—and sent them to all the parents.   But the pupils had to
pay for the stamps.   And my dear mother cried dreadfully,
first because she was so sorry for the boy, and secondly
because she ever had felt uncharitably towards Mr.
Crayshaw.

Crayshaw's cruelty crushed others, it made liars and
sneaks of boys naturally honest, and it produced in
Lorraine an unchildlike despair that was almost grand, so
far was the spirit above the flesh in him.   But I think its
commonest and strangest result was to make the boys bully
each other.

One of the least cruel of the tyrannies the big boys put
upon the little ones, sometimes bore very hardly on those
who were not strong.   They used to ride races on our
backs and have desperate mounted battles and tourna-
ments.   In many a playground and home since then I
have seen boys tilt and race, and steeplechase, with smaller
boys upon their backs, and plenty of wholesome rough-
and-tumble in the game ; and it has given me a twinge of
heartache to think how, even when we were at play,
Crayshaw's baneful spirit cursed us with its example, so
that the big and strong could not be happy except at the
expense of the little and weak.

For it was the big ones who rode the little ones, with
neatly-cut ash-sticks and clumsy spurs.   I can see them
now, with the thin legs of the small boys tottering under
them, like a young donkey overridden by a coalheaver.

I was a favourite horse, for I was active and nimble, and
(which was more to the point) well made.   It was the

shambling, ill-proportioned lads who suffered most. The biggest boy in school rode me, as a rule, but he was not at all a bad bully, so I was lucky. He never spurred me, and he boasted of my willingness and good paces. I am sure he did not know, I don't suppose he ever stopped to think, how bad it was for me, or what an aching lump of prostration I felt when it was over. The day I fainted after winning a steeplechase, he turned a bucket of cold water over me, and as this roused me into a tingling vitality of pain, he was quite proud of his treatment, and told me nothing brought a really good horse round after a hard day like a bucket of clean water. And (so much are we the creatures of our conditions!) I remember feeling something approaching to satisfaction at the reflection that I had " gone till I dropped," and had been brought round after the manner of the best-conducted stables.

It was not that that made Jem and me run away. (For we did run away.) Overstrain and collapse, ill-usage short of torture, hard living and short commons, one got a certain accustomedness to, according to the merciful law which within certain limits makes a second nature for us out of use and wont. The one pain that knew no pause, and allowed of no revival, the evil that overbore us, mind and body, was the evil of constant dread. Upon us little boys fear lay always, and the terror of it was that it was uncertain. What would come next, and from whom, we never knew.

It was I who settled we should run away. I did it the night that Jem gave in, and would do nothing but cry noiselessly into his sleeve and wish he was dead. So I settled it and told Lorraine. I wanted him to come too, but he would not. He pretended that he did not care, and he said he had nowhere to go to. But he got into Snuffy's very own room at daybreak whilst we stood outside and heard him snoring ; and very loud he must have snored too, for I could hear my heart thumping so I should not

"SO WE TOOK EACH OTHER'S HANDS, AND FOR NEARLY A MILE WE RAN AS HARD AS WE COULD GO."

Page 105

have thought I could have heard anything else. And Lorraine took the back-door key off the drawers, and let us out, and took it back again. He feared nothing. There was a walnut-tree by the gate, and Jem said, " Suppose we do our faces like gipsies, so that nobody may know us." (For Jem was terribly frightened of being taken back.) So we found some old bits of peel and rubbed our cheeks, but we dared not linger long over it, and I said, " We'd better get further on, and we can hide if we hear steps or wheels." So we took each other's hands, and for nearly a mile we ran as hard as we could go, looking back now and then over our shoulders, like the picture of Christian and Hopeful running away from the Castle of Giant Despair.

We were particularly afraid of the milkman, for milkmen drive about early, and he had taken a runaway boy back to Crayshaw's years before, and Snuffy gave him five shillings. They said he once helped another boy to get away, but it was a big one, who gave him his gold watch. He would do anything if you paid him. Jem and I had each a little bundle in a handkerchief, but nothing in them that the milkman would have cared for. We managed very well, for we got behind a wall when he went by, and I felt so much cheered up I thought we should get home that day, far as it was. But when we got back into the road, I found that Jem was limping, for Snuffy had stamped on his foot when Jem had had it stuck out beyond the desk, when he was writing ; and the running had made it worse, and at last he sat down by the roadside, and said I was to go on home and send back for him. It was not very likely I would leave him to the chance of being pursued by Mr. Crayshaw ; but there he sat, and I thought I never should have persuaded him to get on my back, for good-natured as he is, Jem is as obstinate as a pig. But I said, " What's the use of my having been first horse with the heaviest weight in school, if I can't carry you ?" So he got up and I carried him a long way, and then a cart overtook us, and we got a lift home. And they knew us quite well, which shows how little use walnut-juice is, and it is disgusting to get off.

I think, as it happened, it was very unfortunate that we had discoloured our faces ; for though my mother was horrified at our being so thin and pinched-looking, my father said that of course we looked frights with brown daubs all over our cheeks and necks. But then he never did notice people looking ill. He was very angry indeed, at first, about our running away, and would not listen to what we said. He was angry too with my dear mother, because she believed us, and called Snuffy a bad man and a brute. And he ordered the dog-cart to be brought round, and said that Martha was to give us some break-fast, and that we might be thankful to get that instead of a flogging, for that when *he* ran away from school to escape a thrashing, his father gave him one thrashing whilst the dog-cart was being brought round, and drove him straight back to school, where the schoolmaster gave him another.

"And a very good thing for me," said my father, buttoning his coat, whilst my mother and Martha went about crying, and Jem and I stood silent. If we were to go back, the more we told, the worse would be Snuffy's revenge. An unpleasant hardness was beginning to creep over me. "The next time I run away," was my thought, " I shall not run home." But with this came a rush of regret for Jem's sake. I knew that " Crayshaw's " did more harm to him than to me, and almost involuntarily I put my arms round him, thinking that if they would only let him stay, I could go back and bear anything, like Lewis Lorraine. Jem had been crying, and when he hid his face on my shoulder, and leaned against me, I thought it was for comfort, but he got heavier and heavier, till I called out, and he rolled from my arms and was caught in my father's. He had been standing about on the bad foot, and pain and weariness and hunger and fright overpowered him, and he had fainted.

The dog-cart was counter-ordered, and Jem was put to bed, and Martha served me a breakfast that would have served six full-grown men. I ate far more than satisfied me, but far less than satisfied Martha, who seemed to hope that cold fowl and boiled eggs, fried bacon and pickled beef, plain cakes and currant cakes, jam and marmalade, buttered toast, strong tea and unlimited sugar and yellow cream, would atone for the past in proportion to the amount I ate, if it did not fatten me under her eyes. I really think I spent the rest of the day in stupor. I am sure it was not till the following morning that I learned the decision to which my father had come about us.

Jem was too obviously ill to be anywhere at present but at home; and my father decided that he would not send him back to Crayshaw's at all, but to a much more expensive school in the south of England, to which the parson of our parish was sending one of his sons. I was to return to Crayshaw's at once; he could not afford the expensive school for us both, and Jem was the eldest. Besides which, he was not going to countenance rebellion in any school to which he sent his sons, or to insult a man so highly recommended to him as Mr. Crayshaw had been. There certainly seemed to have been some severity, and the boys seemed to be a very rough lot; but Jem would fight, and if he gave he must take. His great-grandfather was just the same, and *he* fought the Putney Pet when he was five-and-twenty, and his parents thought he was sitting quietly at his desk in Fetter Lane.

I loved Jem too well to be jealous of him, but I was not the less conscious of the tender tone in which my father always spoke even of his faults, and of the way it stiffened and cooled when he added that I was not so ready with my fists, but that I was as fond of my own way as Jem

was of a fight; but that setting up for being unlike other
people didn't do for school life, and that the Woods had
done me no kindness by making a fool of me. He added,
however, that he should request Mr. Crayshaw, as a
personal favour, that I should receive no punishment for
running away, as I had suffered sufficiently already.

We had told very little of the true history of Crayshaw's
before Jem fainted, and I felt no disposition to further
confidences. I took as cheerful a farewell of my mother
as I could, for her sake ; and put on a good deal of
swagger and "don't care" to console Jem. He said,
"You're as plucky as Lorraine," and then his eyes shut
again. He was too ill to think much, and I kissed his
head and left him. After which I got stoutly into the
dog-cart, and we drove back up the dreary hills down
which Jem and I had run away.

That Snuffy was bland to cringing before my father did
not give me a hope that I should escape his direst revenge;
and the expression of Lorraine's face showed me, by its
sympathy, what *he* expected. But we were both wrong,
and for reasons which we then knew nothing about.

Cruelty was, as I have said, Mr. Crayshaw's ruling
passion, but it was not his only vice. There was a
whispered tradition that he had once been in jail for a
misuse of his acquirements in the art of penmanship; and
if you heard his name cropping up in the confidential
conversation of such neighbours as small farmers, the
postman, the parish overseer, and the like, it was sure to
be linked with unpleasingly suggestive expressions, such
as—"a dirty bit of business," "a nasty job that," "an
awkward affair," "very near got into trouble," "a bit
of bother about it, but Driver and Quills pulled him
through; theirs isn't a nice business, and they're men of
t' same feather as Crayshaw, so I reckon they're friends."
Many such hints have I heard, for the "White Lion" was
next door to the sweetshop, and in summer, refreshment of

a sober kind, with conversation to match, was apt to be enjoyed on the benches outside. The good wives of the neighbourhood used no such euphuisms as their more prudent husbands, when they spoke of Crayshaw's. Indeed one of the whispered anecdotes of Snuffy's past was of a hushed-up story that was just saved from becoming a scandal, but in reference to which Mr. Crayshaw was even more narrowly saved from a crowd of women who had taken the too-tardy law into their own hands. I remember myself the retreat of an unpaid washerwoman from the back premises of Crayshaw's on one occasion, and the unmistakable terms in which she expressed her opinions.

" Don't tell me! I know Crayshaw's well enough; such folks is a curse to a country side, but judgment overtakes 'em at last."

"Judgment," as the good woman worded it, kept threatening Mr. Crayshaw long before it overtook him, as it is apt to disturb scoundrels who keep a hypocritical good name above their hidden misdeeds. As it happened, at the very time Jem and I ran away from him, Mr. Crayshaw himself was living in terror of one or two revelations, and to be deserted by two of his most respectably connected boys was an ill-timed misfortune. The countenance my father had been so mistaken as to afford to his establishment was very important to him, for we were the only pupils from within fifty miles, and our parents' good word constituted an "unexceptionable reference."

Thus it was that Snuffy pleaded humbly (but in vain) for the return of Jem, and that he not only promised that I should not suffer, but to my amazement kept his word.

Judgment lingered over the head of Crayshaw's for two years longer, and I really think my being there had something to do with maintaining its tottering reputation. I was almost the only lad in the school whose parents were alive and at hand and in a good position, and my father's name stifled scandal. Most of the others were orphans, being cheaply educated by distant relatives or guardians, or else the sons of poor widows who were easily bamboozled by Snuffy's fluent letters, and the religious leaflets which it was his custom to enclose. (In several of these cases, he was "managing" the poor women's "affairs" for them.) One or two boys belonged to people living abroad. Indeed, the worst bully in the school was a half-caste, whose smile, when he showed his gleaming teeth, boded worse than any other boy's frown. He was a wonderful acrobat, and could do extraordinary tricks of all sorts. My being nimble and ready made me very useful to him as a confederate in the exhibitions which his intense vanity delighted to give on half-holidays, and kept me in his good graces till I was old enough to take care of myself. Oh, how every boy who dreaded him applauded at these entertainments ! And what dangerous feats I performed, every other fear being lost in the fear of him ! I owe him no grudge for what he forced me to do (though I have had to bear real fire without flinching when he failed in a conjuring-trick, which should only have simulated the real thing) ; what I learned from him has come in so useful since, that I forgive him all.

I was there for two years longer. Snuffy bullied me less, and hated me the more. I knew it, and he knew that I knew it. It was a hateful life, but I am sure the influence of a good home holds one up in very evil paths. Every time we went back to our respective schools my father gave us ten shillings, and told us to mind our books, and my mother kissed us and made us promise we would say our prayers every day. I could not bear to break my promise, though I used to say them in bed (the old form we learnt from her), and often in such a very unfit frame of mind, that they were what it is very easy to call "a mockery."

GOD knows (Who alone knows the conditions under which each soul blunders and spells on through life's hard lessons) if they were a mockery. *I* know they were unworthy to be offered to Him, but that the habit helped to keep me straight I am equally sure. Then I had a good home to go to during the holidays. That was everything, and it is in all humbleness that I say that I do not think the ill experiences of those years degraded me much. I managed to keep some truth and tenderness about me ; and I am thankful to remember that I no more cringed to Crayshaw than Lorraine did, and that though I stayed there till I was a big boy, I never maltreated a little one.

———◆———

CHAPTER XI.

Whose powers shed round him in the common strife
Or mild concerns of ordinary life,
A constant influence, a peculiar grace ;
　　*　　　　*　　　　*　　　　*　　　　*
Or if an unexpected call succeed,
Come when it will, is equal to the need.
　　　　　Wordsworth's " Happy Warrior."

JUDGMENT came at last. During my first holidays I had posted a letter from Lewis Lorraine to the uncle in India to whom he had before endeavoured to appeal. The envelope did not lack stamps, but the address was very imperfect, and it was many months in reaching him. He wrote a letter, which Lewis never received, Mr. Crayshaw probably knew why. But twelve months after that Colonel Jervois came to England, and he lost no time in betaking himself to Crayshaw's. From Crayshaw's he came to my father, the only "unexceptionable reference" left to Snuffy to put forward.

The Colonel came with a soldier's promptness, and,

with the utmost courtesy of manner, went straight to the point. His life had not accustomed him to our neighbourly unwillingness to interfere with anything that did not personally concern us, nor to the prudent patience with which country folk will wink long at local evils. In the upshot what he asked was what my mother had asked three years before. Had my father personal knowledge or good authority for believing the school to be a well-conducted one, and Mr. Crayshaw a fit man for his responsible post? Had he ever heard rumours to the man's discredit ?

Replies that must do for a wife will not always answer a man who puts the same questions. My great-grandfather's memory was not evoked on this occasion, and my father frankly confessed that his personal knowledge of Crayshaw's was very small, and that the man on whose recommendation he had sent us to school there had just proved to be a rascal and a swindler. Our mother had certainly heard rumours of severity, but he had regarded her maternal anxiety as excessive, etc., etc. In short, my dear father saw that he had been wrong, and confessed it, and was now as ready as the Colonel to expose Snuffy's misdeeds.

No elaborate investigation was needed. An attack once made on Mr. Crayshaw's hollow reputation, it cracked on every side ; first hints crept out, then scandals flew. The Colonel gave no quarter, and he did not limit his interest to his own nephew.

"A widow's son, ma'am," so he said to my mother, bowing over her hand as he led her in to dinner, in a style to which we were quite unaccustomed; "a widow's son, ma'am, should find a father in every honest man who can assist him."

The tide having turned against Snuffy, his friends (of the Driver and Quills type) turned with it. But they gained nothing, for one morning he got up as early as we had done, and ran away, and I never heard of him again.

And before nightfall the neighbours, who had so long tolerated his wickedness, broke every pane of glass in his windows.

During all this, Lewis Lorraine and his uncle stayed at our house. The Colonel spent his time between holding indignant investigations, writing indignant letters (which he allowed us to seal with his huge signet), and walking backwards and forwards to the town to buy presents for the little boys.

When Snuffy ran away, and the school was left to itself, Colonel Jervois strode off to the nearest farm, requisitioned a waggon, and having packed the boys into it, bought loaves and milk enough to breakfast them all, and transported the whole twenty-eight to our door. He left four with my mother, and marched off with the rest. The Woods took in a large batch, and in the course of the afternoon he had for love or money quartered them all. He betrayed no nervousness in dealing with numbers, in foraging for supplies, or in asking for what he wanted. Whilst other people had been doubting whether it might not "create unpleasantness" to interfere in this case and that, the Colonel had fought each boy's battle, and seen most of them off on their homeward journeys. He was used to dealing with men, and with emergencies, and it puzzled him when my Uncle Henry consulted his law-books and advised caution, and my father saw his agent on farm business, whilst the fate of one of Crayshaw's victims yet hung in the balance.

When all was over the Colonel left us, and took Lewis with him, and his departure raised curiously mixed feelings of regret and relief.

He had quite won my mother's heart, chiefly by his energy and tenderness for the poor boys, and partly by his kindly courtesy and deference towards her. Indeed all ladies liked him—all, that is, who knew him. Before they came under the influence of his pleasantness and politeness, he shared the half-hostile reception to which any person or anything that was foreign to our daily experience was subjected in our neighbourhood. So that the first time Colonel Jervois appeared in our pew, Mrs. Simpson (the wife of a well-to-do man of business who lived near us) said to my mother after church, " I see you've got one of the military with you," and her tone was more critical than congratulatory. But when my mother, with un-conscious diplomacy, had kept her to luncheon, and the Colonel had handed her to her seat, and had stroked his moustache, and asked in his best manner if she meant to devote her son to the service of his country, Mrs. Simpson undid her bonnet-strings, fairly turned her back on my father, and was quite unconscious when Martha handed the potatoes ; and she left us wreathed in smiles, and resolved that Mr. Simpson should buy their son Horace a commission instead of taking him into the business. Mr. Simpson did not share her views, and I believe he said some rather nasty things about swaggering, and not having one sixpence to rub against another. And Mrs. Simpson (who was really devoted to Horace and could hardly bear him out of her sight) reflected that it was possible to get shot as well as to grow a moustache if you went into the army ; but she still maintained that she should always remember the Colonel as a thorough gentleman, and a wonderful judge of the character of boys.

The Colonel made great friends with the Woods, and he was deeply admired by our rector, who, like many parsons, had a very military heart, and delighted in exciting tales of the wide world which he could never explore. It was perhaps natural that my father should hardly be devoted to a stranger who had practically reproached his negligence, but the one thing that did draw him towards the old Indian officer was his habit of early rising. My father was always up before any of us, but he generally found the Colonel out before him, enjoy-

ing the early hours of the day as men who have lived in
hot climates are accustomed to do. They used to come
in together in very pleasant moods to breakfast ; but with
the post-bag Lorraine's uncle was sure to be moved to
voluble indignation, or pity, or to Utopian plans to which
my father listened with puzzled impatience. He did not
understand the Colonel, which was perhaps not to be
wondered at.

His moral courage had taken away our breath, and
physical courage was stamped upon his outward man. If
he was anything he was manly. It was because he was
in some respects very womanly too, that he puzzled my
father's purely masculine brain. The mixture, and the
vehemence of the mixture, were not in his line. He
would have turned "Crayshaw's" matters over in his
own mind as often as hay in a wet season before grappling
with the whole bad business as the Colonel had done.
And on the other hand, it made him feel uncomfortable
and almost ashamed to see tears standing in the old
soldier's eyes as he passionately blamed himself for what
had been suffered by "my sister's son."

The servants one and all adored Colonel Jervois. They
are rather acute judges of good breeding, and men and
maids were at one on the fact that he was a visitor who
conferred social distinction on the establishment. They
had decided that we should "dine late so long as The
Gentleman" was with us, whilst my mother was thinking
how to break so weighty an innovation to such valuable
servants. They served him with alacrity, and approved
of his brief orders and gracious thanks. The Colonel did
unheard-of things with impunity—threw open his bedroom shutters at night, and more than once unbarred and
unbolted the front door to go outside for a late cigar.
Nothing puzzled Martha more than the nattiness with
which he put all the bolts and bars back into their places,
as if he had been used to the door as long as she had.

Indeed he had all that power of making himself at home, which is most fully acquired by having had to provide for yourself in strange places, but he carried it too far.

One day he penetrated into the kitchen (having previously been rummaging the kitchen-garden) and insisted upon teaching our cook how to make curry. The lesson was much needed, and it was equally well intended, but it was a mistake. Everything cannot be carried by storm, whatever the military may think. Jane said, " Yes, sir," at every point that approached to a pause in the Colonel's ample instructions, but she never moved her eyes from the magnificent moustache which drooped above the stew-pan, nor her thoughts from the one idea produced by the occasion—that The Gentleman had caught her without her cap. In short our curries were no worse, and no better, in consequence of the shock to kitchen-etiquette (for that was all) which she received.

And yet we modified our household ways for him, as they were never modified for anyone else. On Martha's weekly festival for cleaning the bedrooms (and if a room was occupied for a night, she scrubbed after the intruder as if he had brought the plague in his portmanteau) the smartest visitor we ever entertained had to pick his or her way through the upper regions of the house, where soap and soda were wafted on high and unexpected breezes along passages filled with washstands and clothes-baskets, cane-seated chairs and baths, mops, pails and brooms. But the Colonel had "given such a jump" on meeting a towel-horse at large round a sharp corner, and had seemed so uncomfortable on finding everything that he thought was inside his room turned outside, that for that week Martha left the lower part of the house uncleaned, and did not turn either the dining or drawing rooms into the hall on their appointed days. She had her revenge when he was gone.

On the day of his departure, my lamentations had met

with the warmest sympathy as I stirred toffy over Jane's kitchen fire, whilst Martha lingered with the breakfast things, after a fashion very unusual with her, and gazed at the toast-rack and said, " the Colonel had eaten nothing of a breakfast to travel on." But next morning, I met her in another mood. It was a mood to which we were not strangers, though it did not often occur. In brief, Martha (like many another invaluable domestic) " had a temper of her own ;" but to do her justice her ill feelings generally expended themselves in a rage for work, and in taking as little ease herself as she allowed to other people. I knew what it meant when I found her cleaning the best silver when she ought to have been eating her breakfast ; but my head was so full of the Colonel, that I could not help talking about him, even if the temptation to tease Martha had not been overwhelming. No reply could I extract ; only once, as she passed swiftly to the china cupboard, with the whole Crown Derby tea and coffee service on one big tray (the Colonel had praised her coffee), I heard her mutter—" Soldiers is very upsetting." Certainly, considering what she did in the way of scolding, scouring, black-leading, polishing and sand-papering that week, it was not Martha's fault if we did not " get straight again," furniture and feelings. I've heard her say that Calais sand would " fetch anything off," and I think it had fetched the Colonel off her heart by the time that the cleaning was done.

It had no such effect on mine. Lewis Lorraine himself did not worship his uncle more devoutly than I. Colonel Jervois had given me a new ideal. It was possible, then, to be enthusiastic without being unmanly ; to live years out of England, and come back more patriotic than many people who stayed comfortably at home ; to go forth into the world and be the simpler as well as the wiser, the softer as well as the stronger for the experience ? So it seemed. And yet Lewis had told me,

with such tears as Snuffy never made him shed, how
tender his uncle was to his unworthiness, what allowances
he made for the worst that Lewis could say of himself,
and what hope he gave him of a good and happy future.

"He cried as bad as I did," Lewis said, "and begged
me to forgive him for having trusted so much to my other
guardian. Do you know, Jack, Snuffy regularly forged a
letter like my handwriting, to answer that one Uncle
Eustace wrote, which he kept back? He might well do
such good copies, and write the year of Our Lord with a
swan at the end of the last flourish! And you remember
what we heard about his having been in prison—but, oh,
dear! I don't want to remember. He says I am to
forget, and he forbade me to talk about Crayshaw's, and
said I was not to trouble my head about anything that
had happened there. He kept saying, "Forget, my boy,
forget! Say GOD help me, and look forward. While
there's life there's always the chance of a better life for
everyone. Forget! forget!'"

Lewis departed with his uncle. Charlie went for two
nights to the moors. Jem's holidays had not begun, and
in our house we were "cleaning down" after the Colonel
as if he had been the sweeps.

I went to old Isaac for sympathy. He had become
very rheumatic the last two years, but he was as intelligent as ever, and into his willing ear I poured all that I
could tell of my hero, and much that I only imagined.

His sympathy met me more than half-way. The
villagers as a body were unbounded in their approval of
the Colonel, and Mrs Irvine was even greedier than old
Isaac for every particular I could impart respecting him.

"He's a *handsome* gentleman," said the beemaster's
wife, "and he passed us (my neighbour, Mrs. Mettam,
and me) as near, sir, as I am to you, with a gold-headed
stick in his hand, and them lads following after him, for
all the world like the Good Shepherd and his flock."

I managed not to laugh, and old Isaac added, " There's a many in this village, sir, would have been glad to have taken the liberty of expressing themselves to the Colonel, and a *depitation* did get as far as your father's gates one night, but they turned bashful and come home again. And I know, for one, Master Jack, that if me and my missus had had a room fit to offer one of them poor young gentlemen, I'd have given a week's wage to do it, and the old woman would have been happy to her dying day."

CHAPTER XII.

"GOD help me ! save I take my part
Of danger on the roaring sea,
A devil rises in my heart,
Far worse than any death to me."
Tennyson's " Sailor-boy."

THE fact that my father had sent me back against my will to a school where I had suffered so much and learnt so little, ought perhaps to have drawn us together when he discovered his mistake. Unfortunately it did not. He was deeply annoyed with himself for having been taken in by Snuffy, but he transferred some of this annoyance to me, on grounds which cut me to the soul, and which I fear I resented so much that I was not in a mood that was favourable to producing a better understanding between us. The injustice which I felt so keenly was, that my father reproached me with having what he called "kept him in the dark" about the life at Crayshaw's. At my age I must have seen how wicked the man and his system were.

I reminded him that I had run away from them once, and had told all that I dared, but that he would not hear me then. He would not hear me now.

" I don't wish to discuss the subject. It is a very
painful one," he said (and I believe it was as physically
distressing to him as the thought of Cripple Charlie's
malformation). " I have no wish to force your confidence
when it is too late," he added (and it was this which i felt
to be so hard). " I don't blame you ; you have other friends
who suit you better, but you have never been fully open
with me. All I can say is, if Mr. Wood was better informed than I have been, and did not acquaint me, he has
behaved in a manner which——. There—don't speak !
we'll dismiss the subject. You have suffered enough, if
you have not acted as I should have expected you to act.
I blame myself unutterably, and I hope I see my way to
such a comfortable and respectable start in life for you
that these three years in that vile place may not be to
your permanent disadvantage."

I was just opening my lips to thank him, when he got
up and went to his tall desk, where he took a pinch of
snuff, and then added as he turned away, " Thank GOD, I
have *one* son who is frank with his father !"

My lips were sealed in an instant. This, then, was my
reward for that hard journey of escape, with Jem on my
back, which had only saved him ; for having stifled envy
in gladness for his sake, when (in those bits of our different
holidays which overlapped each other) I saw and felt the
contrast between our opportunities ; for having suffered
my harder lot in silence that my mother might not fret,
when I felt certain that my father would not interfere !
My heart beat as if it would have pumped the tears into
my eyes by main force, but I kept them back, and said
steadily enough, " Is that all, sir ?"

My father did not look up, but he nodded his head and
said, " Yes ; you may go."

As I went he called me back.

" Are you going to the farm this afternoon ?"

To my own infinite annoyance I blushed as I answered,

"I was going to sit with Charlie a bit, unless you have any objection."

"Not at all. I only asked for information. I have no wish to interfere with any respectable friends you may be disposed to give your confidence to. But I should like it to be understood that either your mother or I must have some knowledge of your movements."

"Mother knew quite well I was going!" I exclaimed. "Why, I've got a parcel to take to Mrs. Wood from her."

"Very good. There's no occasion to display temper. Shut the door after you."

I shut it very gently. (If three years at Crayshaw's had taught me nothing else, it had taught me much self-control). Then I got away to the first hiding-place I could find, and buried my head upon my arms. Would not a beating from Snuffy have been less hard to bear? Surely sore bones from those one despises are not so painful as a sore heart from those one loves.

Our household affections were too sound at the core for the mere fact of displeasing my father not to weigh heavily on my soul. But I could not help defending myself in my own mind against what I knew to be injustice.

Jem "frank with his father"? Well he might be, when our father's partiality met him half way at every turn. *That* was no fancy of mine. I had the clearest of childish remembrances of an occasion when I wanted to do something which our farming man thought my father would not approve, and how when I urged the fact that Jem had already done it with impunity, he shook his head wiseacrely, and said, "Aye, aye, Master Jack. But ye know they say some folks may steal a horse, when other folks mayn't look over the hedge."

The vagueness of "some folks" and "other folks" had left the proverb dark to my understanding when I heard it, but I remembered it till I understood it.

I never was really jealous of Jem. He was far too good.

natured and unspoilt, and I was far too fond of him. Besides which, if the mental tone of our country lives was at rather a dull level, it was also wholesomely unfavourable to the cultivation of morbid grievances, or the dissection of one's own hurt feelings. If I had told anybody about me, from my dear mother down to our farming-man, that I was misunderstood and wanted sympathy, I should probably have been answered that many a lad of my age was homeless and wanted boots. As a matter of reasoning the reply would have been defective, but for practical purposes it would have been much to the point. And it is fair to this rough-and-ready sort of philosophy to defend it from a common charge of selfishness. It was not that I should have been the happier because another lad was miserable, but that an awakened sympathy with his harder fate would tend to dwarf egotistic absorption in my own. Such considerations, in short, are no justification of those who are responsible for needless evil or neglected good, but they are handy helps to those who suffer from them, and who feel sadly sorry for themselves.

I am sure the early-begun and oft-reiterated teaching of daily thankfulness for daily blessings was very useful to me at Crayshaw's and has been useful to me ever since. With my dear mother herself it was merely part of that pure and constant piety which ran through her daily life, like a stream that is never frozen and never runs dry. In me it had no such grace, but it was an early-taught good habit (as instinctive as any bodily habit) to feel—" Well, I'm thankful things are not so with me ;" as quickly as " Ah, it might have been thus !" Looking at the fates and fortunes and dispositions of other boys, I had, even at Snuffy's, " much to be thankful for " as well as much to endure, and it was a good thing for me that I could balance the two. For if the grace of thankfulness does not solve the riddles of life, it lends a willing shoulder to its common burdens.

I certainly had needed all my philosophy at home as well as at school. It was hard to come back, one holiday-time after another, ignorant except for books that I devoured in the holidays, and for my own independent studies of maps, and an old geography book at Snuffy's from which I was allowed to give lessons to the lowest form ; rough in looks, and dress, and manners (I knew it, but it requires some self-respect even to use a nail-brush, and self-respect was next door to impossible at Crayshaw's) ; and with my north-country accent deepened, and my conversation disfigured by slang which, not being fashionable slang, was as inadmissible as thieves' lingo. It was hard, I say, to come back thus, and meet dear old Jem, and generally one at least of his schoolfellows whom he had asked to be allowed to invite—both of them well dressed, well-cared for, and well mannered, full of games that were not in fashion at Crayshaw's, and slang as " correct " as it was unintelligible.

Jem's heart was as true to me as ever, but he was not so thin-skinned as I am. He was never a fellow who worried himself much about anything, and I don't think it struck him I could feel hurt or lonely. He would say, " I say, Jack, what a beastly way your hair is cut. I wish Father would let you come to our school :" or, " Don't say it was a dirty trick—say it was a beastly chouse, or something of that sort. We're awfully particular about talking at ——'s, and I don't want Cholmondley to hear you."

Jem was wonderfully polished-up himself, and as pugnacious on behalf of all the institutions of his school as he had once been about our pond. I got my hair as near right as one cutting and the town hair-cutter could bring it, and mended my manners and held my own with good temper. When it came to feats of skill or endurance, I more than held my own. Indeed, I so amazed one very " swell " little friend of Jem's, whose mother (a titled lady)

had allowed him to spend part of the summer holidays
with Jem for change of air, that he vowed I must go and
stay with him in the winter, and do juggler and acrobat
at their Christmas theatricals.   But he may have reported
me as being rough as well as ready, for her ladyship never
ratified the invitation.   Not that I would have left home
at Christmas, and not that I lacked pleasure in the
holidays.   But other fashions of games and speech and
boyish etiquette lay between me and Jem ; hospitality,
if not choice, kept him closely with his schoolfellows,
and neither they nor he had part in the day-dreams of my
soul.

For the spell of the Penny Numbers had not grown
weaker as I grew older.   In the holidays I came back to
them as to friends.   At school they made the faded maps
on Snuffy's dirty walls alive with visions, and many a night
as I lay awake with pain and over-weariness in the stifling
dormitory, my thoughts took refuge not in dreams of home
nor in castles of the air, but in phantom ships that sailed
for ever round the world.

The day of the interview with my father I roused myself
from my grievances to consider a more practical question.
Why should I not go to sea?   No matter whose fault it
was, there was no doubt that I was ill-educated, and that
I did not please my father as Jem did.   On the other hand
I was strong and hardy, nimble and willing to obey ; and
I had roughed it enough, in all conscience.   I must have
ill-luck indeed, if I lit upon a captain more cruel than Mr.
Crayshaw.   I did not know exactly how it was to be accomplished, but I knew enough to know that I could not
aim at the Royal Navy.   Of course I should have preferred
it.   I had never seen naval officers, but if they were like
officers in the army, like Colonel Jervois, for instance, it
was with such a port and bearing that I would fain have
carried myself when I grew up to be a man.   I guessed,
however, that money and many other considerations might

make it impossible for me to be a midshipman ; but I had heard of boys being apprenticed to merchant-vessels, and I resolved to ask my father if he would so apprentice me.

He refused, and he accompanied his refusal with an unfavourable commentary on my character and conduct, which was not the less bitter because the accusations were chiefly general.

This sudden fancy for the sea—well, if it were not a sudden fancy, but a dream of my life, what a painful instance it afforded of my habitual want of frankness !— This long-concealed project which I had suddenly brought to the surface—I had talked about it to my mother years ago, had I, but it had distressed her, and even to my father, but he had snubbed me?—then I had been deliberately fostering aims and plans to which I had always known that my parents would be opposed. My father didn't believe a word of it. It was the old story. I must be peculiar at any price. I must have something new to amuse me, and be unlike the rest of the family. It was always the same. For years I had found more satisfaction from the conversation of a man who had spent ten years of his life in the hulks than from that of my own father. Then this Indian Colonel had taken my fancy, and it had made him sick to see the womanish—he could call it no better, the *weak-womanish*—way in which I worshipped him. If I were a daughter instead of a son, my caprices would distress and astonish him less. He could have sent me to my mother, and my mother might have sent me to my needle. In a son, from whom he looked for manly feeling and good English common-sense, it was painful in the extreme. Vanity, the love of my own way, and want of candour—(my father took a pinch of snuff between each count of the indictment)—these were my besetting sins, and would lead me into serious trouble. This new fad, just, too, when he had made most favourable arrangements for my admission into my Uncle Henry's office as the first

step in a prosperous career. I didn't know; didn't I?
Perhaps not. Perhaps I had been at the Woods' when he
and my mother were speaking of it. But now I did know.
The matter was decided, and he hoped I should profit by
my opportunities. I might go, and I was to shut the door
after me.

I omit what my father said of the matter from a religious
point of view, though he accused me of flying in the face
of Providence as well as of the Fifth Commandment. The
piety which kept a pure and GOD-fearing atmosphere about
my home, and to which I owe all the strength I have found
against evil since I left it, was far too sincere in both my
parents for me to speak of any phase of it with disrespect.
Though I may say here that I think it is to be wished that
more good people exercised judgment as well as faith in
tracing the will of Heaven in their own. Practically I did
not even then believe that I was more "called" to that
station of life which was to be found in Uncle Henry's
office, than to that station of life which I should find on
board a vessel in the Merchant Service, and it only discredited truth in my inmost soul when my father put his
plans for my career in that light. Just as I could not help
feeling it unfair that a commandment which might have
been fairly appealed to if I had disobeyed him, should be
used against me in argument because I disagreed with
him.

I did disagree with him utterly. Uncle Henry's office
was a gloomy place, where I had had to endure long
periods of waiting as a child when my mother took us in
to the dentist, and had shopping and visiting of uncertain
length to do. Uncle Henry himself was no favourite with
me. He was harder than my father if you vexed him, and
less genial when you didn't. And I wanted to go to sea.
But it did not seem a light matter to me to oppose my
parents, and they were both against me. My dear mother
was thrown into the profoundest distress by the bare

notion. In her view to be at sea was merely to run an imminent and ceaseless risk of shipwreck ; and even this jeopardy of life and limb was secondary to the dangers that going ashore in foreign places would bring upon my mind and morals.

So when my father spoke kindly to me at supper, and said that he had arranged with Mr. Wood that I should read with him for two hours every evening, in preparation for my future life as an articled clerk, my heart was softened. I thanked him gratefully, and resolved for my own part to follow what seemed to be the plain path of duty, though it led to Uncle Henry's office, and not out into the world.

The capacity in which I began life in Uncle Henry's office was that of office boy, and the situation was attended in my case with many favourable conditions. Uncle Henry wished me to sleep on the premises, as my predecessor had done, but an accidental circumstance led to my coming home daily, which I infinitely preferred. This was nothing less than an outbreak of boils all over me, upon which every domestic application having failed, and gallons of herb tea only making me worse, Dr. Brown was called in, and pronounced my health in sore need of restoration. The regimen of Crayshaw's was not to be recovered from in a day, and the old doctor would not hear of my living altogether in the town. If I went to the office at all, he said, I must ride in early, and ride out in the evening. So much fresh air and exercise were imperative, and I must eat two solid meals a day under no less careful an eye than that of my mother.

She was delighted. She thought (even more than usual) that Doctor Brown was a very Solomon in spectacles, and I quite agreed with her. The few words that followed gave a slight shock to her favourable opinion of his wisdom, but I need hardly say that it confirmed mine.

He had given me a kindly slap on the shoulder, which

happened at that moment to be the sorest point in my body, and I was in no small pain from head to foot. I only tightened my lips, but I suppose he bethought himself of what he had done, and he looked keenly at me and said, " You can bear pain, Master Jack ?"

" Oh, Jack's a very brave boy," said my dear mother. " Indeed, he's only too brave. He upset his father and me terribly last week by wanting to go to sea instead of to the office."

" And much better for him, ma'am," said the old doctor, promptly ; " he'll make a first-rate sailor, and if Crayshaw's is all the schooling he's had, a very indifferent clerk."

" That's just what I think !" I began, but my mother coloured crimson with distress, and I stopped, and went after her worsted ball which she had dropped, whilst she appealed to Doctor Brown.

" Pray don't say so, Doctor Brown. Jack is *very* good, and it's all *quite* decided. I couldn't part with him, and his father would be *so* annoyed if the subject——"

" Tut, tut, ma'am !" said the doctor, pocketing his spectacles ; " I never interfere in family affairs, and I never repeat what I hear. The first rules of the profession, young gentleman, and **very** good general rules for anybody."

I got quite well again, and my new life began. I rode in and out of the town every day on Rob Roy, our red-haired pony. After tea I went to the farm to be taught by Mr. Wood, and at every opportunity I devoured such books as I could lay my hands on. I fear I had very little excuse for not being contented now. And yet I was not content.

It seems absurd to say that the drains had anything to do with it, but the horrible smell which pervaded the office added to the distastefulness of the place, and made us all feel ill and fretful, except my uncle, and Moses Benson, the Jew clerk. He was never ill, and he said he smelt

"I GOT QUITE WELL AGAIN, AND MY NEW LIFE BEGAN.
I RODE IN AND OUT OF THE TOWN EVERY DAY ON ROB ROY,
OUR RED-HAIRED PONY."

Page 128.

nothing; which shows that one may have a very big nose to very little purpose.

My uncle pooh-poohed the unwholesome state of the office, for two reasons which certainly had some weight. The first was that he himself had been there for five and twenty years without suffering by it ; and the second was, that the defects of drainage were so radical that (the place belonging to that period of house-building when the system of drainage was often worse than none at all) half the premises, if not half the street, would have to be pulled down for any effectual remedy. So it was left as it was, and when Mr. Burton, the head clerk, had worse headaches than usual, he used to give me sixpence for chloride of lime, which I distributed at my discretion, and on those days Moses Benson used generally to say that he "fancied he smelt something."

Moses Benson was an articled clerk to my uncle, but he had no pretensions to be considered a gentleman. His father kept a small shop where second-hand watches were the most obvious goods ; but the old man was said to have money, though the watches did not seem to sell very fast, and his son had duly qualified for his post, and had paid a good premium. Moses was only two or three years older than I, not that I could have told anything about his age from his looks. He was sallow, and had a big nose ; his hands were fat, his feet were small, and I think his head was large, but perhaps his hair made it look larger than it was, for it was thick and very black, and though it was curly, it was not like Jem's ; the curls were more like short ringlets, and if he bent over his desk they hid his forehead, and when he put his head back to think, they lay on his coat-collar. And I suppose it was partly because he could not smell with his nose, that he used such very strong hair-oil, and so much of it. It used to make his coat-collar in a horrid state, but he always kept a little bottle of "scouring drops" on the ledge of

K

his desk, and when it got very bad, I knelt behind him on
the corner of his stool and scoured his coat-collar with a
little bit of flannel.   Not that I did it half so well as he
could.   He wore very odd-looking clothes, but he took
great care of them, and was always touching them up,
and " reviving " his hat with one of Mrs. O'Flannagan's
irons.   He used to sell bottles of the scouring drops to
the other clerks, and once he got me to get my mother to
buy some.   He gave me a good many little odd jobs to do
for him, but he always thanked me, and from the beginning
to the end of our acquaintance he was invariably kind.

I remember a very odd scene that happened at the
beginning of it.

Mr. Burton (the other clerk, whose time was to expire
the following year, which was to make a vacancy for me)
was a very different man from Moses Benson.   He was respectably connected, and looked down on " the Jew-boy,"
but he was hot-tempered, and rather slow-witted, and I
think Moses could manage him ; and I think it was he
who kept their constant " tiffs " from coming to real
quarrels.

One day, very soon after I began office-life, Benson
sent me out to get him some fancy note-paper, and
when I came back I saw the red-haired Mr. Burton
standing by the desk and looking rather more sickly and
cross than usual.   I laid down the paper and the change,
and asked if Benson wanted anything else.   He thanked
me exceedingly kindly, and said " No," and I went out of
the enclosure and back to the corner where I had been
cutting out some newspaper extracts for my uncle.   At
the same time I drew from under my overcoat which was
lying there, an old railway volume of one of Cooper's
novels which Charlie had lent me.   I ought not to have
been reading novels in office-hours, but I had had to
stop short last night because my candle went out just
at the most exciting point, and I had had no time to see

what became of everybody before I started for town in the morning. I could bear suspense no longer, and plunged into my book.

How it was in these circumstances that I heard what the two clerks were saying, I don't know. They talked constantly in these open enclosures, when they knew I was within hearing. On this occasion I suppose they thought I had gone out, and it was some minutes before I discovered that they were talking of me. Burton spoke first, and in an irritated tone.

"You treat this young shaver precious different to the last one."

The Jew spoke very softly, and with an occasional softening of the consonants in his words. " How obsherving you are ! " said he.

Burton snorted. " It don't take much observation to see that. But I suppose you have your reasons. You Jews are always so sly. That's how you get on so, I suppose."

"You Gentiles," replied Moses (and the Jew's voice had tones which gave him an infinite advantage in retaliating scorn), "you Gentiles would do as well as we do if you were able to foresee and knew how to wait. You have all the selfishness for success, my dear, but the gifts of prophecy and patience are wanting to you."

"That's nothing to do with your little game about the boy," said Burton ; "however, I suppose you can keep your own secrets."

"I have no secrets," said Moses gently. "And if you take my advice, you never will have. If you have no secrets, my dear, they will never be found out. If you tell your little designs, your best friends will be satisfied, and will not invent less creditable ones for you."

"If they did, you'd talk 'em down," said Burton roughly. " Short of a woman I never met such a hand at jaw. You'll be in Parliament yet——" (" It is poshible !"

K 2

said the Jew hastily,) " with that long tongue of yours
But you haven't told us about the boy, for all you've
said."

" About this boy," said Moses, " a proverb will be shorter
than my jaw. 'The son of the house is not a servant for
ever.' As to the other—he was taken for charity and
dismissed for theft, is it not so ? He came from the dirt,
and he went back to the dirt. They often do. Why should
I be civil to him ?"

What reply Mr. Burton would have made to this question I had no opportunity of judging. My uncle called
him, and he ran hastily upstairs. And when he had gone,
the Jew came slowly out, and crossed the office as if he
were going into the street. By this time my conscience
was pricking hard, and I shoved my book under my coat
and called to him : " Mr. Benson."

" You ?" he said.

" I am very sorry," I stammered, blushing, " but I
heard what you were saying. I did not mean to listen.
I thought you knew that I was there."

" It is of no importance," he said, turning away ; " I
have no secrets."

But I detained him.

" Mr. Benson ! Tell me, please. You *were* talking
about me, weren't you ? What did you mean about the
son of the house not being a servant for ever ?"

He hesitated for an instant, and then turned round and
came nearer to me.

" It is true, is it not ?" he said. " Next year you may
be clerk. In time you may be your uncle's confidential
clerk, which I should like to be myself. You may
eventually be partner, as I should like to be ; and in the
long run you may succeed him, as I should like to do.
It is a good business, my dear, a sound business, a
business of which much, very much, more might be made.
You might die rich, very rich. You might be mayor, you

might be member, you might—but what is the use. *You will not.* You do not see it, though I am telling you. You will not wait for it, though it would come. What is that book you hid when I came in ?"

" It is about North American Indians," said I, dragging it forth. " I am very sorry, but I left off last night at such an exciting bit."

The Jew was thumbing the pages, with his black ringlets close above them.

" Novels in office-hours !" said he ; but he was very good-natured about it, and added, " I've one or two books at home, if you're fond of this kind of reading, and will promise me not to neglect your duties."

" Oh, I promise !" said I.

" I'll put them under my desk in the corner," he said ; " indeed, I would part with some of them for a trifle."

I thanked him warmly, but what he had said was still hanging in my mind, and I added, " Are there real prophets among the Jews nowadays, Mr. Benson ?"

" They will make nothing by it, if there are," said he ; and there was a tone of mysteriousness in his manner of speaking which roused my romantic curiosity. " A few of ush (very few, my dear !) mould our own fates, and the lives of the rest are moulded by what men have within them rather than by what they find without. If there were a true prophet in every market-place to tell each man of his future, it would not alter the destinies of seven men in thish wide world."

As Moses spoke the swing door was pushed open, and one of my uncle's clients entered. He was an influential man, and a very tall one. The Jew bent his ringlets before him, almost beneath his elbow, and slipped out as he came in.

CHAPTER XIII.

"Then, hey for boot and horse, lad,
And round the world away !
Young blood must have its course, lad,
And every dog his day."

C. Kingsley.

MOSES BENSON was as good as his word in the matter of books of adventure. Dirty books, some without backs, and some with very greasy ones (for which, if I bought them, I seldom paid more than half-price), but full of dangers and discoveries, the mightiness of manhood, and the wonders of the world. I read them at odd moments of my working hours, and dreamed of them when I went home to bed. And it was more fascinating still to look out, with Charlie's help, in the Penny Numbers, for the foreign places, and people, and creatures mentioned in the tales, and to find that the truth was often stranger than the fiction.

To live a fancy-life of adventure in my own head, was not merely an amusement to me at this time—it was a refuge. Matters did not really improve between me and my father, though I had obeyed his wishes. It was by his arrangement that I spent so much of my time at home with the Woods, and yet it remained a grievance that I liked to do so. Whether my dear mother had given up all hopes of my becoming a genius I do not know, but my father's contempt for my absorption in a book was un-abated. I felt this if he came suddenly upon me with my head in my hands and my nose in a tattered volume ; and if I went on with my reading it was with a sense of being in the wrong, whilst if I shut up the book and tried to throw myself into outside interests, my father's manner showed me that my efforts had only discredited my candour.

As is commonly the case, it was chiefly little things that pulled the wrong way of the stuff of life between us, but they pulled it very much askew. I was selfishly absorbed in my own dreams, and I think my dear father made a mistake which is a too common bit of tyranny between people who love each other and live together. He was not satisfied with my *doing* what he liked, he expected me to *be* what he liked, that is, to be another person instead of myself. Wives and daughters seem now and then to respond to this expectation as to the call of duty, and to become inconsistent echoes, odd mixtures of severity and hesitancy, hypocrites on the highest grounds ; but sons are not often so self-effacing, and it was not the case with me. It was so much the case with my dear mother, that she never was of the slightest use (which she might have been) when my father and I misunderstood each other. By my father's views of the moment she always hastily set her own, whether they were fair or unfair to me ; and she made up for it by indulging me at every point that did not cross an expressed wish of my father's, or that could not annoy him because he was not there. She never held the scales between us.

And yet it was the thought of her which kept me from taking my fate into my own hands again and again. To have obeyed my father seemed to have done so little towards making him satisfied with me, that I found no consolation at home for the distastefulness of the office ; and more than once I resolved to run away, and either enlist or go to Liverpool (which was at no great distance from us) and get on board some vessel that was about to sail for other lands. But when I thought of my mother's distress, I could not face it, and I let my half-formed projects slide again.

Oddly enough, it was Uncle Henry who brought matters

to a crisis. I think my father was disappointed (though he did not blame me) that I secured no warmer a place in Uncle Henry's affections than I did. Uncle Henry had no children, and if he took a fancy to me and I pleased him, such a career as the Jew-clerk had sketched for me would probably be mine. This dawned on me by degrees through chance remarks from my father and the more open comments of friends. For good manners with us were not of a sensitively refined order, and to be clapped on the back with—" Well, Jack, you've got into a good berth, I hear. I suppose you look to succeed your uncle some day ? " was reckoned a friendly familiarity rather than an offensive impertinence.

I learned that my parents had hoped that, as I was his nephew, Uncle Henry would take me as clerk without the usual premium. Indeed, when my uncle first urged my going to him, he had more than hinted that he should not expect a premium with his brother's son. But he was fond of his money (of which he had plenty), and when people are that, they are apt to begin to grudge, if there is time, between promise and performance. Uncle Henry had a whole year in which to think about foregoing two or three hundred pounds, and as it drew to a close, it seemed to worry him to such a degree, that he proposed to take me for half the usual premium instead of completely remitting it ; and he said something about my being a stupid sort of boy, and of very little use to him for some time to come. He said it to justify himself for drawing back, I am quite sure, but it did me no good at home.

My father had plenty of honourable pride, and he would hear of no compromise. He said that he should pay the full premium for me that Uncle Henry's other clerks had had to pay, and from this no revulsion of feeling on my uncle's part would move him. He was quite bland with Uncle Henry, and he was not quite bland towards me.

When I fairly grasped the situation (and I contrived to get a pretty clear account of it from my mother), there rushed upon me the conviction that a new phase had come over my prospects. When I put aside my own longings for my father's will ; and every time that office-life seemed intolerable to me, and I was tempted to break my bonds, and thought better of it and settled down again, this thought had always remained behind : " I will try ; and if the worst comes to the worst, and I really cannot settle down into a clerk, I can but run away then." But circumstances had altered my case. I felt that now I must make up my mind for good and all. My father would have to make some little sacrifices to find the money, and when it was once paid, I could not let it be in vain. Come what might, I must stick to the office then, and for life.

Some weeks passed whilst I was turning this over and over in my mind. I was constantly forgetting things in the office, but Moses Benson helped me out of every scrape. He was kinder and kinder, so that I often felt sorry that I could not feel fonder of him, and that his notions of fun and amusement only disgusted me instead of making us friends. They convinced me of one thing. My dear mother's chief dread about my going out of my own country was for the wicked ways I might learn in strange lands. A town with an unpronounceable name suggested foreign iniquities to her tender fears, but our own town, where she and everybody we knew bought everything we daily used, did not frighten her at all. I did not tell her, but I was quite convinced myself that I might get pretty deep into mischief in my idle hours, even if I lived within five miles of home, and had only my uncle's clerks for my comrades.

During these weeks Jem came home for the holidays. He was at a public school now, which many of our friends regarded as an extravagant folly on my father's part. We had a very happy time together, and this would have gone

far to keep me at home, if it had not, at the same time,
deepened my disgust with our town, and my companions
in the office.   In plain english, the training of two good
schools, and the society of boys superior to himself, had
made a gentleman of Jem, and the contrast between his
looks and ways, and manners, and those of my uncle's
clerks was not favourable to the latter.   How proud my
father was of him !   With me he was in a most irritable
mood (and one grumble to which I heard him give
utterance, that it was very inconvenient to have to pay
this money just at the most expensive period of Jem's
education), went heavily into the scale for running away.
And that night, as it happened, Jem and I sat up late, and
had a long and loving chat.   He abused the office to my
heart's content, and was very sympathetic when I told him
that I had wished to go to sea, and how my father had
refused to allow me.

"I think he made a great mistake," said Jem ; and he
told me of "a fellow's brother" that he knew about, who
was in the Merchant Service, and how well he was doing.
"It's not even as if Uncle Henry were coming out
generously," he added.

Dear, dear !   How pleasant it was to hear somebody
else talk on my side of the question.   And who was I that
I should rebuke Jem for calling our worthy uncle a
curmudgeon, and stigmatizing the Jew-clerk as a dirty
beast ?   I really dared not tell him that Moses grew more
familiar as my time to be articled drew near ; that he
called me Jack Sprat, and his dearest friend, and offered
to procure me the "silver-top" (or champagne)—which he
said I must "stand" on the day I took my place at the
fellow desk to his—of the first quality and at less than cost
price ; and that he had provided me gratis with a choice
of "excuses" (they were unblushing lies) to give to our
good mother, for spending that evening in town, and
"having a spree."

From **my** affairs we came to talk of Jem's, and I
found that even he, poor chap! was not without his
troubles.   He confided to me, with many expressions of
shame and vexation, that he had got into debt, but
having brought home good reports and even a prize on
this occasion, he hoped to persuade my father to pay what
he owed.

"You see, Jack, he's awfully good to me, but he will
do things his own way, and what's worse, the way they
were done in his young days.   You remember the row we
had about his giving me an allowance?   He didn't want
to, because he never had one, only tips from his governor
when the old gentleman was pleased with him.   And he
said it was quite enough to send me to such a good and
expensive school, and I ought to think of that, and not
want more because I'd got much.   We'd an awful row,
for I thought it was so unfair his making out I was greedy
and ungrateful, and I told him so, and I said I was quite
game to go to a cheap school if he liked, only wherever I
was I did want to be 'like the other fellows.'   I begged
him to take me away and to let me go somewhere cheap
with you; and I said, if the fellows there had no allowances,
we could do without.   As I told him, it's not the beastly
things that you buy that you care about, only of course
you don't like to be the only fellow who can't buy 'em.
So then he came round, and said I should have an
allowance, but I must do with a very small one.   So I
said, very well, then I musn't go in for the games.   Then
he wouldn't have that ; so then I made out a list of what
the subscriptions are to cricket, and so on, and then your
flannels and shoes, and it came to double what he offered
me.   He said it was simply disgraceful that boys shouldn't
be able to be properly educated, and have an honest
game at cricket for the huge price he paid, without the
parents being fleeced for all sorts of extravagances at
exorbitant prices.   And I know well enough its disgrace-

ful, what we have to pay for school books and for things of all sorts you have to get in the town; but, as I said to the governor, why don't you kick up a dust with the head master, or write to the papers—what's the good of rowing us? One must have what other fellows have, and get 'em where other fellows get 'em. But he never did— I wish he would. I should enjoy fighting old Pompous if I were in his place. But they're as civil as butter to each other, and then old Pompous goes on feathering his nest, and backing up the tradespeople, and the governor pitches into the young men of the present day."

"He did give you the bigger allowance, didn't he?" said I, at this pause in Jem's rhetoric.

" Yes, he did. He's awfully good to me. But you know, Jack, he never paid it quite all, and he never paid it quite in time. I found out from my mother he did it on purpose to make me value it more, and be more careful. Doesn't it seem odd he shouldn't see that I can't pay the subscriptions a few shillings short or a few days late? One must find the money somehow, and then one has to pay for that, and then you're short, and go on tick, and it runs up, and then they dun you, and you're cleaned out, and there you are!"

At which climax old Jem laid his curly head on his arms, and I began to think very seriously.

"How much do you owe?"

Jem couldn't say. He thought he could reckon up, so I got a pencil and made a list from his dictation, and from his memory, which was rather vague. When it was done (and there seemed to be a misty margin beyond), I was horrified. "Why, my dear fellow!" I exclaimed, "if you'd had your allowance ever so regularly, it wouldn't have covered this sort of thing."

" I know, I know," said poor Jem, clutching remorsefully at his curls. " I've been a regular fool! Jack! whatever you do—never tick It's the very mischief. You never

know what you owe, and so you feel vague and order more.
And you never know what you don't owe, which is worse,
for sometimes you're in such despair, it would be quite a
relief to catch some complaint and die. It's like going
about with a stone round your neck, and nobody kind
enough to drown you. I can't stand any more of it. I
shall make a clean breast to Father, and if he can't set me
straight, I won't go back ; I'll work on the farm sooner,
and let him pay my bills instead of my schooling—and
serve old Pompous right."

Poor Jem! long after he had cheered up and gone to
bed, I sat on and thought. When my premium was paid
where was the money for Jem's debts to come from?
And would my father be in the humour to pay them? If
he did not, Jem would not go back to school. Of that I
was quite certain. Jem had thought over his affairs,
which was an effort for him, but he always thought in
one direction. His thoughts never went backwards and
forwards as mine did. If he had made up his mind, there
was no more prospect of his changing it than if he had
been my father. And if the happy terms between them
were broken, and Jem's career checked when he was
doing so well !——the scales that weighed my own future
were becoming very uneven now.

I clasped my hands and thought. If I ran away, the
money would be there for Jem's debts, and his errors
would look pale in the light of my audacity, and he would
be dearer than ever at home, whilst for me were freedom,
independence (for I had not a doubt of earning bread and
cheese, if only as a working man); perhaps a better understanding with my father when I had been able to prove
my courage and industry, or even when he got the
temperate and dutiful letter I meant to post to him when
I was fairly off ; and beyond all, the desire of my eyes,
the sight of the world.

Should I stay now? And for what? To see old Jem

at logger-heads with my father, and perhaps demoralised by an inferior school? To turn my own back and shut my eyes for ever on all that the wide seas embrace; my highest goal to be to grow as rich as Uncle Henry or richer, and perhaps as mean or meaner? Should I choose for life a life I hated, and set seals to my choice by drinking silver-top with the Jew-clerk?—No, Moses, no, no!

*   *   *   *   *   *   *

I got up soon after dawn and was in the garden at sunrise the morning that I ran away. I had made my plans carefully, and carried them out, so far with success.

Including the old miser's bequest which his lawyer had paid, there were thirteen pounds to my name in the town savings-bank, and this sum I had drawn out to begin life with. I wrapped a five-pound note in a loving letter to Jem, and put both into the hymn-book on his shelf—I knew it would not be opened till Sunday. Very few run-aways have as much as eight pounds to make a start with: and as one could not be quite certain how my father would receive Jem's confession, I thought he might be glad to have a few pounds of his own, and I knew he had spent his share of the miser's money long ago.

I meant to walk to a station about seven miles distant and there take train for Liverpool. I should be clumsy, indeed, I thought, if I could not stow away on board some vessel, as hundreds of lads had done before me, and make myself sufficiently useful to pay my passage when I was found out.

When I got into the garden I kicked my foot against something in the grass. It was my mother's little gardening-fork. She had been tidying her pet perennial border, and my father had called her hastily, and she had left it half finished, and had forgotten the fork. A few minutes more or less were of no great importance to me, for it was very early, so I finished the border quite neatly, and took the fork indoors.

I put it in a corner of the hall where the light was growing stronger and making familiar objects clear. In a house like ours and amongst people like us, furniture was not chopped and changed and decorated as it is now. The place had looked like this ever since I could remember, and it would look like this to-morrow morning, though my eyes would not see it. I stood stupidly by the hall table where my father's gloves lay neatly one upon the other beside his hat. I took them up, almost mechanically, and separated them, and laid them together again finger to finger, and thumb to thumb, and held them with a stupid sort of feeling, as if I could never put them down and go away.

What would my father's face be like when he took them up this very morning to go out and look for me? and when —oh when!—should I see his face again?

I began to feel what one is apt to learn too late, that in childhood one takes the happiness of home for granted, and kicks against the pricks of its grievances, not having felt the far harder buffetings of the world. Moreover (which one does not think of then), that parental blunders and injustices are the mistakes and tyrannies of a special love that one may go many a mile on one's own wilful way and not meet a second time. Who—in the wide world— would care to be bothered with my confidence, and blame me for withholding it? Should I meet many people to whom it would matter if we misunderstood each other? Would anybody hereafter love me well enough to be disappointed in me? Would other men care so much for my fate as to insist on guiding it by lines of their own ruling?

I pressed the gloves passionately against my eyes to keep in the tears. If my day-dreams had been the only question, I should have changed my mind now. If the home grievances had been all, I should have waited for time and patience to mend them. I could not have broken all these heart-strings. I should never have run away. But there was much more, and my convictions were not changed, though I felt as if I might have managed better as regards my father.

Would he forgive me? I hoped and believed so. Would my mother forgive me? I knew she would—as GOD forgives. And with the thought of her, I knelt down, and put my head on the hall table and prayed from my soul—not for fair winds, and prosperous voyages, and good luck, and great adventures; but that it might please GOD to let me see Home again, and the faces that I loved ah, so dearly, after all!

And then I got up, and crossed the threshold, and went out into the world.

CHAPTER XIV.

" A friend in need is a friend indeed.*"*
Old Proverb.

I HAVE often thought that the biggest bit of good luck (and I was lucky), which befell me on my outset into the world, was that the man I sat next to in the railway-carriage was not a rogue. I travelled third-class to Liverpool for more than one reason—it was the cheapest way, besides which I did not wish to meet any family friends—and the man I speak of was a third-class passenger, and he went to Liverpool too.

At the time I was puzzled to think how he came to guess that I was running away, that I had money with me, and that I had never been to Liverpool before; but I can well imagine now how my ignorance and anxiety must have betrayed themselves at every station I mistook for the end of my journey, and with every question which I put, as I flattered myself, in the careless tones of common conversation. I really wonder I had not thought beforehand about my clothes, which fitted very badly on the character I assumed, and the company I chose; but it was not perhaps to be expected that I should know then, as I know now, how conspicuous all over me must have been the absence of those outward signs of hardship and poverty, which they who know poverty and hardship know so well.

I wish *I* had known them, because then I should have given the man some of my money when we parted, instead of feeling too delicate to do so. I can remember his face too well not to know now how much he must have needed it, and how heroic a virtue honesty must have been in him.

It did not seem to strike him as at all strange or unnatural that a lad of my age should be seeking his own fortune, but I feel sure that he thought it was misconduct on my part which had made me run away from home. I had no grievance to describe which he could recognise as grievous enough to drive me out into the world. However, I felt very glad that he saw no impossibility in my earning my own livelihood, or even anything very unusual in my situation.

" I suppose lots of young fellows run away from home and go to sea from a place like this ?" said I, when we had reached Liverpool.

"And there's plenty more goes that has no homes to run from," replied he sententiously.

Prefacing each fresh counsel with the formula, " You'll excuse *me*," he gave me some excellent advice as we threaded the greasy streets, and jostled the disreputable-looking population of the lower part of the town. General counsels as to my conduct, and the desirableness of turning over a new leaf for "young chaps" who had been wild and got into scrapes at home. And particular counsels which were invaluable to me, as to changing my

L

dress, how to hide my money, what to turn my hand to
with the quickest chance of bread-winning in strange
places, and how to keep my own affairs to myself among
strange people.

It was in the greasiest street, and among the most disreputable-looking people, that we found the "slop-shop"
where, by my friend's orders, I was to "rig out" in clothes
befitting my new line of life.   He went in first, so he did
not see the qualm that seized me on the doorstep.   A
revulsion so violent that it nearly made me sick then and
there ; and if someone had seized me by the nape of my
neck, and landed me straightway at my desk in Uncle
Henry's office, would, I believe, have left me tamed for life.
For if this unutterable vileness of sights and sounds and
smells which hung around the dark entry of the slop-shop
were indeed the world, I felt a sudden and most vehement
conviction that I would willingly renounce the world for
ever.   As it happened, I had not at that moment the
choice.   My friend had gone in, and I dared not stay
among the people outside.   I groped my way into the
shop, which was so dark as well as dingy that they had
lighted a small oil-lamp just above the head of the man
who served out the slops.   Even so the light that fell on
him was dim and fitful, and was the means of giving me
another start in which I gasped out—" Moses Benson ! "

The man turned and smiled (he had the Jew-clerk's exact
smile), and said softly :

" Cohen, my dear, not Benson."

And as he bent at another angle to the oil-lamp I saw
that he was older than the clerk, and dirtier ; and though
his coat was quite curiously like the one I had so often
cleaned, he had evidently either never met with the invaluable "scouring drops," or did not feel it worth while
to make use of them in such a dingy hole.

One shock helped to cure the other.   Come what might,
I could not sneak back now to the civil congratulations of

that other Moses, and the scorn of his eye. But I was so nervous that my fellow-traveller transacted my business for me, and when the oil-lamp flared and I caught Moses Cohen looking at me, I jumped as if Snuffy had come behind me. And when we got out (and it was no easy matter to escape from the various benevolent offers of the owner of the slop-shop), my friend said :

" You'll excuse me telling you—but whatever you do don't go near that there Jew again. He's no friend for a young chap like you."

" I should have got your slops cheaper," he added, " if I could have taken your clothes in without you."

My "slops" were a very loose suit of clothes made of much coarser material than my own, and I suppose they were called "slops" because they fitted in such a peculiarly sloppy manner. The whole "rig out" (it included a strong clasp-knife, and a little leathern bag to keep my money in, which I was instructed to tie round my neck) was provided by Mr. Cohen in exchange for the clothes I had been wearing before, with the addition of ten shillings in cash. I dipped again into the leathern bag to provide a meal for myself and my friend ; then, by his advice, I put a shilling and come coppers into my pocket, that I might not have to bring out my purse in public, and with a few parting words of counsel he wrung my hand, and we parted—he towards some place of business where he hoped to get employment, and I in the direction of the docks, where the ships come and go.

" I hope you *will* get work," were my last words.

" The same to you, my lad," was his reply, and it seemed to acknowledge me as one of that big brotherhood of toilers who, when they want " something to do," want it not to pass time but to earn daily bread.

CHAPTER XV.

"Deark d'on Dearka." (*"Beg of a Beggar."*)
Irish Proverb.

**".... From her way of speaking they also saw imme-
diately that she too was an Eirisher . . . . They must be a
bonny family when they are all at home!"**—*The Life of Mansie
Wauch, Tailor in Dalkeith.*

"DOCK" (so ran the 536th of the 'Penny Numbers') is
"a place artificially formed for the reception of ships,
the entrance of which is generally closed by gates. There
are two kinds of docks, dry-docks and wet-docks. The
former are used for receiving ships in order to their being
inspected and repaired. For this purpose the dock must
be so contrived that the water may be admitted or ex-
cluded at pleasure, so that a vessel can be floated in when
the tide is high, and that the water may run out with the
fall of the tide, or be pumped out, the closing of the gates
preventing its return. Wet-docks are formed for the
purpose of keeping vessels always afloat. . . . One of the
chief uses of a dock is to keep a uniform level of water, so
that the business of loading and unloading ships can be
carried on without any interruption. . . . The first wet-
dock for commercial purposes made in this kingdom was
formed in the year 1708 at Liverpool, then a place of no
importance."

*The business of loading and unloading ships can 'e
carried on without any interruption.* If everything that
the 'Penny Numbers' told of were as true to the life as
that, the world's wonders (at least those of them which
begin with the first four letters of the alphabet) must be
all that I had hoped; and perhaps that bee-hive about
which Master Isaac and I had had our jokes, did really

yield a "considerable income" to the fortunate French beemaster!

Loading and unloading, coming and going, lifting and lowering, shouting and replying, swearing and retorting, creaking and jangling, shrieking and bumping, cursing and chaffing, the noise and restlessness of men and things were utterly bewildering. I had often heard of a Babel of sounds, but I had never before heard anything so like what one might fancy it must have been when that great crowd of workmen broke up, and left building their tower, in a confounding of language and misunderstanding of speech. For the men who went to and fro in these docks, each his own way, jostling and yelling to each other, were men of all nations, and the confusion was of tongues as well as of work. At one minute I found myself standing next to a live Chinaman in a pigtail, who was staring as hard as I at some swarthy supple-bodied sailors with eager faces, and scant clothing wrapped tightly round them, chatting to each other in a language as strange to the Chinaman as to me, their large lustrous eyes returning our curiosity with interest, and contrasting strangely with the tea-caddy countenance of my elbow neighbour. Then a turbaned Turk went by, and then two grinning negroes, and there were lots of men who looked more like Englishmen, but who spoke with other tongues, and amongst those who loaded and unloaded in this busy place, which was once of no importance, Irish brogue seemed the commonest language of all.

One thing made me hopeful—there were plenty of boys no bigger than myself who were busy working, and therefore earning wages, and as I saw several lads who were dressed in suits the very counterpart of my own, I felt sure that my travelling companion had done me a good turn when he rigged me out in slops. An incident that occurred in the afternoon made me a little more doubtful about this.

I really had found much to counterbalance the anxieties of my position in the delightful novelty and variety of life around me, and not a little to raise my hopes ; for I had watched keenly for several hours as much as I could see from the wharf of what was going on in this ship and that, and I began to feel less confused. I perceived plainly that a great deal of every-day sort of work went on in ships as well as in houses, with the chief difference, in dock at any rate, of being done in public. In the most free and easy fashion, to the untiring entertainment of crowds of idlers besides myself, the men and boys on vessel after vessel lying alongside, washed out their shirts and socks, and hung them up to dry, cooked their food, cleaned out their pots and pans, tidied their holes and corners, swept and brushed, and fetched and carried, and did scores of things which I knew I could do perfectly, for want of something better to do.

" It's clear there's plenty of dirty work to go on with till one learns seamanship," I thought ; and the thought was an honest satisfaction to me.

I had always swept Uncle Henry's office, and that had been light work after cleaning the schoolroom at Snuffy's. My hands were never likely to be more chapped at sea than they had been with dirt and snow and want of things to dry oneself with at school ; and as to coal-carrying——

Talking of coals, on board the big ship, out of which great white bales, strapped with bars of iron, were being pulled up by machinery, and caught and flung about by the "unloaders," there was a man whose business seemed to be to look after the fires, and who seemed also to have taken a roll in the coal-hole for pleasure ; and I saw him find a tin basin and a square of soap, and a decent rough towel to wash his face and hands, such as would have been reckoned luxurious in a dormitory at Snuffy's. Altogether, when a heavy hand was laid suddenly on my shoulder, and a gruff voice said :

"Well, my young star-gazing greenhorn, and what do you want?"

I replied with alacrity, as well as with more respect than the stranger's appearance was calculated to inspire, "Please, sir, I want to go to sea, and I should like to ship for America."

He was not a nice-looking man by any means—far too suggestive of Snuffy, when Snuffy was partly drunk. But after a pause, he said:

"All right. Where are your papers? What was your ship, and why did ye run?"

"I have not served in a ship yet, sir," said I, "but I'm sure——"

He did not allow me to go on. With a sudden fierce look that made him more horribly like Snuffy than before, he caught me by my sleeve and a bit of my arm, and shoved me back from the edge of the dock till we stood alone. "Then where did ye steal your slops?" he hissed at me with oaths. "Look here, ye young gallows-bird, if ye don't stand me a liquor, I'll run ye in as a run-away apprentice. So cash up, and look sharp."

"I was startled, but I was not quite such a fool as I looked, mind or body. I had once had a hardish struggle with Snuffy himself when he was savage, and I was strong and agile beyond my seeming. I dived deeply into my trousers-pocket, as if feeling for the price of a "liquor," and the man having involuntarily allowed me a little swing for this, I suddenly put up my shoulders, and ran at him as if my head were a battering-ram, and his moleskin waistcoat the wall of a beleaguered city, and then wrenching myself from his grasp, and dodging the leg he had put out to trip me, I fled blindly down the quay.

No one can take orange-peel into account, however. I slipped on a large piece and came headlong, with the aggravation of hearing my enemy breathing hoarsely

close above me.   As regards him, I suppose it was lucky
that my fall jerked the shilling and the penny out of my
pocket, for as the shilling rolled away he went after it, and
I saw him no more.   What I did see when I sat up was
the last of my penny (which had rolled in another direction), as it gave one final turn and fell into the dock.

I could have cried with vexation, and partly with
fatigue, for it was getting late, and I was getting tired.   I
had fallen soft enough, as it happened, for I found myself
on a heap of seeds, some kind of small bean, and the
yielding mass made a pleasant resting-place.   There was
no one very near, and I moved round to the back of the
heap to be still more out of sight, and sat down to try and
think what it was best to do.   If my slops were really a
sort of uniform to which I was not entitled, they would do
me more harm than good.   But whom could I ask?   If
there were an honest, friendly soul in all this crowd, and I
could come across him, I felt that (without telling too
much of my affairs) I could explain that I had exchanged
some good shore clothes of my own for what I had been
told were more suitable to the work I was looking out for,
and say further that though I had never yet been at sea, I
was hardy, and willing to make myself useful in any way.
But how could I tell whom to trust?   I might speak fair
to some likely-looking man, and he might take me somewhere and strip me of my slops, and find my leather
money-bag, and steal that too.   When I thought how
easily my fellow-traveller might have treated me thus, I
felt a thrill of gratitude towards him, and then I wondered
how he had prospered in his search for work.   As for me,
it was pretty clear that if I hoped to work my way in this
wicked world, I must suspect a scoundrel in every man I
met, and forestall mischief by suspicion.   As I sat and
thought, I sifted the beans through my fingers, and saw
that there were lots of strange seeds mixed with them,
some of very fantastic shapes ; and I wondered what

"I WAS WAKENED BY A TOUCH ON MY HEAD, AND A VOICE JUST ABOVE ME."

countries they came from, and with what shape and scent and colour the plants blossomed, and thought how Charlie would like some of them to sow in pots and watch. As I drove my hands deeper into the heap, I felt that it was quite warm inside, and then I put my head down to smell if there was any fragrance in the seeds, and I did not lift it up again, for I fell fast asleep.

I was wakened by a touch on my head, and a voice just above me, saying : " He's alive annyhow, thank GOD ! " and sitting up among the beans I found that it was dark and foggy, but a lamp at some distance gave me a pretty good view of an old woman who was bending over me.

She was dressed, apparently, in several skirts of unequal lengths, each one dingier and more useless-looking than the one beneath it. She had a man's coat, with a short pipe in the breast-pocket ; and what her bonnet was like one could not tell, for it was comfortably tied down by a crimson handkerchief with big white spots, which covered it completely. Her face was as crumpled and as dirty as her clothes, but she had as fine eyes and as kind eyes as mine have ever met. And every idea of needful wariness and of the wickedness of the world went quite naturally out of my head, and I said, " Did you think I was dead, mother ? "

" I did not ; though how would I know what would be the matter wid ye, lying there those three hours on your face, and not a stir out o' ye ? "

" You're very kind," I said, dusting the bean-dust off my trousers, and I suppose I looked a little puzzled, for the old woman (helping me by flicking at my sleeve) went on : " I'll not deceive ye, my dear. It was my own Micky that was on my mind : though now you've lifted your face, barring the colour of his hair, there's no likeness betwixt ye, and I'm the disappointed woman again, GOD help me ! "

" Is Micky your son ? " I asked.

" He is, and a better child woman never had, till he tired of everything I would do for him, being always the boy for change, and went for a stow-away from this very port."

" Sit down, mother ; stow-aways are lads that hide on board ship, and get taken to sea for nothing, aren't they ? "

" They are, darlin' ; but it's not for nothing they get kept at sea, ye may take your oath. And many's the one that leaves this in the highest of expictations, and is glad enough to get back to it in a tattered shirt and a whole skin, and with an increase of contintment under the ways of home upon his mind."

" And you hope Micky'll come back, I suppose ? "

" Why wouldn't I, acushla ? Sure it was by reason o that I got bothered with the washin' after me poor boy left me, from my mind being continually in the docks, instead of with the clothes. And there I would be at the end of the week, with the captain's jerseys gone to old Miss Harding, and *his* washing no corricter than *hers*, though he'd more good nature in him over the accidents, and iron-moulds on the table-cloths, and pocket-handker-chers missin', and me ruined entirely with making them good, and no thanks for it, till a good-natured sowl of a foreigner that kept a pie-shop larned me to make the coffee, and lint me the money to buy a barra, and he says : ' Go as convanient to the ships as ye can, mother ; it'll aise your mind. My own heart,' says he, laying his hand to it, ' knows what it is to have my body here, and the whole sowl of me far away.' "

" Did you pay him back ? " I asked. I spoke without thinking, and still less did I mean to be rude; but it had suddenly struck me that I was young and hearty, and that it would be almost a duty to share the contents of my leather bag with this poor old woman, if there were no chance of her being able to repay the generous foreigner.

"Did I pay him back?" she screamed. "Would I be the black-hearted thief to him that was kind to me? Sorra bit nor sup but dry bread and water passed me lips till he had his own agin, and the heart's blessings of owld Biddy Macartney along with it."

I made my peace with old Biddy as well as I could, and turned the conversation back to her son.

"So you live in the docks with your coffee-barrow, mother, that you may be sure not to miss Micky when he comes ashore?"

"I do, darlin'. Fourteen years all but three days. He'll be gone fifteen if we all live till Wednesday week."

"*Fifteen?* But, mother, if he were like me when he went, he can't be very like me now. He must be a middle-aged man. Do you think you'd know him?"

This question was more unfortunate than the other, and produced such howling and weeping, and beating of Biddy's knees as she rocked herself among the beans, that I should have thought every soul in the docks would have crowded round us. But no one took any notice of us, and by degrees I calmed her, chiefly by the assertion—

"He'll know you, mother, anyhow."

"He will so, GOD bless him!" said she. "And haven't I gone over it all in me own mind, often and often, when I'd see the vessels feelin' their way home through the darkness, and the coffee staymin enough to cheer your heart wid the smell of it, and the laste taste in life of something betther in the stone bottle under me petticoats. And then the big ship would be coming in with her lights at the head of her, and myself sitting alone with me patience, GOD helping me, and one and another strange face going by. And then he comes along, cold maybe, and smells the coffee. 'Bedad, but that's a fine smell with it,' says he, for Micky was mighty particular in his aitin' and drinkin'. 'I'll take a dhrop of that,' says he, not noticing me particular, and if ever I'd the saycret of a good cup he gets it, me consayling me face. 'What will it be?' says he, setting down the mug. 'What would it be, Micky, from your mother?' says I, and I lifts me head. Arrah, but then there's the heart's delight between us. 'Mother!' says he. 'Micky!' says I. And he lifts his foot and kicks over the barra, and dances me round in his arms. 'Ochone!' says the spictators; 'there's the fine coffee that's running into the dock.' ' Let it run,' says I, in the joy of me heart, ' and you after it, and the barra on the top of ye, now Micky me son's come home!'"

"Wonderfully jolly!" said I. "And it must be pleasant even to think of it."

But Biddy's effort of imagination seemed to have exhausted her, and she relapsed into the lowest possible spirits, from which she suddenly roused herself to return to her neglected coffee-stall.

"Bad manners to me, for an old fool! sitting here whineging and lamenting, when there's folks, maybe, waiting for their coffee, and yourself would have been the betther of some this half-hour. Come along wid ye."

And giving a tighter knot to the red kerchief, which had been disordered by her lamentations, the old woman went down the dock, I following her.

We had not to go far. Biddy's coffee barrow was placed just as the pieman had advised. It was as neaɪ the ships as possible. In fact it was actually under the shadow of a big black-looking vessel which loomed large through the fog, and to and from which men were coming and going as usual. With several of these the old woman interchanged some good-humoured chaff as she settled herself in her place, and bade me sit beside her.

" Tuck your legs under ye, agra! on that bit of an ould sack. 'Tis what I wrap round me shoulders when the nights do be wet, as it isn't this evening, thank GOD! And there's the coffee for ye."

" Mother," said I, "do you think you could sit so as to
hide me for a few minutes? All the money I have is
in a bag round my neck, and I don't want strangers to
see it."

" Ye'll just keep it there, then," replied Biddy, irately,
" and don't go an' insult me wid the show of it."

And she turned her back on me, whilst I drank my
coffee, and ate some excellent cakes, which formed part
of her stock-in-trade. One of these she insisted on my
putting into my pocket "against the hungry hour." I
thanked her warmly for the gift, whereupon she became
mollified, and said I was kindly welcome; and whilst she
was serving some customers, I turned round and looked at
the ship. Late as it was, people seemed very busy about
her, rather more so than about any I had seen. As I sat,
I was just opposite to a yawning hole in the ship's side,
into which men were noisily running great bales and
boxes, which other men on board were lowering into
the depths of the vessel with very noisy machinery and
with much shouting in a sort of uncouth rhythm, to
which the grating and bumping of the crane and its
chains was a trifle. I was so absorbed by looking, and
it was so impossible to hear anything else unless one
were attending, that I never discovered that Biddy and I
were alone again, till the touch of her hand on my head
made me jump.

" I beg your pardon, mother," I said; " I couldn't think
what it was."

" I ax yours, dear. It's just the curls, and I'm the
foolish woman to look at 'em. Barrin' the hair, ye don't
favour each other the laste."

I had really heard a good deal about Micky, and was
getting tired of him, and inclined to revert to my own
affairs.

" Mother, do you know where this ship comes from?"

" I do not. But she sails with the morning for Halifax,

I'm told. And that's America way, and I insensed the cook—that was him that axed me where I bought my coffee—to have an eye out for Micky, in case he might come across him anywhere."

America way! To-morrow morning! A storm of thoughts rushed through my head, and in my passionate longing for help I knelt up by the old Irishwoman and laid my hand upon hers.

"Mother dear, do help me! You are so kind, and you've a boy of your own at sea. I want to go to America, and I've no papers or anything. Couldn't I stow away as Micky did? Couldn't I stow away on this one? I can work well enough when they find me out, if I could only hide so as to get off; and you know the ships and the docks so well, you could tell me how, if only you would."

I am always ashamed to remember the feeble way in which I finished off by breaking down, though I do not know that I could have used any argument that would have gone so far with Biddy. If it had been a man who had been befriending me, I'm sure I shouldn't have played the fool, but it was a woman, so I felt doubly helpless in having to depend on her, and she felt doubly kind, and in short, I put my face in my hands and sobbed.

For quite four hours after this I was puzzled to death by smelling stale bad tobacco about myself; then I discovered that by some extraordinary jerk in the vehemence of the embrace which was Biddy's first response to my appeal, the little black pipe had got out of her coat-pocket and tumbled down the breast of my slops.

I hope my breakdown was partly due to the infectious nature of emotion, of which Biddy was so lavish that my prospects were discussed in a sadly unbusinesslike fashion. My conscience is really quite clear of having led her to hope that I would look out for Micky on the other side of the Atlantic, but I fear that she had made up her mind that

we should meet, and that this went far towards converting
her to my views for stowing away on the vessel lying
alongside of us. However, that important point once
reached, the old woman threw herself into the enterprise
with a practical knowledge of the realities of the under-
taking and a zest for the romance of it which were alike
invaluable to me.

" The botheration of it is," said Biddy, after some talk,
tangling her bonnet and handkerchief over her face till
I felt inclined to beg her to let me put her straight—" the
botheration of it is, that it's near to closing-time, and when
the bell rings ivery soul'll be cleared out, labourers and
idlers, and myself among 'em. Ye'll have to hide, me
darlin', but there'll be no mighty difficulty in that, for I
see a fine bit of tarpaulin yonder that'd consale a dozen of
the likes of you. But there's that fool of a watchman
that'll come parading and meandering up and down wid
all the airs of a sentry on him and none of the good looks,
and wid a sneaking bull's-eye of a lantern in his hand.
He's at the end of the wharf now, purshuin' to him!
Maybe I'll get him to taste a dhrop of me coffee before the
bell rings. Many's the cup I gave to the old watchman
before him, peace to his sowl, the kindly craythur! that
never did a more ill-natured thing on his beat than sleep
like a child. Hide now, darlin', and keep the tail of your
eye at a corner where ye'll see the ship. Maybe he'll
take a nap yet, for all his airs, and then there's the chance
for ye! And mind now, keep snug till the pilot's gone as
I warned ye, and then it's the bold heart and the civil
tongue, and just the good-nature of your ways, that'll be
your best friends. The cook tells me the captain's as
dacent a man as iver he served with, so you might aisy do
worse, and are not likely to do better. Are ye hid now?
Whisht! Whisht! "

I heard most of this through a lifted corner of the
tarpaulin, under which I had the good luck to secrete

myself without observation and without difficulty. In the same manner I became witness to the admirable air of indifference with which Biddy was mixing herself a cup of coffee as the watchman approached. I say *mixing* advisedly, for as he came up she was conspicuously pouring some of the contents of the stone bottle into her cup. Whether this drew the watchman's attention in an unusual degree, of course I do not know, but he stopped to say, " Good evening, Biddy."

" Good evening to ye, me dear, and a nasty damp evening it is."

" You're taking something to keep the damp out, I see, missus."

" I am, dear ; but it's not for a foine milithrary-looking man like yourself to be having the laugh at a poor old craythur with nothin' but the wind and weather in her bones."

" The wind and weather get into my bones, I can tell you," said the watchman ; "and I begin my work in the fog just when you're getting out of it."

" And that's thrue, worse luck. Take a dhrop of coffee, allanna, before I lave ye."

" No, thank ye, missus ; I've just had my supper."

" And would that privint ye from takin' the cup I'd be offering ye, wid a taste of somethin' in it against the damps, barrin' the bottle was empty ? "

" Well, I'm not particular—as you are so pressing. Thank ye, mum ; here's your good health."

I heard the watchman say this, though at the moment I dared not peep, and then I heard him cough.

" My sakes, Biddy, you make your—coffee—strong."

" Strong, darlin'? It's pure, ye mane. It's the rale craythur, that, and bedad ! there's a dhrop or two left that's not worth the removing, and we'll share it annyhow. Here's to them that's far—r away."

" Thank you, thank you, woman."

"Thim that's *near*, and thim that's far away!" said Biddy, improving upon her toast.

There was a pause. I could hear the old woman packing up her traps, and then the man (upon whom the coffee and whisky seemed to produce a roughening rather than a soothing effect) said coarsely, "You're a rum lot, you Irish!"

"We are, dear," replied Biddy blandly; "and that's why we'd be comin' all the way to Lancashire for the improvement of our manners." And she threw the sacking round her neck, and lifted the handles of her barrow.

"Good-night, me darlin'!" said she, raising her voice as she moved off. "*We'll meet again*, GOD willing."

"Safe enough, unless you tumble into the dock," replied the watchman. "Go steady, missus. I hope you'll get safe home with that barra o' yours."

"GOD send all safe home that's far from it!" shouted Biddy, in tones that rose above the rumbling of the wheel and the shuffling of her shoes.

"Haw! haw!" laughed the watchman, and with increased brutalness in his voice he reiterated, "You're a rum lot, Biddy! and free of most things, blessings and all."

I was not surprised that the sound of the wheel and the shoes ceased suddenly. Biddy had set down her barrow to retort. But it was with deep gratitude that I found her postpone her own wrath to my safety, and content herself with making her enemy "a prisint of the contimpt of a rogue."

"And what would I be doing but blessing ye?" she cried, in a voice of such dramatic variety as only quick wits and warm feelings can give, it was so full at once of suppressed rage, humorous triumph, contemptuous irony, and infinite tenderness. And I need hardly say that it was raised to a ringing pitch that would have reached my ears had they been buried under twenty tarpaulins. "GOD bless ye for ivermore! Good luck to ye! fine weather to

M

ye ! health and strength to ye ! May the knaves that would harm ye be made fools for your benefit, and mav niver worse luck light on one hair of your head than the best blessings of Biddy Macartney !"

Something peculiar in the sound of Biddy's retreating movements made me risk another glance from an angle of the tarpaulin.

And upon my honour it is strictly true that I saw the old Irish woman drive her barrow down the dock till she passed out of sight, and that she went neither walking nor running, but *dancing;* and a good high stepping dance too, that showed her stockings, and shook the handkerchief on her head. And when she reached the end of the wharf she snapped her fingers in the air.

Then I drew my head back, and I could hear the watchman guffaw as if he would have split his sides. And even after he began to tramp up and down I could hear him still chuckling as he paced by.

And if I did not hear Biddy chuckle, it was perhaps because the joke on her side lay deeper down.

----◆----

CHAPTER XVI.

" The mariners shout,
The ships swing about,
The yards are all hoisted,
The sails flutter out."
The Saga of King Olaf.

THE docks were very quiet now. Only a few footfalls broke the silence, and the water sobbed a little round the piles, and there was some creaking and groaning and grinding, and the vessels drifted at their moorings, and bumped against the wharves.

The watchman paced up and down, and up and down.
I did not hear him very clearly from under the tarpaulin,
and sometimes when he went farther away I did not hear
him at all. At last I was so long without hearing him
that I peeped cautiously out. What Biddy had said might
be, seemed really to have happened. The watchman was
sitting in a sort of armchair of ironbound cotton-bales ;
his long coat was tucked between his legs, his hat was
over his nose, and he was fast asleep.

I did not need any one to tell me that now was my time ;
but it was with limbs that almost refused their office from
sheer fright, that I crept past the sleeping man, and
reached the edge of the wharf. There was the vessel
moving very slightly, and groaning dismally as she moved,
and there was the hole, and it was temptingly dark. But—
the gangway that had been laid across to it from the
wharf was gone ! I could have jumped the chasm easily
with a run, but I dared not take a run. If I did it at all
it must be done standing. I tried to fetch a breath free
from heart-throbs, but in vain ; so I set my teeth, and
pulled nerves and sinews together and jumped.

It was too much for me, and I jumped short and fell.
Then my training under the half-caste told in my favour.
I caught the edge of the hole with my hands, and swung
suspended over the water, with quite presence of mind
enough to hear and think of what was going on about me.
What I heard was the watchman, who roused up to call
out, " Who's there ? " and then he shot a sharp ray of light
from his lantern right into the hole. It was very lucky for
me that I was so low, for the light went over my head,
and he saw nothing of me, my dark clothes making no
mark against the ship's black hull.

My head was cool enough now, and my heart steady,
and I listened with an intensity that postponed fear,
though my predicament was not a pleasant one, and the
rippling water below me was confusing.

M 2

The suspense was no doubt shorter than it seemed, before the light disappeared, and with a thankful heart I distinctly heard the watchman flop down again among the cotton-bales. Then I drew myself up over the edge and crept noiselessly into the ship. I took care to creep beyond range of the lantern, and then the swaying of the vessel made me feel so giddy that I had to lie still for a while where I was, before I could recover myself enough to feel about for a suitable hiding-place.

As I afterwards learnt, I was on the lower deck, which was being used for cargo instead of passengers. The said cargo seemed so tightly packed, that in spite of creeping, and groping, and knocking myself pretty hard, I could feel no nook or corner to my mind. Then I turned giddy again and reeled against the door of a cabin, which gave way so far as to let me fall inwards on to a heap of old sails, ropes, and other softish ship lumber stowed away within. As I fell my hand struck something warm, which I fancied gave a writhe out of my grasp. I groped and seized it again, and now there was no mistake. It was somebody's arm, who said in a quick undertone, " Gently, gently, sirs ; I'm coming along with ye. I'll gie ye my word I'm after no harm."

I was taken aback, but thought it well to keep up my position, which appeared to be one of advantage. The young man (for it was a youngster's voice) was evidently no ship's officer. If he were a dockyard-pilferer, it was a nuisance, and a complication in my affairs, but I might pull through the difficulty with presence of mind.

" Speak low ! " I whispered sharply. " What's your name, and where do you come from ? "

" Alister Auchterlay, they call me " (the whisper was a reluctant one, but I jogged his arm rather fiercely to shake the truth out of him). " I come from Aberdeenshire. But, man ! if ye're for having me up in court, for GOD'S sake let me plead in another name, for my mother taks the papers."

"What are you doing here?" I whispered in a not very steady whisper, as I think my prisoner detected.

"I'm just stowing away," he said eagerly; "I'm no harming a thing. Eh, sir, if you're a ship's 'prentice, or whatever may be your duties on this vessel, let me bide! There's scores of stowaways taken every day, and I'll work as few could."

"Do, *do* try and speak low," I whispered; "or we shall both be found out. *I'm stowing away myself!*"

"Whew, laddie! How long will ye have been in Liverpool?"

"Only to-day. How long have you been here?"

"A week, and a sore week too."

"You've no friends here, have you?"

"Freens, did ye say? I've no freens nearer than Scotland."

"You must have had a hard time of it," I whispered.

"Ye may say so. I've slept four nights in the docks, and never managed to stow till to-night. There's a watchman about."

"I know," said I.

"I shouldn't have got in to-night, but the misconducted body's asleep, though I'll say it's the first time I saw him sleeping these four days. Eh, sirs! there's an awful indifference to responsibility, when a man does a thing like yon. But it'll be whisky, I'm thinking; for I heard him at clishmaclavers with one of these randy, drucken old Eirishers."

My blood boiled. "She was *not* drunk!" said I. "And she's—she's a great friend of mine."

"Whisht! whisht, man! We'll be heard. I ask your pardon, I'm sure."

I made no reply. The Scotchman's tone was unpleasantly dry. Besides it is very difficult to give vent to one's just indignation in whispers, and I still felt giddy, though I was resting my back against some of the lumber, rather comfortably.

" You'll no be Eirish, yourself?" the Scotchman asked in his own accent, which was as strong in its way as Biddy's.

" I'm English," I said.

" Just so.   And edyucated, I dare to say?"

" I suppose so."

" Ye've not forgiven me that I wronged the old lady? Indeed, but I ask your pardon, and hers no less.   It's not for the best of us to sit in judgment on the erring, as my mother has often said to me, unless it comes in the plain path of duty.   But maybe your own temper would be a bit soored if your head were as light and your heart as sick as mine with starvation and hope deferred——"

" Are you hungry?" I interrupted.

" I'll not be sorry when we get a meal."

" What have you had to-day?" I asked.

" I've been in the dock all day," he answered evasively, "but I'm no great eater at the best of times, and I chewed two bits of orange-peel, not to speak of a handful of corn where there was a big heap had been spilt by some wasteful body or another, that had small thoughts of it's coming to use.   Now hoo in this world's a man to make honest profit on a commodity he entrusts——"

" Sh! sh!   You're raising your voice again," said I. " Where's your hand?   It's only a cake, but it'll be better than nothing."   And I held out the cake Biddy had made me put in my pocket.

" I'll no take it from ye.   Keep it for your own needs; I'm harder than yourself, it's likely," he said, pushing my hand aside, and added almost peevishly, " but keep the smell of it from me."

" I can spare it perfectly," I whispered.   " I've had plenty to eat quite lately."

I shall never forget how he clutched it then.   I could hear his teeth clash with the eagerness of his eating.   It almost frightened me in the darkness.

" Eh! man, that was good!" he gasped.   " Are ye

sure indeed and in truth ye could spare it all? I didn't think they made such bannocks out of Scotland. But we've much to learn in all matters, doubtless. Thank ye a thousand times."

"The old Irishwoman gave it me!" I said with some malice. "She made me put it in my pocket, though she had given me a good meal before, for which she would take nothing."

"It was leeberal of her," said Alister Auchterlay. "Verra leeberal; but there are good Christians to be met with, amongst all sorts, there's not a doot aboot it."

I should probably have pursued my defence of Biddy against this grudging—not to say insulting—tribute to her charity, if I had not begun to feel too tired to talk, and very much teased by the heaving of the vessel.

"I wish the ship would be quiet till we start," I said. "We're not at sea yet."

In reply to this Alister at some length, and with as much emphasis as whispering permitted, explained to me that a ship could not, in the nature of things, keep still, except in certain circumstances, such as being in dry dock for repairs or lying at anchor in absolutely still water.

"Good gracious!" I interrupted. "Of course I know all that. You don't suppose I expect it not to move."

"I understood ye to say that ye wushed it," he replied with dignity, if not offence.

"I don't know what I wish!" I moaned.

My companion's reply to this was to feel about for me and then to begin scrambling over me; then he said—"Move on, laddie, to your right, and ye'll find space to lie on the flat of your back, close by the ship's side. I'm feared you're barely fit for the job ye've undertaken, but ye'll be easier if ye lie down, and get some sleep."

I moved as he told me, and the relief of lying flat was

great—so great that I began to pull myself together again, and made ready in my mind to thank my unseen companion for the generosity with which he had evidently given me the place he had picked for himself. But whilst I was thinking about it I fell fast asleep.

When I woke, for the first minute I thought I was at home, and I could not conceive what Martha could be doing, that there should be, as far as one could hear, chimney - sweeping, cinder - riddling, furniture - moving, clock-winding, and spring-cleaning, of the most awful nature, all going on at once, and in a storm of yelling and scolding, which was no part of our domestic ways. But in another minute I knew where I was, and by the light coming through a little round porthole above me, I could see my companion.

He was still sleeping, so that I could satisfy my keen curiosity, without rudeness. He had indeed given up the only bit of space to me, and was himself doubled up among lumber in a fashion that must have been very trying to the length of his limbs. For he was taller than I, though not, I thought, much older; two years or so, perhaps. The cut of his clothes (not their raggedness, though they were ragged as well as patched) confirmed me in my conviction that he was " not exactly a gentleman "; but I felt a little puzzled about him, for, broad as his accent was, he was even less exactly of the Tim Binder and Bob Furniss class.

He was not good-looking, and yet I hardly know any word that would so fittingly describe his face in the repose of sleep, and with that bit of light concentrated upon it, as the word "noble." It was drawn and pinched with pain and the endurance of pain, and I never saw anything so thin, except his hands, which lay close to his sides— both clenched. But I do think he would have been handsome if his face had not been almost aggressively intelligent when awake, and if his eyebrows and eyelashes had had any colour. His hair was fair but not bright, and it was straight without being smooth, and tossed into locks that had no grace or curl. And why he made me think of a Bible picture—Jacob lying at the foot of the ladder to heaven, or something of that sort—I could not tell, and did not puzzle myself to wonder, for the ship was moving, and there was a great deal to be seen out of the window, tiny as it was.

It looked on to the dock, where men were running about in the old bewildering fashion. To-day it was not so bewildering to me, because I could see that the men were working with some purpose that affected our vessel, though the directions in which they ran, dragging ropes as thick as my leg, to the grinding of equally monstrous chains, were as mysterious as the figures of some dance one does not know. As to the noises they made, men and boys anywhere are given to help on their work with sounds of some sort, but I could not have believed in anything approaching to these, out of a lunatic asylum, unless I had heard them.

I could hear quite well, I could hear what was said, and a great deal of it, I am sorry to say, would have been better unsaid. But the orders which rang out interested me, for I tried to fit them on to what followed, though without much result. At last the dock seemed to be moving away from me—I saw men, but not the same men —and every man's eye was fixed on us. Then the thick brown rope just below my window quivered like a bow-string, and tightened (all the water starting from it in a sparkling shower) till it looked as firm as a bar of iron, and I held on tight, for we were swinging round. Suddenly the voice of command sang out—(I fancied with a touch of triumph in the tone)—"Let go the warp!" The thick rope sprang into the air, and wriggled like a long snake, and it was all I could do to help joining in the shouts that rang from the deck above and from the dock below. Then the very heart of the ship began to beat with a new sound, and the Scotch lad leaped like a deer-hound to the window, and put his arm round my shoulder, and whispered, " That's the screw, man ! *we're off !* "

———♦———

CHAPTER XVII.

"He that tholes o'ercomes."
"Tak' your venture, as mony a gude ship has done."

Scotch Proverbs.

I AM disposed to think that a ship is a place where one has occasional moments of excitement and enthusiasm that are rare elsewhere, but that it is not to be beaten (if approached) for the deadliness of the despondency to be experienced therein.

For perhaps a quarter of an hour after our start I felt much excited, and so, I think, did my companion. Shoulder to shoulder we were glued to the little round window, pinching each other when the hurrying steps hither and thither threatened to come down our way. We did not talk much, we were too busy looking out, and listening to the rushing water, and the throbbing of the screw. The land seemed to slip quickly by, countless ships, boats and steamers barely gave us time to have a look at them, though Alister (who seemed to have learned a good deal during his four days in the docks) whispered little bits of information about one and another. Then the whole shore seemed to be covered by enormous sheds, and later on it got farther off, and then the land lay distant, and it was very low and marshy and most dreary-looking, and I fancied it was becoming more difficult to keep my footing at the window ; and just when Alister had been pointing out a queer red ship with one stumpy mast crowned by a

sort of cage, and telling me that it was a light-ship, our
own vessel began to creak and groan worse than ever, and
the floor under our feet seemed to run away from them,
and by the time you had got used to going down, it caught
you and jerked you up again, till my head refused to think
anything about anything, and I half dropped and was half
helped by Alister on to the flat of my back as before.

As to him, I may as well say at once, that I never knew
him affected at sea by the roughest wind that could blow,
and he sat on a box and looked at me half pityingly, and
half, I suppose, with the sort of curiosity I had felt about
him.

" I'm feared the life'll be a bit overrough for ye," he
said kindly. " Would ye think of going up and disclosing
yourself before we're away from all chance of getting
ashore ?"

" No, no !" said I, vehemently, and added more feebly,
" I daresay I shall be all right soon."

" Maybe," said the Scotchman.

He went back to the window and gazed out, seeing, I
have no doubt, plenty to interest him ; though my eyes, if
opened for a moment, only shrank back and closed again
instinctively, with feelings of indescribable misery. So
indefinite time went on, Alister occasionally making
whispered comments which I did not hear, and did not
trouble myself to ask questions about, being utterly
indifferent to the answers. But I felt no temptation to
give in. I only remember feeling one intense desire and
it amounted to a prayer, that if these intolerable sensations did not abate, I might at any rate become master
enough of them to do my duty in their teeth. The
thought made me more alert, and when the Scotch lad
warned me that steps were coming our way, I implored
him to hide deeper under the sails, if he wished, without
consideration for me, as I had resolved to face my fate
at once, and be either killed or cured.

" Thank ye kindly," said Alister, " but there's small use
in hiding now.   They can but pitch us overboard, and I've
read that drowning is by far an easier death than being
starved, if ye come to that."

It was in this frame of mind that a sailor found us, and
took us prisoners with so little difficulty that he drew the
scarcely fair conclusion that we were the cheekiest, coolest
hands of all the nasty, sneaking, longshore loafers he had
ever had to deal with in all his blessed and otherwise than
blessed born days.   And wrathful as this outburst was, it
was colourless to the indignation in his voice, when (replying to some questions from above) he answered—

" Two on 'em !"

Several other sailors came to the help of our captor,
and we were dragged up the ladder and on deck, where the
young Scotchman looked to better advantage than down
below, and where I made the best presentment of myself
that my miserable condition would allow.   We were soon
hauled before the captain, a sensible-faced, red-bearded
man, with a Scotch accent rather harsher than Alister's, in
which he harangued us in very unflattering phrases for
our attempt to " steal a passage," and described the evil
fate of which we were certain, if we did not work uncommonly hard for our victuals.

With one breath I and my companion asserted our
willingness to do anything, and that to get a free passage
as idlers was our last wish and intention.   To this, amid
appreciating chuckles from the crew, the captain replied,
that, so sneaks and stowaways always *said ;* a taunt which
was too vulgar as repartee to annoy me, though I saw
Alister's thin hands clenching at his side.   I don't know
if the captain did, but he called out—" Here ! you lankey
lad there, show your hands."

" They're no idle set," said Alister, stretching them
out.   He lifted his eyes as he said it, and I do not
think he could have repressed the flash in them to save

his life. Every detail of the scene was of breathless
interest to me, and as I watched to see if the captain took
offence, I noticed that (though they were far less remarkable from being buried in a fat and commonplace countenance) his eyes, like Alister's were of that bright, cold,
sea-blue common among Scotchmen. He did not take
offence, and I believe I was right in thinking that the boy's
wasted hands struck him much as they had struck me.

"Don't speak unless I question you. How long will ye
have been hanging round the docks before ye'd the
impudence to come aboard here?"

"I slept four nights in the docks, sir."

"And where did ye take your meals?"

A flush crept over Alister's bony face. "I'm no' a great
eater, sir," he said, with his eyes on the deck : and then
suddenly lifting a glance at me out of the corner of them,
he added, "the last I had was just given me by a freen."

"That'll do. Put your hands down. Can you sew?"

"I ask your pardon, sir?"

"Is the fool deaf? Can ye use a needle and thread?"

"After a rough fashion, sir, and I can knit a bit."

"Mr. Waters?"

A man with a gold band round his cap stepped forward
and touched it.

"Take him to the sailmaker. He can help to patch the
old fore-stay-sail on the forecastle. And you can——"

The rest of the order was in a low voice, but Mr. Waters
saluted again and replied, "Yes, sir."

The captain saluted Mr. Waters, and then as Alister
moved off, he said, "You're not sick, I see. Have you
sailed before?"

"From Scotland, sir."

Whether, being a Scotchman himself, the tones of
Alister's voice, as it lingered on the word "Scotland,"
touched a soft corner in the captain's soul, or whether the
blue eyes met with an involuntary feeling of kinship, or

whether the captain was merely struck by Alister's power-ful-looking frame, and thought he might be very useful when he was better fed, I do not know ; but I feel sure that as he returned my new comrade's salute, he did so in a softened humour.   Perhaps this made him doubly rough to me, and I have no doubt I looked as miserable an object as one could (not) wish to see.

" *You're* sick enough," he said ; " stand straight, sir ! we don't nurse invalids here, and if you stop you'll have to work for your food, whether you can eat it or not."

" I will, sir," said I.

" Put out your hands."

I did, and he looked keenly, first at them, and then, from head to foot, at me.   And then to my horror, he asked the question I had been asked by the man who robbed me of my shilling.

" Where did you steal your slops ? "

I hastened to explain.   " A working-man, sir, in Liverpool, who was kind enough to advise me, said that I should have no chance of getting work on board-ship in the clothes I had on.   So I exchanged them, and got these, in a shop he took me to," and being anxious to prove the truth of my tale, and also to speak with the utmost respect of everybody in this critical state of my affairs, I added : " I don't remember the name of the street, sir, but the shop was kept by a—by a Mr. Moses Cohen."

" By Mister—*who* ? "

" Mr. Moses Cohen, sir."

When I first uttered the name, I fancied I heard some sniggering among the sailors who still kept guard over me, and this time the captain's face wrinkled, and he turned to another officer standing near him and re-peated—

" Mister Moses Cohen ! " and they both burst into a fit of laughter, which became a roar among the subordinates, till the captain cried—" Silence there ! " and still chuckling sardonically, added, " Your suit must have been a very spic and span one, young gentleman, if *Mister* Moses Cohen accepted it in lieu of that rig out."

" I paid ten shillings as well," said I.

The laughter recommenced, but the captain looked wrathful. " Oh, you paid ten shillings as well, did you ? And what the thunder and lightning have you tried to steal a passage for when you'd money to pay for one ? "

" I didn't mean to steal a passage, sir," said I, " and I don't mean it now. I tried to get taken as a sailor-lad, but they seemed to expect me to have been to sea before, and to have some papers to show it. So I stowed away, and I'm very sorry if you think it dishonest, sir, but I meant to work for my passage, and I will work hard."

" And what do you suppose an ignorant landlubber like you can do, as we don't happen to be short of public speakers ! "

" I thought I could clean things, and carry coals, and do rough work till I learnt my trade, sir."

" Can you climb ? " said the captain, looking at the rigging.

" I've never climbed on board-ship, sir, but I was good at athletics when I was at school, and I believe I could."

" We'll see," said the captain significantly. " And supposing you're of no use, and we kick ye overboard, can ye swim ? "

" Yes, sir, and dive. I'm at home in the water."

" It's more than you are *on* it. Bo'sun ! "

" Yes, sir."

" Take this accomplished young gentleman of fortune, and give him something to do. Give him an oil rag and let him rub some of our brass, and stow his own. And, bo'sun ! "

" Yes, sir."

" Take him first to Mr. Johnson, and say that I

request Mr. Johnson to ascertain how much change
Mister Moses Cohen has left him, and to take charge of
it."

" Yes, sir."

" The captain's witticisms raised renewed chuckling
among the crew, as I followed the boatswain, duly saluting
my new master as I passed him, and desperately trying to
walk easily and steadily in my ordinary boots upon the
heaving deck.

Mr. Johnson was the third mate, and I may as well
say at once that his shrewdness and kindness, his untiring
energy and constant cheerfulness, make his memory very
pleasant to me and to all who served with him, and whose
reasons for being grateful to him belong to all hours of
the day and night, and to every department of our work
and our play.

I was far too giddy to hear what the boatswain said to
Mr. Johnson, but I was conscious that the third mate's
eyes were scanning me closely as he listened. Then he
said, " *Have* you got any money, youngster ? "

" Here, sir," said I ; and after some struggles I got the
leather bag from my neck, and Mr Johnson pocketed it.

" Ran away from school, I suppose ? "

I tried to reply, and could not. Excitement had kept
me up before the captain, but the stress of it was subsiding, and putting my arms up to get my purse had
aggravated the intense nausea that was beginning to
overpower me. I managed to shake my head instead
of speaking, after which I thought I must have died
then and there of the agony across my brow. It seemed
probable that I should go far to pay for my passage by
the amusement I afforded the crew. Even Mr. Johnson
laughed, as he said, " He seems pretty bad. Look after
him, and then let him try his hand on those stanchions—
they're disgraceful. Show him how, and see that he lays
on——"

" Aye, aye, sir."

" And, bo'sun ! don't be too rough on him just yet.
We've all of us made our first voyage."

" Very true, sir."

I could have fallen at the man's feet for those few kind
words, but his alert step had carried him far away ; and
the boatswain had gripped me by the arm, and landed
me on a seat, before I could think of how to express my
thanks.

" Stay where ye are, young stowaway," said he, " and I'll
fetch the oil and things. But don't fall overboard ! for
we can't afford to send a hexpedition on a voyage of
discovery harter ye."

Off went the boatswain, and by the time he came back
with a bundle of brass rods under his arm, and an old
sardine-tin full of a mixture of oil, vinegar, and sand, and
a saturated fragment of a worn-out worsted sock, I had
more or less recovered from a violent attack of sickness,
and was trying to keep my teeth from being chattered
out of my aching head in the fit of shivering that suc-
ceeded it.

" Now, my pea-green beauty !" said he, " pull yourself
together, and bear a hand with this tackle. I'll carry the
stanchions for you." I jumped up, thanked him, and took
the oil tin and etceteras, feeling very grateful that he did
carry the heavy brass rods for me on to the poop, where I
scrambled after him, and after a short lesson in an art the
secret of which appeared to be to rub hard enough and
long enough, he left me with the pointed hint that the
more I did within the next hour or two, the better it would
be for me. " And *wicee the worser*—hif ye learnt what
hat means when ye wos at school," he added.

Fully determined to do my best, I rubbed for the dear
life, my bones and teeth still shuddering as I did so ; but
whatever virtue there was in my efforts was soon its own
reward, for the vigorous use of my arms began to warm me.

N

so greatly to the relief of my headache and general misery, that I began to hold myself up, and drink in the life-giving freshness of the salt breezes with something that came quite close to hope, and was not far off enjoyment. As to the stanchions, I was downright proud of them, and was rubbing away, brightening the brass, and getting the blood comfortably circulated through my body, when with the usual running and shouting, a crowd of men poured on to the poop with long-handled scrubbing-brushes, and big tubs, &c., followed by others dragging a fire-hose. No time was lost in charging the hose with water (a plentiful commodity !), and this was squirted into every hole and cranny in all directions, whilst the first lot of men rubbed and scrubbed and brushed most impartially all over the place.

I went quietly on with my work, but when the stream threatened a group of stanchions, so highly polished that I could not endure the notion of a speck on their brightness, I lifted them out of harm's way, and with the clatter of this movement drew the attention of the plier of the hose.

" Why, bless my stars, garters, and hornaments of hall sorts ! " said he ; " if 'ere ain't the young gentleman of fortin' on the poop deck in his Sunday pumps ! " and without more ado he let fly the water, first at my feet and then upwards, till I was soused from head to foot, and the scrubbers and swabbers laughed at my gasps as I know I could not have moved their sense of humour if I had had the finest wit in the world. However, I suppose they had had to take as well as give such merriment in their time ; and I keenly remembered Biddy's parting hint that the " good-nature of my ways " would be my best friend in this rough society. So I laughed and shook myself, and turning up my sleeves to my elbows, and my trousers to my knees, I also denuded myself of boots and socks and put them aside.

" Is this the correct fashion ? " I inquired—a joke which

passed muster for very good humour ; and I was squirted at no more on that occasion. The chill had made me feel most miserable again, but I had found by experience that the great thing was to keep my blood circulating, and that rubbing-up the ship's brass answered this purpose exceedingly well. I rubbed it so bright, that when the boatswain came to summon me to dinner, he signified his approval in his own peculiar fashion, which appeared to be that of an acknowledged wit.

"H'm!" said he, " I'll say that for ye, young shore-loafer, ' that you've learnt that the best part of polishing-paste is elbow-grease. It wasn't all *parley-voo* and the pianner where you was at boarding-school ! "

I said I hoped not, and laughed as respectfully as it becomes the small to do at the jokes of the great.

But when I was fairly squatted in a corner of the forecastle, with my plate on my lap, in friendly proximity to Alister, I received a far worse shock than the ship's hose had given me. For under cover of the sailors' talk (and they were even noisier at their dinner than at their work) my comrade contrived to whisper in my ear, " The pilot is still on board."

I got what comfort I could out of hearing the sailmaker praise Alister as "an uncommon handy young chap," a compliment which he enforced by a general appeal to some one to " give him " a lad that had been brought up to make himself useful, and anybody else was welcome "for him " to fine gentlemen with no learning but school learning. For this side attack on me roused the boatswain to reproduce his jokes about elbow-grease *versus parley-voo* and the *pianner*, and to add a general principle on his own account to the effect that it was nothing to him if a lad had been " edicated " in a young ladies' boarding-school, so long as he'd been taught to rub brass till you could " see something more of your face than thumbmarks in it." The general and satisfactory conclusion being (so I hoped) that we were neither of us quite useless, and might possibly be spared the ignominy of a return voyage with the pilot.

About an hour and a half after dinner, when I was "rubbing-up" some "bright things" in the cook's galley, Alister looked in, and finding me alone, said, "Would ye dare to come on deck? We're passing under bonny big rocks, with a lighthouse perched up on the height above our heads, for all the world like a big man keeping his outlook with glowering eyes."

"I don't think I dare," said I. "The cook told me not to stir till these were done. Are we going slower? That pumping noise is slower than it was, I'm sure."

"We are so," said Alister; "I'm wondering if——" He ran out without finishing his sentence, but soon returned with a face rather more colourless than usual with repressed excitement. "Jack!" he gasped, "they're lowering a boat. *The pilot's going ashore.*"

He remained with me now, sitting with his head on his hands. Suddenly a shout of two or three voices from the water was answered by a hearty cheer from the deck. By one impulse, Alister and I sprang to our feet and gripped each other by the hand; and I do not believe there were any two sailors on board who sped the parting pilot with more noise than we two made in the cook's galley.

It was gloriously true. They had kept us both. But, though I have no doubt the captain would have got rid of us if we had proved feckless, I think our being allowed to remain was largely due to the fact that the vessel had left Liverpool short of her full complement of hands. Trade was good at the time, and one man who had joined had afterwards deserted, and another youngster had been taken to hospital only the day before we sailed. He had epileptic fits, and though the second mate (whose chief quality seemed to be an impartial distrust of everybody but himself, and a burning desire to trip up his fellow-creatures at their weak points and jump upon them accordingly) expressed in very strong language his wish that the captain had not sent the lad off, but had kept him for him (the second mate) to cure, the crew seemed all of opinion that there was no "shamming" about it, and that the epileptic sailor-boy would only have fallen from one of the yards in a fit, and given more trouble than his services were worth over picking him up.

The afternoon was far from being as fine as the morning had been. Each time I turned my eyes that way it seemed to me that the grey sea was looking drearier and more restless, but I stuck steadily to some miscellaneous and very dirty work that I had been put to down below; and, as the ship rolled more and more under me, as I ran unsteadily about with buckets and the like, I began to wonder if this was the way storms came gradually on, and whether, if the ship went down to-night "with all on board," I should find courage to fit my fate.

I was meditating gloomily on this subject, when I heard a shrill whistle, and then a series of awful noises, at the sound of which every man below left whatever he was at, and rushed on deck. I had read too many accounts of shipwrecks not to know that the deck is the place to make for, so I bolted with the rest, and caught sight of Alister flying in the same direction as we were. When we got up I looked about me as well as I could, but I saw no rocks or vessels in collision with us. The waves were not breaking over us, but four or five men standing on the bulwarks, were pulling things like monstrous grubs out of a sort of trough, and chucking them with more or less accuracy at the heads of the sailors who had gathered round.

"What is it, Alister?" I asked.

"It's just the serving out of the hammocks that they sleep in," Alister replied. "I'm thinking we'll not be entitled to them."

" What's that fellow yelling about?"

" He's crying to them to respond to their names and numbers.   Whisht, man ! till I hear his unchristian lingo, and see if he cries on us."

But in a few minutes the crowd had dispersed, and the hammock-servers with them, and Alister and I were left alone.   I felt foolish, and I suppose looked so, for Alister burst out laughing and said—" Hech, laddie ! it's a small matter.   We'll find a corner to sleep in.   And let me tell ye, I've tried getting into a hammock myself, and——"

" Hi ! you lads !"

In no small confusion at having been found idle and together, we started to salute the third mate, who pointed to a sailor behind him, and said—" Follow Francis, and he'll give you hammocks and blankets, and show you how to swing and stow them."

We both exclaimed—" Thank you, sir !" with such warmth that as he returned our renewed salutations he added—" I hear good accounts of both of you.   Keep it up, and you'll do."

Alister's sentence had been left unfinished, but I learnt the rest of it by experience.   We scrambled down after Francis ; till we seemed to be about at the level where we had stowed away.   I did not feel any the better for the stuffiness of the air and an abominable smell of black beetles, but I stumbled along till we all arrived in a very tiny little office where the purser sat surrounded by bags of ships' biscuits (which they pleasantly call " bread " at sea) and with bins of sugar, coffee, &c., &c.   I daresay the stuffiness made him cross (as the nasty smells used to make us in Uncle Henry's office), for he used a good deal of bad language, and seemed very un-willing to let us have the hammocks and blankets.   How-ever, Francis got them and banged us well with them before giving them to us to carry.   They were just like the others—canvas-coloured sausages wound about with tarred rope ; and warning us to observe how they were fastened up, as we should have to put them away "ship-shape" the following morning, Francis helped us to unfasten and "swing" them in the forecastle. There were hooks in the beams, so that part of the business was easy enough, but, when bedtime came, I found that getting into my hammock was not as easy as getting it ready to get into.

The sailmaker helped Alister out of his difficulties at once, by showing him how to put his two hands in the middle of his hammock and wriggle himself into it and roll his blankets round him in seamanlike fashion. But my neighbours only watched with delight when I first sent my hammock flying by trying to get in at the side as if it were a bed, and then sent myself flying out on the other side after getting in. As I picked myself up I caught sight of an end of thick rope hanging from a beam close above my hammock, and being a good deal nettled by my own stupidity and the jeers of the sailors, I sprang at the rope, caught it, and swinging myself up, I dropped quietly and successfully into my new resting-place. Once fairly in and rolled in my blanket, I felt as snug as a chrysalis in his cocoon, and (besides the fact that lying down is a great comfort to people who are not born with sea-legs), I found the gentle swaying of my hammock a delightful relief from the bumping, jumping, and jarring of the ship. I said my prayers, which made me think of my mother, and cost me some tears in the privacy of darkness ; but, as I wept, there came back the familiar thought that I had "much to be thankful for," and I added the General Thanksgiving with an " especially " in the middle of it (as we always used to have when my father read prayers at home, after anything like Jem and me getting well of scarlet fever, or a good harvest being all carried).

I got all through my "especially," and what with

thinking of the workman, and dear old Biddy, and Alister, and Mr. Johnson, and the pilot, it was a very long one ; and I think I finished the Thanksgiving and said the Grace of our LORD after it. But I cannot be quite sure, for it was such a comfort to be at peace, and the hammock swung and rocked till it cradled me to sleep.

A light sleep, I suppose, for I dreamed very vividly of being at home again, and that I had missed getting off to sea after all ; and that the ship had only been a dream. I thought I was rather sorry it was not real, because I wanted to see the world, but I was very glad to be with Jem, and I thought he and I went down to the farm to look for Charlie, and they told us he was sitting up in the ash-tree at the end of the field. In my dream I did not feel at all surprised that Cripple Charlie should have got into the ash-tree, or at finding him there high up among the branches looking at a spider's web with a magnifying glass. But I thought that the wind was so high I could not make him hear, and the leaves and boughs tossed so that I could barely see him ; and when I climbed up to him, the branch on which I sat swayed so deliciously that I was quite content to rock myself and watch Charlie in silence, when suddenly it cracked, and down I came with a hard bang on my back.

I woke and sat up, and found that the latter part of my dream had come true, as a lump on the back of my head bore witness for some days. Francis had playfully let me down "with a run by the head," as it is called ; that is, he had undone my hammock-cord and landed me on the floor. He left Alister in peace, and I can only think of two reasons for his selecting me for the joke. First that the common sailors took much more readily to Alister from his being more of their own rank in birth and upbringing, though so vastly superior by education. And secondly, that I was the weaker of the two ; for what I have seen of the world has taught me that there are plenty of strong people who will not only let the weaker go to the wall, but who find an odd satisfaction in shoving and squeezing them there.

However, if I was young and sea-sick, I was not quite helpless, happily ; I refastened my hammock, and got into it again, and being pretty well tired out by the day's work, I slept that sleep of the weary which knows no dream.

CHAPTER XVIII.

"Yet more ! The billows and the depths have more ,
High hearts and brave are gathered to thy breast !
*   *   *   *   *   *
Keep thy red gold and gems, thou stormy grave !
Give back the true and brave ! "

Felicia Hemans.

" To them their duty was clear, and they did it successfully ; and the history of the island is written briefly in that little formula !"

Daily Telegraph, Dec. 5, 1878.

I DID not feel as if I had been asleep five minutes, when I was rudely awakened, of course by noise, whistling and inarticulate roaring, and I found that it was morning, and that the boatswain's mate was "turning the hands up" to wash decks. Alister was ready, and I found that my toilet was, if possible, shorter than at Snuffy's in winter.

"We puts hon our togs fust, and takes our shower-baths harterwards," the boatswain humorously explained, as he saw me trying to get the very awkward collar of my "slops" tidy as I followed with the crowd.

The boatswain was a curious old fellow. He was born in London, "within sound of Bow bells," as he told me ;

but though a Cockney by birth, he could hardly be called a
native of anywhere but the world at large. He had sailed
in all seas, and seemed to have tried his hand at most
trades. He had at one time been a sort of man-of-all-work
in a boys' school, and I think it was partly from this, and
partly out of opposition to the sailmaker, that he never
seemed to grudge my not having been born a poor person,
or to fancy I gave myself airs (which I never did), or to
take a pleasure in making me feel the roughest edge of the
menial work I had to do, like so many of the men. But
he knew very well just where things did feel strangest and
hardest to me, and showed that he knew it by many a bit
of not unkindly chaff.

His joke about the shower-bath came very strictly true
to me. We were all on the main deck, bare-armed and
bare-legged, mopping and slopping and swabbing about
in the cold sea-water, which was liberally supplied to us
by the steam-pump and hose. I had been furnished with
a *squeegee* (a sort of scraper made of india-rubber at the
end of a broomstick), and was putting as much "elbow-
grease" into my work as renewed sea-sickness left me
strength for, when the boatswain's mate turned the hose
upon me once more. I happened to be standing rather
loosely, and my thoughts had flown home on the wings of
a wonder what Martha would think of this way of scrubbing a floor—all wedded as the domestic mind is to hairy
flannel and sticky soap and swollen knees,—when the
stream of sea-water came in full force against my neck,
and I and my squeegee went head-over-heels into the lee
scuppers. It was the boatswain himself who picked me
out, and who avenged me on his subordinate by a round
of abuse which it was barely possible to follow, so mixed
were the metaphors, and so cosmopolitan the slang.

On the whole I got on pretty well that day, and began
to get accustomed to the motion of the ship, in spite of the
fact that she rolled more than on the day before. The

sky and sea were grey enough when we were swabbing the decks in the early morning ; as the day wore on, they only took the deeper tints of gathering clouds which hid the sun.

If the weather was dull, our course was not less so. We only saw one ship from the deck, a mail-steamer, as neat and trim as a yacht, which passed us at a tremendous pace, with a knot of officers on the bridge. Some black objects bobbing up and down in the distance were pointed out to me as porpoises, and a good many seagulls went by, flying landwards. Not only was the sky overcast, but the crew seemed to share the depression of the barometer, which, as everybody told everybody else, was falling rapidly. The captain's voice rang out in brief but frequent orders, and the officers clustered in knots on the bridge, their gold cap-bands gleaming against the stormy sky.

I worked hard through the day, and was sick off and on as the ship rolled, and the great green waves hit her on the bows, and ran away along her side, and the wind blew and blew, and most of the sails were hauled in and made fast, and one or two were reefed up close, and the big chimney swayed, and the threatening clouds drifted forwards at a different pace from our own, till my very fingers felt giddy with unrest ; but not another practical joke did I suffer from that day, for every man's hand was needed for the ship.

In the afternoon she had rolled so heavily in the trough of the large waves, that no one made any pretence of finding his sea-legs strong enough to keep him steady without clutching here and there for help, and I had been thankful, in a brief interval when nobody had ordered me to do anything, to scramble into a quiet corner of the forecastle and lie on the boards, rolling as the ship rolled, and very much resigned to going down with her if she chose to go.

Towards evening it was thick and foggy, but as the sun set it began to clear, and I heard the men saying that the moon (which was nearly at the full) would make a clear night of it. It was unquestionably clearer overhead, and the waves ran smoother, as if the sea were recovering its temper, and Alister and I went below at 9 P.M. and turned into our hammocks for a few hours' sleep, before taking our part in the night-watch that lasts from 12 midnight till 4 A.M.

It is astonishing what a prompt narcotic the knowledge that you'll have to be up again in an hour or two is. Alister and I wasted no time in conversation. He told me the fall in the barometer was " by-ordinar " (which I knew as well as he) ; and I told him the wind was undoubtedly falling (which he knew as well as I) : and after this inevitable interchange of the uppermost news and anxieties of the occasion, we bade GOD bless each other, and I said the prayers of my babyhood because they were shortest, and fell fast asleep.

The noises that woke us were new noises, but they made up the whole of that peculiar sound which is the sum of human excitement. " We are going down this time," was my thought, and I found myself less philosophical about it than I had imagined. Neither Alister nor I were long in putting on our clothes, and we rushed up on deck without exchanging a word. By the time we got there, where the whole ship's crew had gone before us, we were as wildly excited as any one of them, though we had not a notion what it was all about. I knew enough now for the first glance to tell me that the ship was in no special danger. Even I could tell that the gale had gone down, the night was clear, and between the scudding of black clouds with silver linings, the moon and stars shone very beautifully though it made one giddy to look at them from the weird way in which the masts and yards seemed to whip across the sky.

We still rolled, and when the side of the ship went up, it felt almost overhead, and I could see absolutely nothing of the sea, which was vexatious, as that was obviously the point of interest. The rigging on that side was as full of men as a bare garden-tree might be of sparrows, and all along the lee bulwarks they sat and crouched like sea-birds on a line of rock. Suddenly we rolled, down went the leeside, and I with it, but I caught hold of the lowest step of the forecastle ladder and sat fast. Then as we dipped I saw all that they were seeing from the masts and rigging— the yet restless sea with fast-running waves, alternately inky black, and of a strange bright metallic lead-colour, on which the scud as it drove across the moon made queer racing shadows. And it was on this stormy sea that every eye from the captain's to the cook's was strained.

Roll ! down we went again to starboard and up went the bulwarks and I could see nothing but the sky and the stars, and the masts and yards whipping across them as before, though the excitement grew till I could bear it no longer, and scrambled up the ladder on to the forecastle, and pushed my way to the edge and lay face downwards, holding on for my life that I might not be blown away, whilst I was trying to see what was to be seen.

I found myself by Alister once more, and he helped me to hold on, and pointed where every one else was pointing. There was a lull in the eager talking of the men, and the knot of captain and officers on the bridge stood still and Alister roared through the wind into my ear—" Bide a wee, the moon'll be out again."

I waited, and the cloud passed from her face or she sailed from beneath it, and at the same instant I saw a streak of light upon the water in which a black object bobbed up and down as the porpoises had bobbed, and all the men burst out again, and a crowd rushed up on to the forecastle.

" It's half a mile aft."—" A bit of wreck."—" An old

sugar hogshead."—" The emperor of the porpoises."—" Is
it the sea sarpint ye're maning ? "—" Will hany gentleman
lend me 'is hopera-glass ? "—" I'm blessed if I don't think
we're going to go half-speed. I sailed seven years in the
'Amiable' with old Savage, and I'm blessed if he ever
put her a point out of her course for anything. 'Every
boat for herself, and the sea for us all,' he used to say,
and allus kept his eyes forwards in foul weather."—
"Aisy, Tom, aisy, ye're out of it entirely. It's the
Humane Society's gold medal we'll all be getting for saving
firewood."—" Stow   your   jaw,   Pat,   *that's*   not   wreck,
it's——"

At this moment the third mate's voice rang through the
ship—

" A boat bottom up ! "

The men passed from chaff to a silence whose eagerness could be felt, through which another voice came
through the wind from the poop—" *there's something on
her !* " and I turned that way, and saw the captain put
down his glass, and put his hand to his mouth ; and when
he sang out " A MAN "! we all sprang to our feet,
and opened our lips, but the boatswain put up his hand,
and cried, " Silence, fore and aft !   Steady, lads !   Look
to the captain ! "

The gold cap-bands glittered close together, and then,
clear to be seen in a sudden gleam of moonlight, the
captain leaned forward and shouted to the crew, " Fo'cs'le
there ! "   And they sang out, " Aye, aye, sir ! "

" Volunteers for the whaleboat ! "

My heart was beating fast enough, but I do not think I
could have counted a dozen throbs, before, with a wild
hurrah, every man had leaped from the forecastle, Alister
among them, and I was left alone.

I was just wondering if I could possibly be of use, when
I heard the captain's voice again. (He had come down,
and was where the whaleboat was hanging, which, I

learned, was fitted like a lifeboat, and the crew were crowding round him.)

" Steady, lads ! Stand back. Come as you're called. Thunder and lightning, we want to man the boat, not sink her. Mr. Johnson ! "

" Aye, aye, sir ! "

" A ! B ! C ! D ! " &c.

" Here, sir ! "   " Here, sir ! "   " Here, sir ! "

" Fall back there ! Thank you all, my lads, but she's manned."

A loud cheer drowned every other sound, and I saw men busy with the boat, and Alister coming back with a dejected air, and the captain jumping up and down, and roaring louder than the wind : " Steward ! rum, and a couple of blankets. Look sharp. Stand back ; in you go ; steady ! Now, mind what I say ; I shall bear up towards the boat. Hi, there ! Stand by the lowering-tackle, and when I say ' Now ! ' lower away handsomely and steadily. Are you ready, Mr. Johnson ? Keep steady, all, and fend her off well when you touch the water. Mr. Waters ! let her go off a point or two to the north'ard. Half speed ; port a little—steady ! All ready in the boat ? "

" Aye, aye, sir ! "

" GOD bless you. Steady—ready—Now ! "

I hardly know which more roused my amazement and admiration—the behaviour of the men or the behaviour of the whaleboat. Were these alert and silent seamen, sitting side by side, each with his oar held upright in his hand, and his eyes upon his captain, the rowdy roughs of the forecastle ? And were those their like companions who crowded the bulwarks, and bent over to cheer, and bless, and *envy* them ?

As to boats—the only one I had been accustomed to used to be launched on the canal with scraping and shoving, and struggling and balancing, and we did oc•

casionally upset her—but when the captain gave the word,
the ship's whaleboat and its crew were smoothly lowered
by a patent apparatus till it all but touched the big black
waves that ran and roared at it.   Then came a few
moments of intense anxiety till the boat was fairly clear of
the ship ; but even when it was quite free, and the men
bending to their oars, I thought more than once that it had
gone down for ever on the other side of the hills and dales
of water which kept hiding it completely from all except
those who were high up upon the masts.   It was a relief
when we could see it, miserable speck as it looked, and
we all strained our eyes after it, through many difficulties
from the spiteful ways of the winds and waves and clouds,
which blinded and buffeted and drenched us when we
tried to look, and sent black veils of shadow to hide our
comrades from our eyes.   In the teeth of the elements,
however, the captain was bearing up towards the other
boat, and it was now and then quite possible to see with
the naked eye that she was upside down, and that a man
was clinging to her keel.   At such glimpses an inarticulate murmur ran through our midst, but for the most part
we, who were only watching, were silent till the whaleboat was fairly alongside of the object of her gallant expedition.   Then by good luck the moon sailed forth and
gave us a fair view, but it was rather a disappointing one,
for the two boats seemed to do nothing but bob about like
two burnt corks in the moonlight, and we began to
talk again.

" What's she doing ? "—" The LORD knows ! "—" Something's gone wrong."—" Why doesn't she go nearer ? "—
" Cos she'd be stove in, ye fool !"—" Gude save us ! they're
both gone."—" Not they, they're to the left ; but what
the winds and waves they're after—— " —" They're trying
to make him hear, likely enough, and they might as well
call on my grandmother.   He's as dead as a herring."—
" Whisht ! whisht ! He's a living soul ! Hech, sirs ! there's

nought but the grip o' despair would haud a man on the
keel of 's boat in waves like yon."—"Silence, all!"

We turned our heads, for a voice rang from the look-
out—

"Man overboard from the whaleboat!"

The men were so excited, and crowded so together, that
I could hardly find a peeping-place.

"He's got him."—"Nay, they're both gone."—"Man!
I'm just thinking that it's ill interfering with the designs
of Providence. We may lose Peter and not save Paul."—
"Stow your discourses, Sandy!"—"They're hauling in
our man, and time they did."

The captain's voice now called to the first mate—

"Do you make it one or both, Mr. Waters?"

"*Both*, sir!"

"Thank GOD!"

We hurrahed again, and the whaleboat-men replied—
but their cheer only came faintly to us, like a wail upon
the wind.

Several men of our group were now called to work, and
I was ordered below to bring up a hammock, and swing
it in the steerage. I was vexed, as I would have given
anything to have helped to welcome the whaleboat back.

When the odd jobs I had been called to were done
with, and I returned to the deck, it was just too late to
see her hauled up. I could not see over the thick
standing group of men, and I did not, of course, dare to
push through them to catch sight of our heroes and the
man they had saved. But a little apart from the rest, two
Irish sailors were standing and bandying the harshest of
brogues with such vehemence that I drew near, hoping at
least to hear something of what I could not see. It was a
spirited, and one would have guessed an angry dialogue,
so like did it sound to the yapping and snapping of two
peppery tempered terriers. But it was only vehement,
and this was the sum of it.

O

" Bedad ! but it's quare ye must have felt at the time."

" I did not, unless it would be when Tom stepped out into the water, GOD bless him ! with the rope aisy round his waist, and the waves drowning him intirely, and the corpse houlding on to the boat's bottom for the dear life."

" Pat ! " said the other in mysterious tones, " would that that's hanging round his neck be the presarving of him, what ? "

" And why wouldn't it ? But isn't he the big fool to be having it dangling where the wash of a wave, or a pick-pocket, or a worse timptation than either might be staling it away from him ? "

" And where else would he put it ? "

" Did ye ever git the sight of mine ? "

" I did not."

" On the back of me ? "

" Whatt ? "

" Look here, now ! " cried Pat, in the tones of one whose patience was entirely exhausted.   His friend drew nearer, and I also ventured to accept an invitation not intended for me, so greatly was my curiosity roused by what the men said.

Pat turned his back to us as rapidly as he had spoken, and stooping at about half-leap-frog-angle, whipped his wet shirt upwards out of his loosely-strapped trousers, baring his back from his waist to his shoulder blades. The moon was somewhat overcast, but there was light enough for us to see a grotesque semblance of the Crucifixion tattooed upon his flesh in more than one colour, and some accompanying symbols and initials which we could hardly distinguish.

" Now am I safe for Christian burial or not, in the case I'd be misfortunate enough to be washed up on the shores of a haythen counthry ? "

" Ye are so ! "

I never saw a funnier sight than Pat craning and twisting his head in futile efforts to look at it under his own arm.

" It's a foine piece of work, I'm told," said he.

" They tould ye no less than the truth that said that, Pat. It's a mighty foine piece of work."

"They all say so that see it," sighed Pat, tucking his shirt in again, " and that'll be ivry soul but meself, worse luck ! "

" Shaughnessy ! "

" Sir ! "

Pat ran off, and as I turned I saw that the crew of the whaleboat were going below with a crowd of satellite , and that a space was cleared through which I could see the man they had saved still lying on the deck, with the captain kneeling at his head, and looking back as if he were waiting for something. And at that moment the moon shone out once more, and showed me a sight that I'll forget when I forget you—Dennis O'Moore !

   *   *   *   *   *   *

It was a lad that they had saved, not a full-grown man, except in the sense of his height, which was nearly an inch beyond Alister's. He was insensible, and I thought he was dead, so deathlike was the pallor of his face in contrast with the dark curls of his head and the lashes of his closed eyes. We were dipping to leeward, his head rolled a little on the rough pillow that had been heaped to raise him, and his white face against the inky waves reminded me of the face of the young lord in Charlie's father's church, who died abroad, and a marble figure of him was sent home from Italy, with his dog lying at his feet. His shoulders were raised as well as his head, and his jacket and shirt had both been washed open by the waves.

And that was how I got the key to the Irishmen's dialogue. For round the lad's throat was a black ribbon, pendant from which a small cross of ebony was clear to be seen upon his naked breast; and on this there glittered in the moonlight a silver image of the Redeemer of the World.

———

CHAPTER XIX.

"Why, what's that to you, if my eyes I'm a wiping?
A tear is a pleasure, d'ye see, in its way ;
'Tis nonsense for trifles, I own, to be piping,
But they that ha'n't pity, why I pities they.
   *   *   *   *   *   *

The heart and the eyes, you see, feel the same motion,
And if both shed their drops, 'tis all the same end ;
And thus 'tis that every tight lad of the ocean
Sheds his blood for his country, his tears for his friend."
Charles Dibdin.

IF one wants to find the value of all he has learned in the way of righteousness, common sense, and real skill of any sort ; or to reap most quickly what he has sown to obedience, industry, and endurance, let him go out and rough it in the world.

There he shall find that a conscience early trained to resist temptation and to feel shame will be to him the instinctive clutch that may now and again—in an ungraceful, anyhow fashion—keep him from slipping down to perdition, and save his soul alive. There he shall find that whatever he has really learned by labour or grasped with inborn talent, will sooner or later come to the surface to his credit and for his good ; but that what he swaggers will not even find fair play. There, in brief, he shall find his level—a great matter for most men. There, in fine, he will discover that there being a great deal of human nature in all men, and a great deal that is common to all lives—

if he has learned to learn and is good-natured withal, he
may live pretty comfortably anywhere—

> " As a rough rule,
> The rough world's a good school,"—

and if there are a few parlour-boarders it is very little
advantage to them.

For my own part I was almost startled to find how
quickly I was beginning to learn something of the ways
of the ship and her crew; and though, when I asked for
information about all the various appliances which come
under the comprehensive sea-name of "tackle," I was
again and again made the victim of a hoax, I soon learned
to correct one piece of information by another, and to feel
less of an April fool and more of a sailor. Reading sea-
novels had not really taught me much, for there was not
one in all that the Jew-clerk lent or sold me which
explained ship's language and customs. But the schoolmaster had given me many useful hints, and experience
soon taught me how to apply them.

The watch in which Alister and I shared just after we
picked up Dennis O'Moore, was naturally very much
enlivened by news and surmises regarding our new
"hand." Word soon came up from below that he was
alive and likely to recover, and for a brief period I found
my society in great request, because I had been employed
in some fetching and carrying between the galley and the
steerage, and had "heard the drowned man groan." We
should have gossiped more than we did if the vessel had
not exacted unusual attention, for the winds and the waves
had "plenty of mischief in 'em" yet, as I was well able
to testify when I was sent aft to help the man at the
wheel.

" That'll take the starch out o' yer Sunday stick-ups ! "
said the boatswain's mate, on hearing where I was bound
for, when he met me clinging to the wet deck with my

stocking-feet, and catching with my hands at every bit of tackle capable of giving support. And as I put out all my strength to help the steersman to force his wheel in the direction he meant it to go, and the salt spray smacked my face and soaked my slops, and every wind of heaven seemed to blow down my neck and up my sleeves and trousers—I heartily agreed with him.

The man I was helping never spoke, except to shout some brief order into my ear or an occasional reply to the words of command which rang over our heads from the captain on the bridge.   Of course I did not speak, I had quite enough to do to keep my footing and take my small part in this fierce bitting and bridling of the elements ; but uncomfortable as it was, I " took a pride and pleasure in it," as we used to say at home, and I already felt that strenuous something which blows in sea-breezes and gives vigour to mind and body even when it chills you to the bone.

That is, to some people; there are plenty of men, as I have since discovered, who spend their lives at sea and hate it to the end.   Boy and man, they do their hard duty and live by its pitiful recompense.   They know the sea as well as other mariners, are used to her uncertain ways, bear her rough usage, control her stormy humours, learn all her moods, and *never feel her charm.*

I have seen two such cases, and I have heard of more, yarned with all their melancholy details during those night watches in which men will tell you the ins and outs of many a queer story that they " never talk about."   And it has convinced me that there is no more cruel blunder than to send a boy to sea, if there is good reason to believe that he will never like it; unless it be that of with-holding from its noble service those sailor lads born, in whose ears the seashell will murmur till they die.

It had murmured in mine, and enticed me to my fate. I thought so now that I knew the roughest of the other

side of the question, just as much as when I sat comfortably on the frilled cushion of the round-backed armchair
and read the ' Penny Numbers' to the beemaster.   Barefoot, bare-headed, cold, wet, seasick, hard worked and
half-rested, would I even now exchange the life I had
chosen for the life I had left?—for the desk next to the
Jew-clerk, for the partnership, to be my uncle's heir, to be
mayor, to be member?   I asked myself the question as I
stood by the steersman, and with every drive of the wheel
I answered it—" No, Moses!   No!   No!"

It is not wise to think hard when you are working hard
at mechanical work, in a blustering wind and a night
watch.   Fatigue and open air make you sleepy, and
thinking makes you forget where you are, and if your work
is mechanical you do it unconsciously, and may fall asleep
over it.   I dozed more than once, and woke with the
horrible idea that I had lost my hold, and was not doing
my work.   That woke me effectually, but even then I had
to look at my hands to see that they were there.   I
pushed, but I could not feel, my fingers were so numb
with cold.

The second time I dozed and started again, I heard
the captain's voice close beside us.   He was bawling
upwards now, to Mr. Waters on the bridge.   Then he
pushed me on one side and took my place at the wheel,
shouting to the steersman—" I meant the Scotch lad, not
that boy."

" He's strong enough, and steady too," was the reply.

They both drove the wheel in silence, and I held on by
a coil of heavy rope, and sucked my fingers to warm
them, and very salt they tasted.   Then the captain left the
wheel and turned to me again.

" Are you cold?"

" Rather, sir."

" You may go below, and see if the cook can spare you
a cup of coffee."

" Thank you, sir."

" But first find Mr. Johnson, and send him here."

" Yes, sir."

Whilst the captain was talking, I began to think of
Dennis O'Moore, and how he groaned, and to wonder
whether it was true that he would get better, and whether
it would be improper to ask the captain, who would not
be likely to humbug me, if he answered at all.

"Well?" said the captain sharply, "what are **you**
standing there like a stuck pig for?"

I saluted. " Please, sir, *will* he get better?"

" What the —— Oh, yes. And hi, you!"

" Yes, sir?"

" He's in the steerage. You may go and see if he
wants anything, and attend on him. You may remain
below at present."

" Thank you, sir."

I lost no time in finding Mr. Johnson, and I got a
delicious cup of coffee and half a biscuit from the cook,
who favoured me in consequence of the conscientious
scouring I had bestowed upon his pans. Then mightily
warmed and refreshed, I made my way to the side of the
hammock I had swung for the rescued lad, and by the
light of a swinging lamp saw his dark head buried in his
arms.

When I said, " Do you want anything?" he lifted his
face with a jerk, and looked at me.

" Not I—much obliged," he said, smiling, and still
staring hard. He had teeth like the half-caste, but the
resemblance stopped there.

" The captain said I might come and look after you,
but if you want to go to sleep, do," said I.

" Why would I, if you'll talk to me a bit?" was his
reply; and resting his head on the edge of his hammock
and looking me well over, he added, " Did they pick you
up as well?"

I laughed and wrung some salt water out of my sleeve.

" No.   I've not been in the sea, but I've been on deck, and it's just as wet.   It always *is* wet at sea," I added in a tone of experience.

His eyes twinkled as if I amused him.   " That, indeed ? And yourself, are ye—a midshipman ? "

It had been taken for granted that our new hand was " a gentleman."   I never doubted it, though he spoke with an accent that certainly recalled old Biddy Macartney; a sort of soft ghost of a brogue with a turn up at the end of it, as if every sentence came sliding and finished with a spring, and I did wish I could have introduced myself as a midshipman—instead of having to mutter, " No, I'm a stowaway."

He raised himself higher in his hammock.

" A stowaway?   What fun!   And what made ye go? Were ye up to some kind of diversion at home, and had to come out of it, eh?   Or were ye bored to extinction, or what?   (Country life in England is mighty dull, so they tell me.)   I suppose it was French leave that ye took, as ye say you're a stowaway?   I'm asking ye a heap of impertinent questions, bad manners to me! "

Which was true.   But he asked them so kindly and eagerly, I could only feel that sympathy is a very pleasant thing, even when it takes the form of a catechism that is all questions, and no room for the answers.   Moreover, I suspect that he rattled on partly to give me time to leave off blushing and feel at ease with him.

" I ran away because of several things,"'said I.   " I always did want to see the world "——("And why wouldn't ye ? " my new friend hastily interpolated).   " But even if I had stayed at home I don't believe I should ever have got to like being a lawyer "—— (" Small chance of it, I should say, the quill-driving thievery! ")   " It was my uncle's office "——(" I ask his pardon and yours.")   " Oh, you may say what you like.   I never could get on with him.

I don't mean that he was cruel to me in the least, though I think he behaved shabbily——"

" Faith, it's a way they have! I've an uncle myself that's a sort of first cousin of my father's, and six foot three in his stockings, without a drop of good-nature in the full length of him."

"Where is your home?" said I, for it certainly was my turn to ask questions.

"Where would it be—but ould Ireland?" And after a moment's pause he added, "They call me Dennis O'Moore. What's *your* name, ye enterprising little stowaway?"

I told him. "And where were you going in your boat, and how did you get upset?" I asked.

He sighed. "It was the old hooker we started in, bad luck to her!"

"Is that the name of the boat you were holding on to?"

"*That* boat? No! We borrowed *her*—and now ye remind me, I wouldn't be surprised if Tim Brady was missing her by this, for I had no leisure to ask his leave at the time, and, as a rule, we take our own coracle in the hooker——"

"What *is* a hooker?" I interrupted, for I was resolved to know.

"What's a hooker? A hooker—what a catechetical little chatterbox ye are! A man can't get a word in edgeways—a hooker's a boat. Ours was a twenty-ton, half-decked, cutter-rigged sort of thing, built for nothing in particular, and always used for everything. It was lucky for me we took Tim Brady's boat instead of the coracle, or I'd be now where—where poor Barney is. Oh, Barney, Barney! How'll I ever get over it? Why did ye never learn to swim, so fond of the water as ye were? Why couldn't ye hold on to me when I got a good grip of ye! Barney, dear, I've a notion in my heart that ye left your hold on purpose, and threw away your own

life that ye mightn't risk mine.   And now I'll never know,
for ye'll never be able to tell me.   Tim Brady's boat would
have held two as easy as one, Barney, and maybe the old
hooker'd have weathered the storm with a few more repairs
about her, that the squire always intended, as no one
knows better than yourself!   Oh, dear! oh, dear!   But—
Heaven forgive us!—putting off's been the ruin of the
O'Moores from time out of mind.   And now you're dead
and gone—dead and gone!   But oh, Barney, Barney, if
prayers can give your soul ease, you'll not want them
while Dennis O'Moore has breath to pray!"

I was beginning to discover that one of the first
wonders of the world is that it contains a great many
very good people, who are quite different from oneself
and one's near relations.   For I really was not conceited
enough to disapprove of my new friend because he
astonished me, though he certainly did do so.   From the
moment when Barney (whoever Barney might be) came
into his head, everything else apparently went out of it.
I am sure he quite forgot me.

For my own part I gazed at him in blank amazement.
I was not used to seeing a man give way to his feelings in
public, still less to seeing a man cry in company, and
least of all to see a man say his prayers when he was
neither getting up nor going to bed, nor at church, nor at
family worship, and before a stranger too !   For, as he
finished his sentence he touched his curls, and then the
place where his crucifix lay, and then made a rapid movement from shoulder to shoulder, and then buried his head
is his hands, and lay silent, praying, I had no manner of
doubt, for " Barney's " soul.

His prayers did not take him very long, and he finished
with a big sigh, and lifted his head again.   When his
eyes met mine he blushed, and said, " I ask your pardon,
Jack ; I'd forgotten ye.   You're a kind-hearted little soul,
and I'm mighty dull company for ye."

"No, you're not," said I. "But—I'm very sorry for you. Was 'Barney' your——?" and I stopped because I really did not know what relationship to suggest that would account for the outburst I had witnessed.

"Ah! ye may well say what was he—for what wasn't he—to me, anyhow? Jack! my mother died when I was born, and never a soul but Barney brought me up, for I wouldn't let 'em. He'd come with her from her old home when she married; and when she lay dead he was let into the room to look at her pretty face once more. Times out of mind has he told me how she lay, with the black lashes on her white cheeks, and the black crucifix on her breast, that they were going to bury with her; the women howling, and me kicking up an indecent row in a cradle in the next apartment, carrying on like a Turk if the nurse came near me, and most outrageously disturbing the peace of the chamber of death. And what does Barney do, when he's said a prayer by the side of the mistress, but ask for the crucifix off her neck, that she'd worn all her girlhood? If the women howled before, they double-howled then, and would have turned him out neck and crop, but my father lifted his head from where he was lying speechless in a kind of a fit at the foot of the bed, and says he, 'Barney Barton! ye knew the sweet lady that lies there long before that too brief privilege was mine. Ye served her well, and ye've served me well for her sake; whatever ye ask for of hers in this hour ye'll get, Barney Barton. She trusted ye—and I may.' 'GOD bless ye, squire,' says Barney; and what does he do but go up to her and unloose the ribbon from her throat with his own hands. And away he went with the crucifix, past the women that couldn't get a sound out of them now, and past my father as silent as themselves, and into the room where I lay kicking up the devil's own din in my cradle. And when he held it up to me, with the light shining on the silver, and the black ribbons hanging down, never

believe him if I didn't stop squalling, and stretch out my
hands with a smile as sweet as sunshine. And Barney
tied it round my neck, and took me into his arms. And
they said he spoke never a word when they told him my
mother was dead, and shed never a tear when he saw her
lie, but he sobbed his heart out over me."

" You may well care for him !" said I.

" Indeed I may. He kept my mother's memory green in
my heart, and he taught me all ever I knew but books. He
taught me to walk, and he taught me to ride, and shooting, and fishing, and such like country diversions ; and
strange to say, he taught me to swim, the way they learn
in my mother's country, with a bundle of bullrushes—for
the old man couldn't swim a stroke himself, or he might
be here now, alive and hearty, please GOD."

" Were there only you and he in the hooker ? "

" That's all. It was altogether sheer madness, for the
old boat was barely fit for a day's fishing in fine weather,
and though Barney nearly killed himself overhauling her,
and patching her sails, I doubt if he knew very well what
he was after. I've been thinking, Jack, that his mind was
not what it was. He was always a bit obstinate, if he got
a notion into his head, but of late the squire himself
couldn't turn him. When he wanted to do a thing about
the place that Barney didn't approve, if he didn't give in
(as he was apt to do, being easy-tempered) I can tell ye
he had to do it on the sly. That was how he ordered the
new ploughs that nearly broke Barney's heart, both because of being new-fangled machines, and ready money
having to be paid for them. ' I'll see the ould place
ruined before ye come to your own, Master Dennis,' he
told me. And—Jack ! that's another thing makes me
think what I tell ye. He was for ever talking as if the
place was coming to me, and I've two brothers older than
myself, let alone my sister. But ye might as well reason
with the rock of Croagh Patrick ! Well, if he didn't ask

my father to let him and me run round in the hooker with
a load of seaweed for Tim Brady's farm, and of course we
got leave, and started as pleasant as could be ; barring
that if Barney'd been a year or two younger, there'd have
been wigs on the green over the cold potatoes, before we
got off."

" *Wigs on the green over cold potatoes ?*" I repeated,
in bewilderment.

" Tst ! tst ! little Saxon !   I mean we'd have had a row
over the provisions. It wasn't two hours' run round to
Tim Brady's, and I found the old man stowing away half
a peck of cold boiled potatoes, and big bottles of tea, and
goodness knows what. ' Is it for ballast ye're using the
potatoes, Barney?' says I. 'Mind your own business,
Master Dennis'—(and I could see he was as cross as two
sticks),—' and leave the provisioning to them that under-
stands it,' says he. ' How many meals d'ye reckon to eat
between this and Tim Brady's ?' I went on, just poking
my fun at him, when—would ye believe it?--the old
fellow fired up like a sky-rocket, and asked me if I
grudged him the bit of food he ate, and Heaven knows
what besides. ' Is it Dennis O'Moore you're speaking
to?' says I, for I've not got the squire's easy temper, GOD
forgive me ! We were mighty near to a quarrel, Jack, I
can tell ye, but some shadow of a notion flitting across
my brain that the dear soul was not responsible entirely,
stopped my tongue, and something else stopped his which
I didn't know till we got to Tim Brady's, and found that
all we wanted with him was to borrow his boat, and that
the seaweed business was no better than a blind ; for
Barney had planned it all out that we were to go down to
Galway and fetch the new ploughs home in the hooker, to
save the cost of the land-carriage. ' Sure it's bad enough
for the squire to be soiling his hands with trumpery made
by them English thieves, that's no more conscience over
bothering a gentleman for money nor if he was one of

themselves,' said Barney ; 'sorra a halfpenny shall the
railway rogues rob him of.' Ah, little stowaway, ye may
guess my delight ! And hadn't we glorious weather at
first, and wasn't the dear old man happy and proud ! I
can tell ye I yelled, and I sang, and I laughed, when I felt
the old hooker begin to bound on the swell when we got
out into the open, but not a look would Barney turn on
me for minding the boat ; but I could hear him chuckling
to himself and muttering about the railway rogues. It
wasn't much time we either of us had for talking, by-and-
bye. I steered and saw to the main sheet, and Barney
did look-out and minded the foresail, Tim Brady's boat
towing astern, getting such a dance as it never had before,
and at last dragging upside down. We'd one thing in our
favour, anyhow. There was no disputing or disturbing of
our minds as to whether we'd turn back or not, for the
gale was at our backs ; and the old hooker was like my
father's black mare—you might guide her, but she was
neither to stop nor turn. How the gallant old boat held
out as she did, Heaven knows ! It was not till the main-
sail had split into ribbons with a noise like a gun going
off, and every seam was strained to leaking, and the sea
came in faster than we could bale it out, that we righted
Tim Brady's tub and got into her, and bade the old
hooker good-bye. The boat was weather-tight enough—
it was a false move of Barney's capsized her,—and I'd a
good hold of her with one hand when I gripped him with
the other. Oh ! Barney dear ! Why would ye always
have your own way ? Oh, why—why did ye loose your
hold ? Ye thought all hope was over, darling, didn't ye ?
Ah, if ye had but known the brave hearts that——"

I suppose it was because I was crying as well as Dennis
that I did not see Mr. Johnson till he was standing by the
Irish boy's hammock. I know I got a sound scolding for
the state of his pulse (which the third mate seemed to
understand, as he understood most other things), and was

dismissed with some pithy hints about cultivating common-sense and not making a fool of myself.   I sneaked off, and was thankful to meet Alister and pour out my tale to him, and ask if he thought that our new friend would have brain-fever, because I had let him talk about his ship-wreck.

Alister was not quite so sympathetic as I had expected. He was so much shocked about the crucifix and about Dennis praying for Barney's soul, that he could think of nothing else.   He didn't seem to think that he would have fever, but he said he feared we had small reason to reckon on the prayers of the idolatrous ascending to the throne of grace.   He told me a long story about the Protestant martyrs who were shut up in a dungeon under the sea, on the coast of Aberdeenshire, and it would have been very interesting if I hadn't been thinking of Dennis.

We had turned in for some sleep, and I was rolling myself in my blanket, when Alister called me:

" Jack! did ye ever read Fox's ' Book of Martyrs ' ? "

" No."

" It's a gran' work, and it has some aweful tales in it. When we've a bit of holiday leesure I'll tell ye some."

" Thank you, Alister."

<hr />

CHAPTER XX.

" A very wise man believed that, if a man were permitted to make all the ballads, he need not care who should make the laws of a nation."—Fletcher of Saltoun in a letter to the Marquis of Montrose.

THE weather was fair enough, and we went along very steadily and pleasantly that afternoon.   I was undoubtedly getting my sea-legs, which was well for me, as they were

"JUMP ON THE BULWARKS, AND THEN FOLLOW ME."

put to the test unexpectedly. I happened to be standing near Alister (we were tarring ropes), when some orders rang out in Mr. Waters' voice, which I found had reference to something to be done to some of the sails. At last came the words " Away aloft! " which were responded to by a rush of several sailors, who ran and leaped and caught ropes and began climbing the rigging with a nimbleness and dexterity which my own small powers in that line enabled me to appreciate, as I gazed upwards after them. The next order bore unexpected and far from flattering reference to me.

" Hi, there. Francis! "

" Aye, aye, sir! "

" Take that gaping booby up with you. I hear he's ' good at athletics.' "

The sailors who were rope-tarring sniggered audibly, and Alister lifted his face with a look of anxiety, that did as much as the sniggering to stimulate me not to disgrace myself.

" Kick off your shoes, and come along," said Francis. " Jump on the bulwarks and then follow me. Look aloft —that's up, ye know—never mind your feet, but keep tight hold of the ratlins—so, with your hands, and when you *are* up aloft, don't let one hand go till you're sure of your hold with the other."

Up we went, gripping the swaying ropes with toes and fingers, till we reached the maintop, where I was allowed to creep through the " Lubber's Hole," and Francis swung himself neatly over the outside edge of the top, and there he and I stood for a few moments to rest.

I cannot say I derived much comfort from his favourable comments on my first attempt. I was painfully absorbed by realising that to climb what is steady, and to climb what is swaying with every wave, are quite different things. Then, in spite of warnings, I was fascinated by the desire to look down ; and when I looked I felt more uncomfort-

P

able than ever; the ship's deck was like a dancing teatray far below; my legs and arms began to feel very light, and my head heavy, and I did not hear what Francis was saying to me, so he pinched my arm and then repeated it.

" Come along—and if the other chaps put any larks on you, keep your eyes open, and never lose a grip by one hand somewhere. So long as you hold on to some of the ship's ropes you're bound to find your way back somehow."

" I'll try," I said.

Then through the confusion in my head I heard a screaming whistle, and a voice from beneath, and Francis pricked his ears, and then suddenly swung himself back on to the ladder of ropes by which we had climbed.

" Lucky for you, young shaver," said he. " Come along! "

I desired no more definite explanation. Francis was going down, and I willingly did the same, but when my foot touched the deck I staggered and fell. It was Mr. Johnson who picked me up by the neck of my slops, saying, as he did so, " Boatswain! The Captain will give an extra lot of grog to drink Mr. O'Moore's good health."

This announcement was received with a cheer, and I heard the boatswain calling to " stow your cleaning-tackle, my lads, and for'ards to the break of the foc'sle. Them that has white ties and kid gloves can wear 'em; and them that's hout of sech articles must come as they can. Pick up that tar-pot, ye fool! Now are ye all coming and bringing your voices along with ye? Hany gentleman as 'as 'ad the misfortin' to leave his music behind, will oblige the ship's company with an ex-tem-por."

" Long life to ye, bo'sun; it's a neat hand at a speech ye are, upon my conscience! " cried Dennis, over my shoulder, and then his arm was around it, shaking with laughter, as we were hurried along by the eager crowd.

"He's a wag, that old fellow, too. Come along, little Jack! You're mighty shaky on your feet, considering the festivities that we're bound for. Step it out, my boy, or I'll have to carry ye."

"Are *you* coming to the foc'sle?" said I, being well aware that this was equivalent to a drawing-room visitor taking tea in the kitchen. "You know it's where the common sailors, and Alister and I have our meals?" I added, for his private ear.

"Thank ye for the hint. I know it's where I hope to meet the men that offered their lives for mine."

"That's true, Dennis, I know; but don't be cross. They'll be awfully pleased to see you."

"And not without reason, I can tell ye! Didn't I beard the lion in his den, the Captain in his cabin, to beg for the grog? And talking of beards, of all the fiery ——, upon my soul he's not safe to be near gunpowder. Jack, is he Scotch?"

"Yes."

"They're bad to blarney, and I did my best, I can tell you, for my own sake as well as for the men. I'm as shy with strangers as an owl by daylight, and I'll never get a thank ye out of my throat, unless we've the chance of a bit of sociability. However, at last he called to that nice fellow—third mate, isn't he?—and gave orders for the rum. 'Two water grog, Mr. Johnson,' says he. 'Ah, Captain,' I said, 'don't be throwing cold water on the entertainment; they got their share of that last night. It's only the rum that's required to complete us now.' But he's as deaf to fun as he is to blarney. Is he good to you, little stowaway?"

"Oh, very," said I. "And you should hear what the men tell about other captains. They all like this one."

"He has an air of uprightness about him; and so has that brother-in-adversity of yours, more polish to him! He must be a noble fellow, though. I can't get over *his*

P 2

volunteering, without the most distant obligation to risk his life for me—not even a sailor. And yet he won't be friendly, do what I will. As formal as you please—that's pride, I suppose—he's Scotch too, isn't he? Blarney's no go with him. Faith, it's like trying to butter short-bread with the thermometer at zero. By Jove, there he is ahead of us. Alister, man! Not the ghost of a look will he give me. He's fine-looking, too, if his hair wasn't so insanely distracted, and his brow ridged and furrowed deep enough to plant potatoes in. What in the name of fortune's he doing to his hands?"

" He's *washing* them with a lump of grease," said I. " I saw Francis give it him. It's to get the tar off."

"That indeed? Alister! *Alister!* Have ye no eyes in the back of ye? Here's Jack and myself."

" I beg your pardon, sir," said Alister stiffly.

" Oh, confound your *sir*-liness!" muttered Dermot, and added aloud, " Is that pomatum for your hair?"

Alister laughed in spite of himself.

"More like hair-*dye*, sir," said he, and rubbing desperately at his fingers, he added, "I can't get them decent."

"Ah, let them rest!" said Dermot. "It's painting the lily to adorn them On ye go; and mind ye keep near to us, and we'll make a land-lubber's parliament in a corner to ourselves."

My first friend had thawed, and went cheerfully ahead of us, as I was very glad to see. Dermot saw it too, but only to relapse into mischief. He held me back, as Alister strode in front, and putting out his thumb and finger, so close to a tuft of hay-coloured hair that stood cocked defiantly up on the Scotchman's crown that I was in all the agony he meant me to be for fear of detection; he chattered in my ear, "Jack, did ye ever study physiognomy, or any of the science of externals? Look at this independent tuft. Isn't the whole character

of the man in it? Could mortal man force it down?
Could the fingers of woman coax it? Would ye appeal
to it with argument? Would hair's grease, bear's
grease——"

But his peroration was suddenly cut short by a rush
from behind, one man tumbling over another on the road
to the forecastle. Dennis himself was thrown against
Alister, and his hand came heavily down on the stubborn
lock of hair.

" It's these fellows, bad manners to them," he explained,
but I think Alister suspected a joke at his expense, and
putting his arms suddenly behind him, he seized Dennis
by the legs and hoisted him on to his back as if he had
been a child. In this fashion the hero of the occasion
was carried to a place of honour, and deposited (not
too gently) on the top of an inverted deck tub, amid the
cheers and laughter of all concerned.

Round another tub—a shallow oak one, tidily hooped
with copper—which served as spittoon, a solemn circle of
smokers was already assembled. They disturbed themselves to salute Dennis, and to make room for others to
join them, and then the enlarged circle puffed and kept
silence as before. I was watching the colour come and
go on the Irish boy's face, and he was making comical
signs to me to show his embarrassment, when Mr.
Johnson shouted for the grog-tub to be sent aft, and
the boatswain summoned me to get it and follow
him.

The smokers were not more silent than we, as the third
mate slowly measured the rum—half a gill a head—into
the grog-tub. But when this solemnity was over and he
began to add the water, a very spirited dialogue ensued ;
Mr. Johnson (so far as I could understand it) maintaining
that " two water grog " was the rule of the ships on their
line, and the boatswain pleading that this being a
" special issue " was apart from general rules, and that it

would be more complimentary to " the young gentleman "
to have the grog a little stronger. How it ended I do not
know ; I know I thought my "tot" very nasty, and
not improved by the reek of strong tobacco in the midst
of which we drank it, to Dennis O'Moore's very good
health.

When the boatswain and I got back to the forecastle,
carrying the grog-tub, we found the company as we had
left it, except that there was a peculiarly bland expression
on every man's face as he listened to a song that the cook
was singing.   It was a very lovelorn, lamentable, and
lengthy song, three qualities which alone would recom-
mend it to any audience of Jack Tars, as I have since had
many occasions to observe.   The intense dolefulness of
the ditty was not diminished by the fact that the cook
had no musical ear, and having started on a note that
was no note in particular, he flattened with every long-
drawn lamentation till the ballad became more of a groan
than a song.   When the grog-tub was deposited, Dennis
beckoned to the boatswain, and we made our way to
his side.

"Your cook's a vocal genius, anyhow, bo'sun," said he.
" But don't ye think we'd do more justice to our ac-
complishments, *and keep in tune*, if we'd an accompani-
ment?   Have ye such a thing as a fiddle about ye ? "

The boatswain was delighted. Of course there was a
fiddle, and I was despatched for it. I should find it
hanging on a hook at the end of the plate-rack, and if the
bow was not beside it it would be upon the shelf, and
there used to be a lump of resin and a spare string or two
in an empty division of the spice-box. The whole kit had
belonged to a former cook, a very musical nigger, who
had died at sea, and bequeathed his violin to his ship.
Sambo had been well liked, and there were some old hands
would be well pleased to hear his fiddle once more.

It took me some little time to find everything, and

when I got back to Dennis another song had begun. A young sailor I did not know was singing it, and the less said about it the better, except that it very nearly led to a row. It was by way of being a comic song, but except for one line which was rather witty as well as very nasty, there was nothing humorous about it, unless that it was funny that any one could have been indecent enough to write it, and any one else unblushing enough to sing it. I am ashamed to say I had heard some compositions of a similar type at Snuffy's, and it filled me with no particular amazement to hear a good deal of sniggering in the circle round the spittoon, though I felt miserably uncomfortable, and wondered what Mr. O'Moore would think. I had forgotten Alister.

I was not likely soon to forget his face as I saw it, the blood swelling his forehead, and the white wrath round his lips, when he gripped me by the shoulder, saying, in broader Scotch than usual, "Come awa' wi' ye, laddie! I'll no let ye stay. Come awa' oot of this accurst hole. I wonder he doesna think black burning shame of himsel, to stand up before greyheided men and fill a callant's ears with filth like yon."

Happily just indignation had choked Alister's voice as well as his veins, and I don't think many of the company heard this too accurate summary of the situation. The boatswain did, but before he could speak, Dennis O'Moore had sprung to the ground between them, and laying the fiddle over his shoulder played a wild sort of jig that most effectually and unceremoniously drowned the rest of the song, and diverted the attention of the men.

"The fiddle's an old friend, so the bo'sun tells me," he said, nodding towards the faces that turned to him.

"Aye, aye, sir."

"Why, I'm blessed if it isn't Sambo's old thing."

"It's your honour knows how to bring the heart out of it, anyhow."

" My eyes, Pat ! You should ha' heerd it at the dignity ball we went ashore for at Barbadoes. Did you ever foot the floor with a black washerwoman of eighteen stun, dressed out in muslin the colour o' orange marmalade, and white kid shoes ? "

" I did not, the darlin' ! "

As the circle gossiped, Dennis tuned the fiddle, talking vehemently to the boatswain between whiles.

" Bo'sun ! ye're not to say a word to the boy (sit down, Alister, I tell ye !). I ask it as a favour. He didn't mince matters, I'll allow, but it was GOD'S truth, and no less that he spoke. Come, bo'sun, who's a better judge of manners than yourself? We'd had enough and to spare of that. (Will ye keep quiet, ye cantankerous Scotchman ! Who's harming ye now ? Jack, if ye move an inch, I'll break this fiddle over your head.) Bo'sun ! we're perishing for our grog, are ye aware ? "

The diversion was successful. The boatswain, with a few indignant mutterings, devoted himself to doling out the tots of grog, and then proposed Dennis O'Moore's health in a speech full of his own style of humour, which raised loud applause ; Dennis commenting freely on the text, and filling up awkward pauses with flourishes on Sambo's fiddle. The boatswain's final suggestion that the ship's guest should return thanks by a song, instead of a sentiment, was received with acclamations, during which he sat down, after casting a mischievous glance at Dennis, who was once more blushing and fidgeting with shyness.

" Ye've taken your revenge, bo'sun," said he.

" Them that blames should do better, sir," replied the boatswain, folding his arms.

" A song ! A song ! Mr. O'Moore ! " shouted the men.

" I only know a few old Irish songs," pleaded Dennis.

" Ould Ireland for ever ! " cried Pat Shaughnessy.

"Hear! hear! Encore, Pat!" roared the men. They were still laughing. Then one or two of those nearest to us put up their hands to get silence. Sambo's fiddle was singing (as only voices and fiddles can sing) a melody to which the heads and toes of the company soon began to nod and beat—

"La, lĕ lā la la, la la la, lā lĕ la, lâ
Lā, le lā la la, la la la, lâ—lĕ la lâ,"

hummed the boatswain. "Lor' bless me, Mr. O'Moore, I heard that afore you were born, though I'm blessed if I know where. But it's a genteel pretty thing!"

"It's all about roses and nightingales!" shouted Dennis, with comical grimaces.

"Hear! hear!" answered the oldest and hairiest-looking of the sailors, and the echoes of his approbation only died away to let the song begin. Then the notes of Sambo's fiddle also dropped off, and I heard Dennis O'Moore's beautiful voice for the first time as he gave his head one desperate toss and began :

"There's a bower of roses by Bendemeer's stream,
And the nightingale sings round it all the night long.
In the time of my childhood 'twas like a sweet dream
To sit in the roses and hear the bird's song."

One by one the pipes were rested on the smoker's knees ; they wanted their mouths to hear with. I don't think the assembled company can have looked much like exiles from flowery haunts of the nightingale, but we all shook our heads, not only in time but in sympathy, as the clear voice rose to a more passionate strain :

"That bower and its music I never forget ;
But oft when alone in the bloom of the year,
I think—is the nightingale singing there yet ?
Are the roses still bright by the calm Bendemeer ?

I and the oldest and hairiest sailor were sighing like furnaces as the melody recommenced with the second verse :

" No, the roses soon withered that hung o'er the wave,
  But some blossoms were gathered while freshly they shone,
And a dew was distilled from their flowers, that gave
  All the fragrance of summer when summer was gone."

If making pot-pourri after my mother's old family recipe had been the chief duty of able-bodied seamen, this could not have elicited more nods of approbation. But we listened spell-bound and immoveable to the passion and pathos with which the singer poured forth the conclusion of his song :

" Thus memory draws from delight, ere it dies,
  An essence that breathes of it many a year ;
Thus bright to my soul—as 'twas then to my eyes—
  Is that bower on the banks of the calm Bendemeer."

And then (as somebody said) the noise we made was enough to scare the seagulls off the tops of the waves.

" You scored that time, Mr. O'Moore," said the boatswain. " You'd make your fortune in a music-hall, sir."

" Thank ye, bo'sun.   Glad I didn't give ye your revenge, anyhow."

But the boatswain meant to strike nearer home. A ship's favourite might have hesitated to sing after Dennis, so Alister's feelings may be guessed on hearing the following speech :

" Mr. O'Moore, and comrades all.   I believe I speak for all hands on this vessel, when I say that we ain't likely to forget sech an agreeable addition to a ship's company as the gentleman who has just given us a taste of the nightingale's quality " (loud cheers).   " But we've been

out-o'-way favoured as I may say, this voyage. We
mustn't forget that there's two other little strangers
aboard" (roars of laughter). "They 'olds their 'eads
rather 'igh p'raps, for *stowaways*" ("Hear! hear!"),
"but no doubt their talents bears 'em out" ("Hear,
hear!" from Dennis, which found a few friendly echoes).
"Anyway, as they've paid us a visit, without waiting to
ask if we was at 'ome to callers, we may look to 'em to
contribute to the general entertainment. Alister Auchterlay will now favour the company with a song."

The boatswain stood back and folded his arms, and
fixed his eyes on the sealine, from which attitude no
appeals could move him. I was very sorry for Alister,
and so was Dennis, I am sure, for he did his best to
encourage him.

"Sing 'GOD save the Queen,' and I'll keep well after
ye with the fiddle," he suggested. But Alister shook his
head. "I know one or two Scotch tunes," Dennis added,
and he began to sketch out an air or two with his fingers
on the strings.

Presently Alister stopped him. "Yon's the Land o'
the Leal?"

"It is," said Dennis.

"Play it a bit quicker, man, and I'll try 'Scots, wha hae.'"

Dennis quickened at once, and Alister stood forward.
He neither fidgeted nor complained of feeling shy, but as
my eyes (I was squatted cross-legged on the deck) were
at the level of his knees, I could see them shaking, and
pitied him none the less, that I was doubtful as to what
might not be before *me*. Dennis had to make two or
three false starts before poor Alister could get a note out
of his throat, but when he had fairly broken the ice with
the word "Scots!" he faltered no more.

The boatswain was cheated a second time of his malice.
Alister could not sing in the least like Dennis, but he had
a strong manly voice, and it had a ring that stirred one's

blood, as he clenched his hands, and rolled his Rs to the rugged appeal :

> "Scots, wha hae wi' Wallace bled,
> Scots, wham Bruce has aften led ;
> Welcome to your gory bed,
> Or to victory !"

Applause didn't seem to steady his legs in the least, and he never moved his eyes from the sea, and his face only grew whiter by the time he drove all the blood to my heart with—

> "Wha will be a traitor knave ?
> Wha can fill a coward's grave ?
> Wha sae base as be a slave ?
> Let him turn and flee !"

"GOD forbid !" cried Dennis impetuously. "Sing that verse again, me boy, and give us a chance to sing with ye !" which we did accordingly ; but as Alister and Dennis were rolling Rs like the rattle of musketry on the word *turn*, Alister did turn, and stopped suddenly short. The Captain had come up unobserved.

"Go on !" said he, waving us back to our places.

By this time the solo had become a chorus. Beautifully unconscious, for the most part, that the song was by way of stirring Scot against Saxon, its deeper patriotism had seized upon us all. Englishmen, Scotchmen, and sons of Erin, we all shouted at the top of our voices, Sambo's fiddle not being silent. And I maintain that we all felt the sentiment with our whole hearts, though I doubt if any but Alister and the Captain knew and sang the precise words :

> "Wha for Scotland's king and law
> Freedom's sword will strongly draw,
> Freeman stand, or freeman fa' ?
> Let him on wi' me !"

CHAPTER XXI.

" 'Tis strange—but true ; for truth is always strange—
Stranger than fiction."

Byron.

" Fair laughs the morn, and soft the zephyr blows."

Gray.

THE least agreeable part of our voyage came near the
end. It was when we were in the fogs off the coast of
Newfoundland. The work that tired one to death was
not sufficient to keep one warm ; the cold mist seemed to
soak through one's flesh as well as one's slops, and cling to
one's bones as it clung to the ship's gear. The deck was
slippery and cold, everything, except the funnel, was sticky
and cold, and the foghorn made day and night hideous
with noises like some unmusical giant trying in vain to hit
the note Fa. The density of the fog varied. Sometimes
we could not see each other a few feet off, at others we
could see pretty well what we were about on the vessel,
but could see nothing beyond.

We went very slowly, and the fog lasted unusually long.
It included a Sunday, which is a blessed day to Jack at
sea. No tarring, greasing, oiling, painting, scraping or
scrubbing but what is positively necessary, and no yarn-
spinning but that of telling travellers' tales, which seamen
aptly describe as spinning yarns. I heard a great many
that day which recalled the schoolmaster's stories, and
filled my head and heart with indefinable longings and
impatience. More and more did it seem impossible that
one could live content in one little corner of this interesting world when one has eyes to see and ears to hear, and
hands for work, and legs to run away with.

Not that the tales that were told on this occasion were
of an encouraging nature, for they were all about fogs
and ice ; but they were very interesting.   One man had
made this very voyage in a ship that got out of her course
as it might be where we were then.   She was too far to the
north'ard when a fog came on, as it might be the very fog
we were in at that moment, and it lasted, lifting a bit and
falling again worse than ever, just the very same as it was
a-doing now.   Cold?   He believed you this fog was cold,
and you might believe him that fog was cold, but the cold
of both together would not be a patch upon what it was
when your bones chattered in your skin and you heard the
ship's keel grinding, and said " Ice ! "   " He'd seen some
queer faces—dead and living—in his time, but when *that*
fog lifted and the sun shone upon walls of green ice on
both sides above our head, and the Captain's face as
cold and as green as them with knowing all was up——"

At this point the narrator was called away, and somebody asked,

" Has any one heard him tell how it ended ? "

" I did," said Pat Shaughnessy, " and it spoilt me dinner
that time."

" Go on, Pat !   What happened to them ? "

" The lowest depths of misfortune.   Sorra a soul but
himself and a boy escaped by climbing to a ledge on the
topmost peak of one of the icebergs just in the nick o
time to see the ship cracked like a walnut between your
fingers.   And the worst was to come, bad luck ! "

" What ?   Go on, Paddy !   What did he and the boy
do ? "

" They just ate each other," faltered Pat.   "But, Heaven
be praised ! a whaler fetched off the survivor.   It was
then that he got the bad fever though, so maybe he
dreamt the worst."

I felt great sympathy with Pat's evident disrelish for
this tale, but the oldest and hairiest sailor seemed hardly to

regard it as worth calling an adventure. If you wanted to
see ice that was ice, you should try the coast of Greenland,
he said. " Hartic Hexploration for choice, but seals or
blubber took you pretty far up. He remembered the
Christmas he lost *them two.* (And cocking one leg over
the other, he drew a worsted sock from his foot, and
displayed the fact that his great toe and the one next to it
were gone.) They lost more than toes that time too.
You might believe it gave you a lonelyish kind of feel
when there was no more to be done for the ship but
get as much firewood out of her timber as you could, and
all you had in the way of a home was huts on an ice-
floe, and a white fox, with a black tip to its tail, for a pet.
It wouldn't have lasted long, except for discipline," we
young 'uns might take notice. " Pleasure's all very well
ashore, where a man may go his own way a long time,
and show his nasty temper at home, and there's other
folks about him doing double duty to make up for it and
keep things together ; but when you come to a handful of
men cast adrift to make a world for themselves, as one
may say, Lord bless you ! there's nothing's any good then
but making every man do as he's bid and be content with
what he gets—and clearing him out if he won't. It was
a hard winter at that. But regularity pulled us through.
Reg'lar work, reg'lar ways, reg'lar rations and reg'lar lime-
juice, as long as it lasted. And not half a bad Christmas
we didn't have neither, and poor Sal's Christmas-tree was
the best part of it. ' What sort of a Christmas-tree, and
why Sal's ? ' Well, the carpenter put it up, and an uncommon neat thing he made too, of pinewood and birch-
broom, and some of the men hung it over with paper
chains. And then the carpenter opened the bundle Sal
made him take his oath he wouldn't open till Christmas,
whatever came, and I'm blessed if there wasn't a pair of
brand-new socks for every soul of the ship's crew. Not
that we were so badly off for socks, but washing 'em

reg'lar, and never being able to get 'em really dry, and
putting 'em on again like stones, was a mighty different
thing to getting all our feet into something dry and warm.
'Who was Sal?' Well poor Sal was a rum 'un, but she's
dead. It's a queer thing, we only lost one hand, and that
was the carpenter, and he died the same day poor Sal
was murdered down Bermondsey way. It's a queer world,
this, no matter where you're cruising! But there's one
thing you'll learn if you live as long as me ; a woman's heart
and the ocean deep's much about the same. You can't
reckon on 'em, and GOD A'mighty as made 'em, alone
knows the depths of 'em ; but as our doctor used to
say (and he was always fetching things out and putting
'em into bottles) it's the rough weather brings the best of
it up."

This was not a cheerful story, but it was soon driven
out of our heads by others. Fog was the prevailing topic ;
yarns of the fogs of the northern seas being varied by "red
fogs" off the Cape de Verd Islands ; and not the least
dismal of the narratives was told by Alister Auchterlay,
of a fog on Ben Nevis, in which his own grandmother's
uncle perished, chiefly, as it appeared, in consequence of
a constitutional objection to taking advice, or to "going
back upon his word," when he had made up his mind
to do something or to go somewhere. And this drew
from the boatswain the sad fate of a comrade of his, who
had sailed twice round the world, been shipwrecked four
times, in three collisions, and twice aboard ships that took
fire, had Yellow Jack in the West Indies, and sunstroke at
the Cape, lost a middle finger from frost-bite in the north
of China, and one eye in a bit of a row at San Francisco,
and came safe home after it all, and married a snug
widow in a pork-shop at Wapping Old Stairs, and got out
of his course steering home through a London fog on Guy
Fawkes Day, and walked straight into the river, and was
found at low tide next morning with a quid of tobacco in

his cheek, and nothing missing about him but his glass eye, which shows, as the boatswain said, that " Fogs is fogs anywhere, and a nasty thing too."

It was towards dark when we had been fourteen days at sea, that our own fog suddenly lifted, and the good news flew from mouth to mouth that we might be "in about mid-night." But the fog came down again, and I do not think that the whole fourteen days put together had felt so long as the hours of that one night through which the fog-horn blew, and we longed for day.

I was leaning against the bulwarks at eight o'clock the next morning. White mist was all around us, a sea with no horizon. Suddenly, like the curtain of a theatre, the mist rose. Gradually the horizon-line appeared, then a line of low coast, which, muddy-looking as it was, made one's heart beat thick and fast. Then lines of dark wood ; then the shore was dotted with grey huts ; then the sun came out, the breeze was soft and mild, and the air became strangely scented, and redolent of pine forests. Nearer the coast took more shape, though it was still low, rather bare and dotted with brushwood and grey stones low down, and always crowned with pines. Then habitations began to sparkle along the shore. Red roofs, cardboard-looking churches, little white wooden houses, and stiffish trees mixed everywhere. And the pine odour on the breeze was sweeter and sweeter with every breath one drew.

Suddenly I found Alister's arm round my shoulder.

" Isn't it glorious ? " I exclaimed.

" Aye, aye," he said, and then, as if afraid he had not said enough, he added with an effort : " The toun's built almost entirely of wood, I'm told, with a population of close on 30,000 inhabitants."

" What a fellow you are ! " I groaned ; " Alister, aren't you glad we're safe here ? Are you ever pleased about anything ? "

He didn't speak, and I turned in his arm to look up at

Q

his face.   His eyes, which always remind me of the sea,
were looking away over it, but he brought them back to
meet mine, and pressed my shoulder.

"It is bonnie," he said, "verra bonnie.   But eh, man !
If strange land shines like yon, hoo'll oor ain shores look
whenever we win Home?"

CHAPTER XXII.

"One, two, three, and away !"

WE three were fast friends when our voyage ended, and in
planning our future we planned to stick together, " Like the
three leaves of the Shamrock," as Dennis O'Moore said.

The Captain would have kept Alister as one of his
crew, but the Scotch lad had definite plans for looking
up a cousin on this side of the Atlantic, and pushing his
fortunes by the help of his relative, so he did not care to
make the return voyage.   The Captain did not offer the
berth to me, but he was very kind, and returned my
money, and gave us a written paper testifying to our good
conduct and capabilities.   He also gave Alister his address, and he and the other officers collected a small sum
of money for him as a parting gift.

That afternoon we three crossed the harbour, and went
for a walk in the pinewoods.   How I longed for Charlie !
I would have given anything if he could have been there,
warmed through by the hot sun, refreshed by the smell
of pines, resting his poor back in the deep moss, and
getting excited over the strange flowers that grew wild all
round our feet.   One never forgets the first time one sees
unknown flowers growing wild ; and though we were not
botanical, like Charlie, we had made ourselves very hot
with gathering nosegays by the time that Dennis summoned

us to sit down and talk seriously over our affairs. Our place of council was by the side of a lake, which reflected a sky more blue than I had ever seen. It stretched out of sight, and all about it were pines—pines. It was very lovely, and very hot, and very sweet, and the little black flies which swarmed about took tiny bits out of our cheeks, and left the blood trickling down, so cleverly, that one did not feel it—till afterwards. We did feel the mosquitos, and fought with them as well as we could, whilst Dennis O'Moore, defending his own face with a big bunch of jack-in-pulpits striped like tabby cats, explained his plans as follows :

Of course we had no notion of going home awhile. Alister and I had come away on purpose ; and for his own part it had always been the longing of his soul to see the world. Times out of mind when he and Barney were on board one of these emigrant ships, that had put into the bay, GOD-speeding an old tenant or acquaintance with good wishes and whisky and what not, he had been more than half-inclined to give old Barney and the hooker the slip, and take his luck with the outward bound And now he was here, and no blame for it, why would he hurry home? The race of the O'Moores was not likely to become extinct for the loss of him, at the worst ; and the Squire wouldn't grudge him a few months' diversion and a peep at the wide world. Far from it ; he'd send him some money, and why not? He (Dennis) was a bit of a favourite for his mother's sake, and the Squire had a fine heart. The real difficulty was that it would be at least a month before the Squire could get a letter and Dennis could get his money ; but if we couldn't keep our heads above water for a month we'd small chance of pushing our way in the world.

It is needless to say that I was willing to fall in with Dennis O'Moore's plans, being only too thankful for such companions in my wanderings. I said so, and added

Q 2

that what little money I had was to be regarded as a common purse so long as it lasted.

When Alister was appealed to, he cast in his lot with no less willingness, but it seemed that he must first look up a relation of his mother's, who lived in Halifax, and to whom his mother had given him a letter of introduction. Alister had never told us his history, and of course we had not asked for it ; but on this occasion some of it crept out.   His father had been the minister of a country parish in Scotland, but he had died young, and Alister had been reared in poverty.   Dennis and I gathered that he had well-to-do relatives on his father's side, but, as Dennis said, " more kinship than kindness about them." " Though I wouldn't wonder if the widow herself had a touch of stiff-neckedness in her," he added.

However that might be, Alister held with his mother, of course, and he said little enough about his paternal relations, except one, whom he described as " a guid man, and *verra* canny, but hard on the failings of the young." What youthful failings in our comrade had helped to snap the ties of home, we did not know, but we knew enough of Alister by this time to feel sure they could not have been very unpardonable.

It was not difficult to see that it was under the sting of this man's reproaches that the lad had taken his fate into his own hands.

" I'm not blaming him," said Alister in impartial tones ; and then he added, with a flash of his eyes, " but I'll no be indebted to him ! "

We had returned to the town and were strolling up the shady side of one of the clean wooden streets when a strange figure came down it with a swinging gait, at a leisurely pace.   She (for, after a moment's hesitation, we decided that it was a woman) was of gipsy colouring, but not of gipsy beauty.   Her black hair was in a loose knot on her back, she wore a curious skull cap of black cloth

embroidered with beads, a short cloth skirt, a pair of old
trousers tucked into leather socks, a small blanket with
striped ends folded cunningly over her shoulders, and on
her breast a gold cross about twice as large as the one
concealed beneath the Irish boy's shirt. And I looked at
her with a curious feeling that my dreams were coming
true. Dark—high-cheeked—a blanket—and (unless the
eyes with which I gazed almost reverentially at the dirty
leather socks deceived me) moccasins—she was, she must
be, a *squaw!*

Probably Dennis had come to the same conclusion,
when, waving the tabby-coloured *arums,* he said, " I'll ask
her what these are," and gaily advanced to carry out his
purpose.

" Ye're daft," said Alister, getting red.

" It's a North American Indian ! " said I.

" It's a woman, anyhow ! " retorted Dennis over his
shoulder, with a twinkle of his eyelashes that drew from
Alister in his broadest accent, " The lad's a pairrfect
libberrteen ! " an expression which he afterwards retracted
and apologised for at considerable length.

Within a few feet of the squaw Dennis lifted the broad-
brimmed hat which I had bought for him directly we
landed, and then advancing with a winning smile, he asked
the name of the flowers in very good Irish. The squaw
smiled too, she touched the flowers, and nodded and said
something in a soft, rapid and unknown tongue, which
only made Dennis shake his head and smile again, on
which she spoke in a language still dark to Alister and
me, but not so to Dennis, who, to our amazement, replied
in the same, and a dialogue so spirited ensued, that they
both seemed to be talking at once. Alister's face was a
study when Dennis put out his hand towards the squaw's
gold cross, and all but touched it, and then (both chattering faster than ever) unbuttoned his throat and drew out
his crucifix to show her. His last act was to give her half
the tabby-striped *arums* as they parted. Then he lifted

the broad hat once more and stood bareheaded, as the squaw came slowly down the wooden causeway, not without one glance at us as she passed. But at the bottom of the street she turned round to look at Dennis. His hat was still in his hand, and he swung it round his head crying, " A Dieu, Madame ! "

" A Dieu ! " said the squaw, and she held up the tabby-striped *arums.* Very mingled feelings seemed to have been working in Alister's mind, but his respect for the fruits of education was stronger even than his sense of propriety. He forgot to scold Dennis for his unseemly familiarity with a stranger, he was so anxious to know in what language he had been speaking.

" French," said Dennis. " There seems to be a French mission somewhere near here. She's a good Catholic too, but she has a mighty queer accent, and awful feet ! "

" It's a grand thing to speak with other tongues ! " said Alister.

" If ye want to learn French, I'll teach ye all I can," said Dennis. " Sh—sh ! No kindness whatever. I wish we mayn't have idle time for any amount of philology ! "

At the top of the hill we parted for a time, and went our ways. Alister to look up his relation, I to buy stationery and stamps for our letters home, and Dennis to convert his gold ring into the currency of the colony. We would not let him pawn his watch, which he was most anxious to do, though Alister and I pointed out how invaluable it might prove to us (it was a good hunting-watch and had been little damaged by the sea), because, as he said, " he would feel as if he was doing *something,* anyhow."

Alister and I were the last to part, and as we did so, having been talking about Dennis O'Moore, I said, " I knew it was French when I got nearer, but I never learnt French, though my mother began to teach me once. You don't really think you'll learn it from him, do you ? "

" With perseverance," replied Alister, simply.

" What good will French be to you ? " I asked.

" Knowledge is a light burden, and it may carry ye yet," was Alister's reply.

When we met again, Dennis was jingling some money in his pocket, which was added to the common fund of which the miser's legacy had formed the base. I had got paper and stamps, and information as to mails, and some more information which was postponed till we found out what was amiss with the Scotch leaf of our Shamrock. For there were deep furrows on Alister's brow, but far deeper was the despondency of his soul. He was in the lowest possible spirits, and with a Scotchman that is low indeed. He had made out his way to his cousin's place of business, and had heard a very satisfactory report of the commercial success, but—the cousin had gone " to the States."

Alister felt himself very much ill-used by fate, and I believe Dennis felt himself very much ill-used by Alister, that evening, but I maintain that I alone was the person really to be pitied, because I had to keep matters smooth between the two. The gloom into which Alister relapsed, his prophecies, prognostications, warnings, raven-like croakings, parallel instances, general reflections and personal applications, as well as his obstinate notion that he would be " a burden and a curse " to " the two of us," and that it would have been small wonder had the sailors cast him forth into the Atlantic, like the Prophet Jonah, as being certain to draw ill-luck on his companions, were trying enough ; but it was no joke that misfortune had precisely the opposite effect upon Dennis. If there was a bit of chaff left unchaffed in all Ireland, from Malin Head to Barley Cove, I believe it came into Dennis's head on this inappropriate occasion, and he forthwith discharged it at Alister's. To put some natures into a desperate situation seems like putting tartaric acid into soda and water—they sparkle up and froth. It certainly was so with Dennis O'Moore ; and if Alister could hardly have been more raven-like upon the crack of doom, the levity of Dennis would, in our present circumstances, have been discreditable to a paroquet.

For it was no light matter to have lost our one hope of a friend in this strange land ; and yet this was practically what it meant, when we knew that Alister Auchterlay's cousin had gone to the States. But the idea of kinship at last suggested something more sensible than jokes to Dennis O'Moore.

"Why, I've a cousin of my own in Demerara, and I'd forgotten him entirely !" he suddenly announced.

"You haven't a cousin in New York, have you?" I asked, and I proceeded to explain, that having done my business, I had been drawn back to the harbour by all the attractions shipping has for me, and had there been accosted by the mate of a coasting-vessel bound for New York with salt fish, who was in want of hands both to load and man her. The Water-Lily had been pointed out to me from a distance, and we might go and see her to-morrow morning if we liked. With the prospect of living for at least a month on our slender stocking, the idea of immediate employment was very welcome, to say nothing of the attraction of further adventures. Alister began to cheer up, and Dennis to sober down. We wrote home, and posted our letters, after which we secured a decent sleeping-room and a good meal of broiled salmon, saffron-coloured cakes, and hot coffee, for a very reasonable sum ; but, moderate as it was, it confirmed us in the conviction that we could not afford to eat the bread of idleness.

Next day we were early at the wharf. The Water-Lily was by no means so white as she was named, and the smell of the salt fish was abominable. But we knew we could not pick and choose when we wanted employment, and wanted to be together ; and to this latter point we had nailed our colours. With Alister and me the mate came to terms at once, but for a time he made difficulties about

Dennis. We "stowaways" had had so much dirty work to do in all weathers for the past fortnight, that we looked sailor-like enough, I dare say; and as it had honestly been our endeavour to learn all we could, and shirk nothing, and as the Captain's paper spoke well of us, I think the mate got a very good bargain—for we were green enough to take lower wages than the customary rate on the strength of a long string of special reasons which he made us swallow. This probably helped towards his giving in about Dennis. The matter about Dennis was that he looked too much of the fine gentleman still, though his homespun suit had seen salt water, and was far from innocent of tar and grease, for he had turned his hand to plenty of rough work during the voyage, partly out of good-nature, and partly to learn all he could get the sailors to teach him. However, his coaxing tongue clinched the bargain at last; indeed the mate seemed a good deal struck by the idea that he would find it " mighty convenient" to have a man on board who was a good scholar and could help him to keep the log. So we signed articles, and went to our duty.

The Water-Lily was loaded, and we sailed in her, and we got to New York. But of all the ill-found tubs that ever put to sea, I should think she might have taken the first prize. We were overhauling her rotten rigging, taking off, putting on, and mending chafing gear every bit of our time, Sunday included. The carpenter used horrible language, but for his vexation I could have forgiven him if he had expressed it more decently, for he never had a moment's rest by day; and though a ship's carpenter is exempt from watches and allowed to sleep at night as a rule, I doubt if he had two nights' rest between Halifax and New York.

As Dennis put it, there was " any amount of chicanery about the whole affair." Some of our pay was " set against " supplying "duds" for Dennis to do dirty work in ; Alister was employed as sailmaker, and then, like the carpenter, was cheated of his rest. As to food, we were nearly starved, and should have fared even worse than we did, but that the black cook was friendly towards us.

"Dis Water-Lily ob ours a leetle ober-blown, Dennis, I'm tinking," said Alfonso, showing all his white teeth. "Hope she not fall to pieces dis voyage."

"Hope not, Alfonso. She hasn't lost her scent anyhow!" At which allusion to our unsavoury cargo Alfonso yelled with laughter.

For our favour with the cook (and it means hot coffee, dry socks, and other little comforts being in favour with the cook) we had chiefly to thank Dennis. Our coal-black comrade loved jokes much, but his own dignity just a little more ; and the instinctive courtesy which was as natural to Dennis as the flow of his fun, made him particularly acceptable to Alfonso.

And for the rest, we came to feel that if we could keep the Water-Lily afloat to the end of her voyage, most other considerations were minor ones.

CHAPTER XXIII.

"May it please GOD not to make our friends so happy as to forget us!"—*Old Proverb.*

THE Water-Lily was re-christened by Dennis, with many flourishes of speech and a deck-tub of salt water long before we reached our journey's end. The 'Slut,' as we now privately called her, defied all our efforts to make her look creditable for New York harbour, but we were glad enough to get her there at all.

We made the lights of Barnegat at about six o'clock one fine morning, took a pilot on board at Sandy Hook, and the 'Slut' being by this time as ship-shape as we could get her, we cleaned ourselves to somewhat better purpose, put on our shore-togs, and were at leisure to enjoy one of the most charming sensations in the world, that of making one's way into a beautiful harbour on a beautiful morning. The fresh breeze that favoured us, the sunshine that—helped by the enchantment of distance —made warehouses look like public buildings, and stone houses like marble palaces, a softening hue of morning mist still clinging about the heights of Brooklyn and over the distant stretch of the Hudson River Islands, the sparkling waves and dancing craft in the bay, and all the dear familiar maze of spars and rigging in the docks ; it is wonderful how such sights, and the knowledge that you are close to the haven where you would be, charm away the sore memories of the voyage past, and incline you to feel that it hasn't been such a bad cruise after all.

"Poor ole Water-Lily !" sighed Alfonso, under the influence of this feeling, " you and me's called her a heap o' bad names, Dennis ; I 'spects we has to have our grumbles, Dennis. Dat's 'bout whar 't is."

" She's weathered the storm and got into port, anyhow," said Dennis, " and I suppose you think the best can do no more. Eh ? "

" Jes so, Dennis."

Alfonso was not far wrong on the subject of grumbling. It is one of a sailor's few luxuries and privileges, and acts as safety-valve for heats of just and unjust indignation, which might otherwise come to dangerous explosion. We three had really learned no mean amount of rough-and-ready seamanship by this time, and we had certainly practised the art of grumbling as well. That "of all the dirty ill-found tubs," the ' Slut ' was the worst we had ever known, our limited experience had made us safe in declaring, and we had also been voluble about the undue length of time during which we had been "humbugging about" between Halifax and New York. But these bygones we

now willingly allowed to be bygones, especially as we had
had duff-pudding the day before, though it was not Sunday
—(Oh, Crayshaws ! that I should have lived to find duff-
pudding a treat—but it *is* a pleasant change from salt meat),
—and as the captain had promised some repairs to the ship
before we returned to Halifax.

We were not long in discovering that the promise was a
safe one, for he did not mean to return to Halifax at all.
Gradually it leaked out, that when the salt-fish was disposed of, we were not going to take in ballast and go back,
as we had thought, but to stow away a " general cargo " of
cheap manufactured articles (chiefly hardware, toys, trumpery pictures, and looking-glasses) and proceed with them
on a trading voyage " down south."—" West Indies," said
the carpenter. " Bermuda for certain," was another opinion;
but Alfonso smiled and said " Demerara."

" Cap'n berry poor sailor, but berry good trader," he
informed us in confidence. " Sell 'm stinking fish and buy
gimcracks cheap ; sell gimcracks dear to Portugee store
in Georgetown, take in sugar—berry good sugar, Demerara sugar—and come back to New York."

Alfonso had made the voyage before on these principles,
and was all the more willing to believe that this was to be
the programme, because he was—at such uncertain inter-
vals as his fate ordained—courting a young lady of colour
in Georgetown, Demerara. I don't think Dennis O'Moore
could help sympathising with people, and as a result of
this goodnatured weakness, he heard a great deal about
that young lady of colour, and her genteel clothes, and
how she played the piano, and belonged to the Baptist
congregation.

" I've a cousin myself in Demerara, Alfonso," said
Dennis.

" Hope she'm kind to you, Dennis. Hope you can
trust her, 'specially if the members walks home with her
after meeting." And Alfonso sighed.

But jokes were far too precious on board the 'Slut' for Dennis to spoil this one by explaining that his cousin was a middle-aged gentleman in partnership with the owner of a sugar estate.

As we had sailed on the understanding that the Water-Lily was bound for New York and back again to Halifax, of course we made a fuss and protested at the change. But we had not really much practical choice in the matter, whatever our strict rights were, and on the whole we found it would be to our advantage to go through with it, especially as we did secure a better understanding about our wages, and the captain promised us more rest on Sundays. On one point we still felt anxious—our home letters ; so Dennis wrote to the postmaster at Halifax, and arranged for them to be forwarded to us at the post-office, George-town, Demerara. For Alfonso was right, we were bound for British Guiana, it being however understood that we three were not under obligation to make the return voyage in the Water-Lily.

An odd incident occurred during our brief stay in New York. It was after the interview in which we came to terms with the captain, and he had given us leave for three hours ashore. You can't see very much of a city when you have no money to spend in it ; but we had walked about till we were very hungry, and yet more thirsty, for it was hot, when we all three caught sight of a small shop (or store, as Americans would call it), and we all spoke at once.

" Cooling drinks ! " exclaimed Dennis.

" There's cakes yonder," said Alister.

" Michael Macartney," muttered I, for that was the name over the door.

We went in as a customer came out, followed by Michael Macartney's parting words in a rich brogue that might have been old Biddy's own. I took a good look at him, which he returned with a civil comment on the heat, and

an inquiry as to what I would take, which Dennis, in the
thirstiness of his throat, answered for me, leaving me a few
moments more of observation. I made a mental calculation,
and decided that the man's age would fit Mickey, and in
the indescribableness of the colour of his clothes and his
complexion he was undoubtedly like Biddy, but if they
had been born in different worlds the expression of his eyes
could not have been more different. I had the clearest
remembrance of hers. One does not so often look into
the eyes of a stranger and see genuine feeling that one
should forget it. For the rest of him, I was glad that Biddy
had allowed that there was no similarity " betwixt us." He
had a low forehead, a broad nose, a very wide mouth, full
of very large teeth, and the humorous twinkle in his eye
did not atone for the complete absence of that steady light
of honest tenderness which shone from Biddy's as freely
and fearlessly as the sun shines. He served Dennis and
Alister and turned to me.

" Have you a mother in Liverpool ?" I asked, before he
had time to ask me which " pop " I wanted.

As I have said, his mouth was big, but I was almost
aghast at the size to which it opened, before he was able
to say, " Murther and ages ! Was ye there lately ? Did ye
know her ?"

" Yes ; I know her. "

" And why would ye be standing out there with the cold
pop, when there's something better within ? Come in, me
boy. So you're acquainted with my mother ? And how
was she ?"

" No, thank you, I don't drink spirits. Yes ; your
mother was well when I saw her."

" GOD be praised ! It's a mighty long time since I
seen the ould craythur."

" Fifteen years," said I.

I looked at Mr. Macartney as I said it, but he had
evasive eyes, and they wandered to the doorway. No

customers appeared, however, and he looked back to
Dennis and Alister, but they had both folded their arms,
and were watching us in silence.

" Murther and ages !" he repeated, " it doesn't feel the
half of it."

" I fancy it seems longer, if anything, to her. But she
has been on the look-out for you every day, you see.
You've a good business, Mr. Macartney, so I dare say
you're a ready reckoner. Fifteen times three hundred and
sixty-five ? Five thousand four hundred and seventy-five,
isn't it ? "

" It's a fine scholar for a sailor-boy that ye are !" said
Mickey ; and there was a touch of mischief in his eye and
voice which showed that he was losing his temper. I
suppose Dennis heard it, too, for he took one bound to
my side in a way that almost made me laugh to feel how
ready he was for a row. But I knew that, after all, I had
no right over the man's private affairs, warm as was my
zeal for old Biddy.

" And you think I might mind my business and leave
you to yours, Mr. Macartney ? " I said. " But you see
your mother was very kind to me, very kind indeed ; and
when I left Liverpool I promised her if ever I came across
you, you should hear of her, and she should hear of you."

" And why not ? " he answered in mollified tones. " It's
mighty good-natured in ye, too. But come in, all the
three of ye, and have somethin' to eat and to drink for the
sake of the old country."

We followed him into a back parlour, where there were
several wooden rocking-chairs, and a strong smell of stale
tobacco. Here he busied himself in producing cold meat,
a squash pie, and a bottle of whisky, and was as voluble
as civil about every subject except the one I wished to
talk of. But the memory of his mother was strong upon
me, and I had no intention of letting it slide.

" I'm so glad to have found you," I said. " I am sure

you can't have knowr. what a trouble it has been to
your mother never to have heard from you all these
years."

"Arrah ! And why should she bother herself over me ?"
he answered impatiently. "Sure I never was anything
but a trouble to her, worse luck !" And before I could
speak again, he went on, "But make your mind aisy, I'll
be writing to her. Many's the time that I've all but
indited the letter, but I'll do it now. Upon me conscience,
ye may dipind upon me."

Could I depend upon his shambling conscience? Every
instinct of an honest man about me answered, No. As he
had done for fifteen years past, so he would do for fifteen
years to come. As long as he was comfortable himself,
his mother would never get a line out of him. Perhaps his
voice recalled hers, but I almost fancied I could hear her
as I sat there.—" I ax your pardon, darlin'. It was my own
Mickey that was on my mind."

"Look here, Mr. Macartney," said I ; " I want you to
do me a favour. I owe your mother a good turn, and it'll
ease my mind to repay it. Sit down whilst we're enjoying
your hospitality, and just write her a line, and let me have
the pleasure of finding a stamp and putting it in the post
with my own hands."

We argued the point for some time, but Mickey found
the writing materials at last, and sat down to write. As
he proceeded he seemed to become more reconciled to
the task ; though he was obviously no great scribe, and
followed the sentiments he was expressing with curious
contortions of his countenance which it was most funny to
behold. By-and-by I was glad to see a tear or two drop
on to the paper, though I was sorry that he wiped them
up with his third finger, and wrote over the place before it
had time to dry.

"Murther and ages ! But it's mighty pleased that
she'll be," said Mr. Macartney when he had finished. He

looked mighty pleased with himself, and he held the letter
out to me.

" Do you mean me to read it ? " I asked.

" I did. And ye can let your friends hear too."

I read it aloud, wondering as I read. If pen and ink
spoke the truth, Biddy's own Mickey's heart was broke
entirely with the parting from his mother. Sorra a bit of
taste had there been in his food, or a drop of natural rest
had he enjoyed for the last fifteen years. " Five thousand
four hundred and seventy-five days—no less." (When I
reached this skilful adoption of my calculations, I involuntarily looked up. There sat Mr. Macartney in his
rocking-chair. He was just lighting a short pipe, but
he paused in the operation to acknowledge what he evidently believed to be my look of admiration, with a nod
and a,wink. I read on.) Times were cruel bad out there
for a poor boy that lived by his industry, but thank GOD
he'd been spared the worst pangs of starvation (I glanced
.round the pop-shop, but as Mickey himself would have
said, No matther !) and didn't it lighten his heart that day
to hear of his dear mother sitting content and comfortable
at her own coffee-stall. It was murderously hot in these
parts, and New York—bad luck to it—was a mighty
different place from the dear old Ballywhack where he
was born. Would they ever see old Ireland again ?
(Here a big blot betrayed how much Mr. Macartney
had been moved by his own eloquence.) The rest of the
letter was rich with phrases both of piety and affection.
How much of the whole composition was conscious
humbug, and whether any of it was genuine feeling, I
have as little idea now as I had then. The shallows of
the human heart are at least as difficult to sound as its
depths, and Mickey Macartney's was quite beyond me.
One thing about the letter was true enough. As he said,
it would " plaze the ould craythur intirely."

By the time I had addressed it " Mrs. Biddy Macartney,

R

coffee-seller," to the care of the Dockgate-keeper, we had not much spare time left in which to stamp and post it, so we took leave of the owner of the pop-shop. He was now very unwilling to let us go. He did not ask another question about his mother, but he was consumed with trivial curiosity about us. Once again he alluded to Biddy. We were standing outside, and his eye fell upon the row of shining pop-taps—

"Wouldn't she be the proud woman now, av she could see me!" he cried.

"Why don't you get her out to live with you?" I asked.

He shook his head. "I'm a married man, Mr.—— bad luck to me, I've forgotten your name now?"

"I didn't trouble you with it. Well, I hope you'll go and see her before she dies."

But when I came to think of it, I did not feel sure if that was what I wished. Not being a woman, how could I balance the choice of pain? How could I tell if it were better for her to be disappointed with every ship and every tide, still having faith in her own Mickey, and hope of his coming, or for the tide and the ship to bring him with all his meanness upon the head she loved, a huge disappointment, once for all!

———◆———

CHAPTER XXIV.

"Roose the fair day at e'en."

Scotch Proverb.

AFTER leaving New York, we no longer hugged the coast. We stood right off, and to my great delight, I found we were going to put in at Bermuda for repairs. I never knew, but I always fancy that these were done cheaper there than at New York. Or it may merely have

been because when we had been at sea two days the
wretched ' Slut ' leaked so that, though we were pumping
day and night, till we were nearly worn out, we couldn't
keep the wet from our gimcrack cargo.

Fortunately for us the weather was absolutely lovely,
and though it was hot by day, we wore uncommonly little
clothing and "carried our change of air with us," as
Dennis said.   As to the nights, I never can forget the
ideal beauty of the last three before we reached Bermuda.
I had had no conception of what starlight can be and
what stars can look like.   These hanging lamps of the vast
heavens seemed so strangely different from the stars that
"twinkle, twinkle," as the nursery book has it, through
our misty skies at home.   We were, in short, approaching
the tropics.   Very beautiful were the strange constellations
of the midnight sky, the magic loveliness of the moonlight,
and the phosphorescence of the warm waves, whilst the
last exquisite touch of delight was given by the balmy air.
By day the heat (especially as we had to work so hard in
it) made one's enjoyment less luxurious, but if my love for
the sea had known no touch of disappointment on the
cold swell of the northern Atlantic, it would have needed
very dire discomfort to spoil the pleasure of living on
these ever-varying blue waters, flecked with white foam
and foam-like birds, through the clearness of which we
now and then got a peep of a peacock-green dolphin,
changing his colour with every leap and gambol, as if
he were himself a wave.

Of living things (and, for that matter, of ships) we saw
far less than I expected, though it was more than a
fortnight from the time of our leaving Sandy Hook to the
night we lay off to the east of the Bermudas—the warm
lights from human habitations twinkling among the islands,
and the cold light of the moon making the surf and coral
reefs doubly clear against the dark waters—waiting, but
scarcely wishing, for the day.

R 2

As I have said, Alfonso was very black, and Alfonso
was very dignified. But his blackness, compared with the
blackness of the pilot who came off at St. George's Island
and piloted us through the Narrows, was as that of a kid-
shoe to a boot that has been polished by blacking. As to
dignity, no comparison can be made. The dignity of that
nigger pilot exceeded anything, regal, municipal, or even
parochial, that I have ever seen. As he came up the ship's
side, Dennis was looking over it, and when the pilot stood
on deck Dennis fled abruptly, and Alister declares it took
two buckets of water to recover him from the fit of hysterics
in which he found him rolling in the forecastle.

The pilot's costume bore even more reference to his
dignity than to the weather. He wore a pea-coat, a tall
and very shiny black hat, white trousers, and neither shoes
nor socks. His feet were like flat-irons turned the wrong
way, and his legs seemed to be slipped into the middle
of them, like the handles of two queer-shaped hoes. His
intense, magnificent importance, and the bombastic way
he swaggered about the deck, were so perfectly absurd,
that we three youngsters should probably have never had
any feeling towards him but that of contempt, if it had not
been that we were now quite enough of seamen to appreciate the skill with which he took us safely on our dangerous and intricate passage into harbour. How we ever got
through the Narrows, how he picked our way amongst the
reefs and islands, was a marvel. We came in so close to
shore that I thought we must strike every instant, and so
we should have done had there been any blundering on
his part.

We went very slowly that day, as became the atmosphere
and the scene, the dangers of our way, and the dignity of
our guide.

"It's an ill wind that blows nobody good," said Dennis,
as we hung over the side. "If it's for repairs we've put into
Paradise, long life to the old tub and her rotten timbers!

I wouldn't have missed *this* for a lady's berth in the West
Indian Mail, and my passage paid ! "

" Nor I."

" Nor I."

This was indeed worth having gone through a good deal
to see. The channel through which we picked our way
was marked out by little buoys, half white and half black,
and on either side the coral was just a-wash. Close at
hand the water was emerald green or rosy purple, according
to its depth and the growths below ; half a mile away it
was deep blue against lines of dazzling surf and coral
sand ; and the reefs and rocks amongst whose deadly
edges our hideous pilot steered for our lives, were like beds
of flowers blooming under water. Red, purple, yellow,
orange, pale green, dark green, in patches quite milky, and
in patches a mass of all sorts of seaweed, a gay garden on
a white ground, shimmering through crystal ! And down
below the crabs crawled about, and the fishes shot hither
and thither ; and over the surface of the water, from reef
to reef and island to island, the tern and sea-gulls skimmed
and swooped about.

We anchored that evening, and the pilot went ashore.
Lovely as the day had been, we were (for some mysterious
reason) more tired at the end of it, than on days when we
had been working three times as hard. This, with Dennis,
invariably led to mischief, and with Alister to intolerance.
The phase was quite familiar to me now, and I knew it
was coming on when 'they would talk about the pilot.
That the pilot was admirably skilful in his trade, and that
he was a most comical-looking specimen of humanity,
were obvious facts. I quite agreed with both Alister and
Dennis, but that, unfortunately, did not make them agree
with each other. Not that Dennis contradicted Alister
(he pretended to be afraid to do so), but he made comments that were highly aggravating. He did not attempt
to deny that it was "**a gran sight to see ony man do his**

wark weel," or that the African negro shared with us "our common humanity and our immortal hopes," but he introduced the quite irrelevant question of whether it was not a loss to the Presbyterian Ministry that Alister had gone to sea. He warmly allowed that the pilot probably had his feelings, and added that even he had his ; that the Hat tried them, but that the Feet were " altogether too many for them intirely." He received the information that the pilot's feet were " as his Creator made them," in respectful silence, and a few minutes afterwards asked me if I was aware of the " curious fact in physiology," that it took a surgical operation to get a joke through a Scotchman's brain-pan.

I was feeling all-overish and rather cross myself towards evening, and found Alister's cantankerousness and Dennis O'Moore's chaff almost equally tiresome. To make matters worse, I perceived that Dennis was now so on edge, that to catch sight of the black pilot made him really hysterical, and the distracting thing was, that either because I was done up, or because such folly is far more contagious than any amount of wisdom, I began to get quite as bad, and Alister's disgust only made me worse. I unfeignedly dreaded the approach of that black hat and those triangular feet, for they made me giggle in spite of myself, and I knew a ship's rules far too well not to know how fearful would be the result of any public exhibition of disrespect.

However, we three were not always together, and we had been apart a good bit when we met (as ill-luck would have it) at the moment when the pilot's boat was just alongside, ready for his departure.

"What's the boat for?" asked Alister, who had been below.

" And who would it be for," replied Dennis, " but the gentleman in the black hat? Alister, dear ! What's the reason I can't tread on a nigger's heels without treading on your toes ? "

"Hush!" cried I, in torment, "he's coming."

We stood at attention, but never can I forget the agony of the next few minutes. That hat, that face, those flat black feet, that strut, that smile. I felt a sob of laughter beginning somewhere about my waist-belt, and yet my heart ached with fear for Dennis. Oh, if only His Magnificence would move a little quicker, and let us have it over!

There's a fish at Bermuda that is known as the toad-fish (so Alfonso told me), and when you tickle it it blows itself out after the manner of the frog who tried to be as big as an ox. It becomes as round as a football, and if you throw it on the water it floats. If you touch it it sounds (according to Alfonso) "all same as a banjo." It will live some time out of water; and if it shows any signs of subsiding, another tickle will blow it out again. "Too muchee tickle him burst," said Alfonso. I had heard this decidedly nasty story just before the pilot's departure, and it was now the culmination of all the foolish thoughts that gibbered in my head. I couldn't help thinking of it as I held my breath to suppress my laughter, and quaked for the yet more volatile Dennis. Oh, dear! Why wouldn't that mass of absurdity walk quicker? His feet were big enough. Meanwhile we stood like mutes—eyes front! To have looked at each other would have been fatal. "Too muchee tickle him burst." I hoped we looked grave (I have little doubt now that we looked as if we were having our photographs taken). The sob had mounted from my waist to my throat. My teeth were set, my eyes watered, but the pilot was here now. In a moment he would be down the side. With an excess of zeal I found strength to raise my hand for a salute.

I fear it was this that pleased him, and made him stop; and we couldn't help looking at him. His hat was a little set back for the heat, his black triangular feet were in the third position of dancing. He smiled.

There was an explosive sound to my right. I knew what it meant. Dennis had " burst."

And then I never felt less like laughing in my life. Visions of insubordination, disrespect, mutiny, flogging, and black-hole, rushed through my head, and I had serious thoughts of falling on my knees before the insulted pilot. With unfeigned gratitude I record that he was as magnanimous as he was magnificent. He took no revenge, except in words. What he said was :

" Me one coloured gentleman. You one dam mean white trash ob common sailor. YAH ! "

And with unimpaired dignity he descended the ladder and was rowed away over the prismatic waters. And Alister and I turned round to look for Dennis and found him sitting in the scuppers, wiping the laughter-tears out of his thick eyelashes.

There was something fateful about that evening, which was perhaps what made the air so heavy. If I had been keeping the log, I should have made the following entry :
" Captain got drunk. A ring round the moon. Alister and Dennis quarrelsome."

I saw the ring round the moon when I was rowing the captain and the mate back from one of the islands, where they had been ashore. Alfonso afterwards pointed it out to me and said, " Tell you, Jack, I'm glad dis ole tub in harbour now ! " From which I concluded that it was an omen of bad weather.

Alister and Dennis were still sparring. I began to think we'd better stretch a rope and let them have it out with their fists, but I could not make out that there was anything to fight about except that Alister had accused Dennis of playing the fool, and Dennis had said that Alister was about as good company as a grave-digger. I felt very feverish and said so, on which they both began to apologise, and we all turned in for some sleep.

Next day we were the best of friends, and we got leave

to go ashore for a few hours. We were anchored in
Grassy Bay, off Ireland Island—that is, off the island
where the hulks are, and where the schoolmaster spent
those ten long years. Alister and Dennis wanted to take
a boat and make for Harrington Sound, a very beautiful
land-locked sheet of water, with one narrow entrance
through which the tide rushes like a mill-race, but when
they heard my reason for wanting to have a look at
my friend's old place of labour and imprisonment, they
decided to stay with me, which, as it happened, was very
lucky for us all.

We were all three so languid, that though there was
much to see and little time in which to see it, when we
found three firm and comfortable resting-places among
the blocks of white stone in the dockyard, we sat down on
them, and contented ourselves with enjoying the beautiful
prospect before us. And it so happened that as Dennis
said, if we'd "taken a box for the Opera" we could not
have placed ourselves better for the marvellous spectacle
that it was our good luck to witness. I must try and tell
it in order.

The first thing we noticed was a change among the sea-
birds. They left their careless, graceful skimming and
swooping, and got into groups, wheeling about like
starlings, and uttering curious cries. And scarcely had
we become conscious of this change among the birds than
a simultaneous flutter ran through the Bermudian "rig-
boats" which had been skimming with equal carelessness
about the bay. Now they were hurriedly thrown up into
the wind, their wide mainsails lowered and reefed, whilst
the impulse spread as if by magic to the men-of-war and
ships in the anchorage. Down came the sails like falling
leaves, the rigging swarmed with men bracing yards,
lowering top-gallant masts, and preparing—we could not
conceive for what.

"What, in the name of fortune ——" said Dennis.

But at this moment Alister cried, "Look behind ye, man!"

We turned round, and this was what we saw—

The sky out to seaward was one great half-circle of blue black, but in what sailors call the eye of the storm, was another very regular patch, with true curved outlines of the arc and the horizon. Under this the sea was dazzlingly white, and then in front of that it was a curious green black, and it was tossing and flopping about as if it did not know what to be at. The wind was scarcely to be felt as wind, but we could hear it moaning in a dull way that was indescribably terrifying. Gradually the blackness seemed to come down over us as if it would swallow us up, and when I looked back to the bay not a bird was to be seen, and every boat was flying into shelter.

And as they fled, there arose from the empty sea and sky a strange hissing sound, which gradually grew so intense that it became almost a roar ; and, as the noise increased, the white line on the horizon widened and widened.

Suddenly there came a lull. It quite startled us. But about half a mile away, I could see over Alister's shoulders that the clouds were blacker, and the sea took up the colour and seemed to heave and rock more sulkily than before. There was no white water here, only a greenish ink. And at the same moment Dennis and Alister each laid a hand upon my arm, but we none of us spoke. We lost ourselves in intense watching.

For by degrees the black water, leaving its natural motion, seemed to pile up under the black cloud, and then, very suddenly, before one could see how it happened, either the cloud stretched out a trunk to the sea, or the sea to the cloud, and two funnel-shaped masses were joined together by a long, twisting, whirling column of water that neither sea nor sky seemed able to break away from. It was a weird sight to see this dark shape writhe

and spin before the storm, and at last the base of it struck
a coral reef, and it disappeared, leaving nothing but a
blinding squall of rain and a tumult of white waves breaking on the reef. And then the water whirled and tossed,
and flung its white arms about, till the whole sea, which
had been ink a few minutes before, had lashed itself into a
vast sheet of foam.

We relaxed our grip of each other, and drew breath, and
Alister stretching his arm seawards after a fashion peculiar
to him in moments of extreme excitement, gave vent to
his feelings in the following words :

" Sirs ! yon's a water-spout."

But before we had time to reply, a convict warder, whom
we had not noticed, called sharply to us, " Lie down, or
you'll be blown down !" and the gale was upon us. We
had quite enough to do to hold on to the ground, and keep
the stone-dust out of our eyes by shutting them. Further
observations were impossible, though it felt as if everything in the world was breaking up, and tumbling about
one's ears.

Luckily nothing did strike us, though not more than a
hundred yards away, a row of fine trees went down like
a pack of cards, each one parallel with its neighbour.
House-tiles flew in every direction, shutters were whipped
off and whirled away ; palm-trees snapped like fishing-rods,
and when the wind squall had passed, and we sat up, and
tried to get the sand out of our ears, we found the whole
place a mass of débris.

But when we looked seaward we saw the black arch
going as fast as it came. All sense of fever and lassitude
had left us. The air was fresh, and calm, and bright, and
within half an hour, the tern and seagulls were fishing
over the reef and skimming and swooping above the
prismatic waters as before.

CHAPTER XXV.

"Be stirring as the time ; be fire with fire ;
   *   *   *   so shall inferior eyes,
That borrow their behaviours from the great,
Grow great by your example, and put on
The dauntless spirit of resolution."
                                King John, **v. I.**

"CREAKY doors" are said to "hang long," and leaky
ships may enjoy a similar longevity. It certainly was a
curious fact that the Water-Lily hardly suffered in that
storm, though the damage done to shipping was very great.
Big and little, men-of-war and merchantmen, very few
escaped scot-free, and some dragged their anchors and
were either on the reef in the harbour, or ran foul of one
another.

Repairs were the order of the day, but we managed to
get ours done and to proceed on our voyage, with very
little extra delay.

I cannot say it was a pleasant cruise, though it brought
unexpected promotion to one of the Shamrock three. In
this wise :

The mate was a wicked brute, neither more nor less. I
do not want to get into the sailor fashion of using strong
terms about trifles, but to call him less than wicked would
be to insult goodness, and if brutality makes a brute, he
was brute enough in all conscience ! Being short-handed,
at Bermuda, we had shipped a wretched little cabin boy of
Portuguese extraction, who was a native of Demerara, and
glad to work his passage there, and the mate's systematic
ill-treatment of this poor lad was not less of a torture to us
than to Pedro himself, so agonising was it to see, and not

dare to interfere ; all we could do was to aid him to the best of our power on the sly.

The captain, though a sneaking, unprincipled kind of man, was neither so brutal nor, unfortunately, so good a seaman as the mate ; and the consequence of this was, that the mate was practically the master, and indulged his Snuffy-like passion for cruelty with impunity, and with a double edge. For, as he was well aware, in ill-treating Pedro, he made us suffer, and we were all helpless alike.

His hold over the captain was not from superior seamanship alone. The Water-Lily was nominally a " temperance " vessel, but in our case this only meant that no rum was issued to the crew. In the captain's cabin there was plenty of " liquor," and the captain occasionally got drunk, and each time that he did so, the influence of the mate seemed riveted firmer than before. Crews are often divided in their allegiance, but the crew of the Water-Lily were of one mind. From the oldest to the youngest we all detested the mate, and a natural manliness of feeling made us like the captain better than we ought otherwise have done, because (especially as regards the drinking) we considered his relations with the mate to be characterised by anything but "fair play." No love was really lost between them, and if the captain came on deck and took the lead, they were almost certain to quarrel ; (and none the less so, that *we* rushed with alacrity to obey the captain's orders, whereas with the mate's it was all " dragging work," as nearly as we dare show unwillingness).

What led to the extraordinary scene I am about to relate, I do not quite know. I suppose a mixture of things. Alister's minute, unbroken study of what was now his profession, the "almost monotonous " (so Dennis said) perseverance with which he improved every opportunity, and absorbed all experience and information on the subject of seamanship, could hardly escape the notice of any intelligent captain. Our captain was not much of a seaman, but he was a 'cute trader, and knew "a good article" in any line. The Scotch boy was soon a better sailor than the mate, which will be the less surprising, when one remembers how few men in any trade give more than about a third of their real powers to their work—and Alister gave all his. This, and the knowledge that he was supported by the public opinion of a small but able-bodied crew, may have screwed the captain's courage to the sticking-point, or the mate may have pushed matters just too far ; what happened was this :

The captain and the mate had a worse quarrel than usual, after which the mate rope's-ended poor Pedro till the lad lost consciousness, and whilst I was comforting him below, the brute fumed up and down deck like a hyena ("sight o' blood all same as drink to the likes of him," said Alfonso, "make he drunk for more")—and vented some of his rage in abuse of the captain, such as we had often heard, but which no one had ever ventured to report. On this occasion Alfonso did report it. As I have said, I only knew results.

At eight o'clock next morning all hands were called aft.

The captain was quite sober, and he made very short work of it. He told us briefly and plainly that the mate was mate no longer, and asked if we had any wish as to his successor, who would be chosen from the crew. We left the matter in his hands, as he probably expected, on which, beckoning to Alister, he said, "Then I select Alister Auchterlay. He has proved himself a good and careful seaman, and I believe you all like and trust him. I beg you to show this now by obeying him. And for the rest of the voyage remember that he is *Mister* Auchterlay."

"Mr. Auchterlay" more than justified the captain's choice. His elevation made no change in our friendship, though the etiquette of the vessel kept us a good deal apart, and Dennis and I were all the "thicker" in consequence Alister was not only absolutely loyal to his

trust, but his gratitude never wearied of displaying
itself in zeal. I often wondered how much of this the
captain had foreseen. As Alfonso said, he was "good
trader."

The latter part of the voyage was, in these altered
circumstances, a holiday to what had gone before. The
captain was never actually drunk again, and the Water-
Lily got to look clean, thanks largely to the way Pedro
slaved at scraping, sweeping, swabbing, rubbing, and
polishing, to please his new master. She was really in
something like respectable harbour trim when we approached the coast of British Guiana.

Georgetown, so Alfonso told me, looks very odd from
the sea. The first thing that strikes you being the tops of
the trees which seem to be growing out of the water, but
as you get nearer you discover that this effect is produced
by the low level of the land which is protected from the
sea by a sea-wall and embankment. I have no doubt
Alfonso was right, but when the time came I forgot all
about it, for it was not in ordinary circumstances that I
first saw Georgetown.

It was one of those balmy, moonlit tropical nights of
which I have spoken ; but when we were within about an
hour's sail of the mouth of the Demerara river, the sky
ahead of us began to redden as if the evening had forgotten
itself and was going back to sunset. We made numberless
suggestions, including that of a display of fireworks in our
honour, but as the crimson spread and palpitated, like an
Aurora Borealis, and then shot up higher and flooded a large
area of sky, Alister sang out, " Fire !" and we all crowded
forward in anxious curiosity.

As might be expected, Alfonso and Pedro were in a
state of the wildest excitement. Alfonso, of course,
thought of his lady-love, and would probably have
collapsed into complete despair, but for the necessity of
keeping up his spirits sufficiently to snub every suggestion
made by the cabin-boy, whose rival familiarity with the

topography of Georgetown he could by no means tolerate ; whiist Pedro, though docile as a spaniel to us, despised Alfonso as only a half-caste can despise a negro somewhat blacker than himself, and burned for safe opportunities of displaying his superiority. But when Pedro expressed a somewhat contemptuous conviction that this glowing sky was the result of rubbish burning on plantations up the country, and skilfully introduced an allu͟s͟ion to relatives of his own who had some property in cane-fieids, Alfonso's wrath became sublime.

"You no listen to dat trash ob cabin-boy," said he. "Wait a bit, and I'se find him dirty work below dat's fit for he. Keep him from troubling gentlemen like us wid him lies. Plantation? Yah ! He make me sick. Tell you, me know Demarary well 'nuff. De town is in flames. Oh, my Georgiana ! "

So much, indeed, was beyond doubt before long, and as the fire seemed perilously close to the wharves and shipping, the captain decided to lie off for the night. The thermometer in his cabin stood at ninety degrees, which perhaps accounted for his having no anxiety to go ashore, but, in spite of the heat, Dennis and I were wild to see what was going on, and when Alister called to us to help to lower the jolly-boat, and we found we were to accompany him, we were not dilatory with the necessary preparations, and were soon rapidly approaching the burning town.

It was a strange sight as we drew nearer and nearer. Before us, on the sea, there was a line where the cold silver of the moonshine met the lurid reflections of the fiery sky, and the same cool light and hot glow changed places over our cheeks as we turned our heads, and contrasted on the two sides of the sail of the jolly-boat. And then we got within ear-shot. A great fire is terrible to see, but it is almost more terrible to hear, and it is curious how like it is to the sound of great waters or a great wind. The roar, the hiss, the crackle, the pitiless approach—as Dennis said——

" I'll tell ye what it is, Jack. These elemental giants, when they do break loose from our service, have one note of defiance amongst them ; and it's that awe-ful roar ! "

When we stood in the street where the fire was, it was deafening, and it kept its own distinctness above all other noises ; and with the fire-bells, the saving and losing of household goods, and the trampling and talking of the crowd, there were noises not a few. Dennis and I were together, for Alister had business to do, but he had given us leave to gratify our curiosity, adding a kindly warning to me to take care of myself, and keep " that feather-brained laddie," Dennis, out of danger's way. We had no difficulty in reaching the point of interest, for, ludicrous to say, the fire was in Water Street ; that is, it was in the street running parallel with the river and the wharves ; the main business-street of Georgetown. We were soon in the thick of the crowd, protecting our eyes from the falling fragments of burning wood, and acquiring information. That heap of smoking embers—so we were told—was the big store where it first broke out, the house yonder, where the engines were squirting away, and the fire putting tongues of flame out of the windows at them, as if in derision, cost two thousand dollars——" Ah ! there goes the roof ! "

It fell in accordingly, and, in the sudden blaze of its destruction, I saw a man come riding along, before whom the people made way, and then someone pulled me back and said :

" The Governor."

He stopped near us, and beckoned some one to his side.

" Is he coming? "

" He's here, sir ; " and then into the vivid glare stepped a tall, graceful, and rather fantastic-looking young gentleman in a white jacket, and with a long fair moustache, who raised his hand with a quick salute, and then stood at the govenor's stirrup.

" I know that fellow, I'm sure," said Dennis.

"Royal Engineers officer," said my neighbour. "Mark my words, that means gunpowder," and the good man, who was stout and steaming with perspiration, seemed to feel like one who has asked for a remedy for toothache and been answered by the dentist—"Gunpowder is what it means! And if our governor had sent for a cobbler, *he'd* have said, 'Nothing like leather,' and mended the hose of the steam-pump. And that store of mine, sir, didn't cost a cent less than——"

But I was watching the engineer officer, and catching fragments of the rapid consultation.

"Quite inevitable, sir, in my opinion."

"Very good. You have full powers—instruct—colonel —magazine—do your best."

The engineer officer had very long white hands, which I noticed as one went rapidly to his forehead, whilst with the other he caressed the dark nose of the governor's horse, which had been rubbing its head against his shoulder. And then the governor rode away and left him.

The word "gunpowder" seemed to have brought soldiers to the spot in a sort of natural sequence. There was more quick saluting and short orders, and then all disappeared but one bronzed-looking sergeant, who followed the engineer stripling up and down as he jerked his head, and pulled his moustache, and seemed to have some design upon the gutters of the house-eaves, which took a good deal of explaining and saluting. Then we heard wheels and running footsteps, and I became sensible of great relief from the pressure of the crowd. The soldiers had come back again, running a hand-cart with four barrels of gunpowder, and the public made way for them even more respectfully than for the governor. As they set it down and wiped their faces, the sergeant began to give orders rather more authoritatively than his superior, and he also pointed to the gutters. On which the soldiers vanished as before.

" Can't we help, I wonder ? " said I.

" That's just what I'm thinking," said Dennis, and he strode up to the officer. But he was busy with his subordinate.

" Well, sergeant ? "

" Not a fuse in the place, sir."

" Pretty state of things ! Get a hatchet."

" They sent one, sir."

" All right. This is the house."

" The roof '*as* caught, you know, sir ? "

" The less time to waste," was the reply, and the young man took up a barrel in his hands and walked in with it, kicking the door open with his foot. The sergeant must almost have trodden on his officer's heels, as he followed with the second, and before I could speak Dennis had shouldered the third.

" Here's diversion ! " said he, and away he went.

There was the fourth barrel and there was I. I confess that I felt a twinge, but I followed the rest, and my barrel behaved as well as if it had been a cask of molasses, though the burning wood fell thickly over us all. As I groped my way in, the sergeant and Dennis came out, and by the time that they and some soldiers returned, dragging pieces of house-gutters after them, the fantastic young officer was pouring the gunpowder into a heap in the middle of the floor, by the light of a corner of the ceiling which was now on fire, and I was holding up a shutter, under his orders, to protect it from premature sparks. When he set down the barrel he shook some dirt from his fingers, and then pushing back his white shirt-sleeves from his wrists, he filled his joined hands as full with gunpowder as they would hold, and separating them very slightly let a tiny stream run out on to the floor as he walked backwards ; and as fast as this train was laid, the thin line was covered from falling embers by the gutters, turned over it upside down. Through the room, down along a passage between two houses, and so into the street, where the crowd had more or less assembled again. Then the officer emptied his hands, dusted them together, and said, " Clear everybody out."

The sergeant saluted—" May I fire it, sir ? "

" No thank you, sergeant, clear everybody out." The sergeant was evidently disappointed, and vented this on the civilian public.—" *That,*" said he, turning a blackened thumb over his shoulder, " is a 'eap of gunpowder. It's just a going to be hexploded." There was no need to " clear everybody out." *They went.* And we found ourselves alone with the soldiers, who were laughing, and saying that the crowd had taken a big cast-iron tank for the heap of gunpowder. We stood a little aside in obedience to a wave of the young officer's arm. Then he crossed the street to pick up a long piece of burning wood, and came back, the moonlight and the firelight playing by turns upon him.

I honestly confess that, fierce as the heat was, I turned cold. The experiences of the next few minutes were as follows : I saw the young engineer fire the train, and I heard a puff, and then I saw him fall, face downwards, behind the tank. I gave a cry, and started forward, and was brought up short by a back-hander on my chest from the sergeant. Then came a scrambling, rushing sound, which widened into a deep roar, shaking the ground beneath our feet, and then the big building at which we were gaping seemed to breathe out a monstrous sigh, and then it fell in, and tumbled to pieces, quietly, swiftly, and utterly, like a house of cards.

And the fantastic-looking young officer got up and shook himself, and worried the bits of charred wood out of his long yellow moustaches.

CHAPTER XXVI.

"Die Welt kann dir nichts darbieten, was sie von dir nicht empfienge."

                   SCHILLER.—*Der Menschenfeind.*

AFTER Alister had done the captain's business, he made his way to the post-office and got our letters, thinking, as he cannily observed, that in widespread misfortunes the big are implicated with the little, that fire spares public buildings no more than private residences, and that if the post-office was overtaken by the flames, we might lose not only words of affection, but perhaps enclosures of value. In short, he had brought our letters, and dearly welcome they were.

I had three ; one from my father, one from my mother (with a postscript by Jem), and a long one from Charlie. I read my father's first ; the others were sure to be tender and chatty, and I could enjoy them at leisure.

My father's letter was, for him, a wonderful effort of composition, and it was far kinder than I had expected or deserved. He blamed me ; but he took some blame to himself for our misunderstandings, which he hoped would never recur. He said (very justly) that if he had spoken harshly, he had acted as he believed to be best for me. Uncle Henry's office was an opening many parents envied for their sons, and he had not really believed that my fancy for the sea was more than a boyish whim. He was the last man in the world to thwart a real vocation, and no doubt (as my Uncle Henry and he had agreed, and, thank GOD, they had had a very pleasant brotherly bit of a chat over old times, and a glass of my grandfather's 1815 port) every Briton had a natural tendency to rule the waves, and it was stronger in some lads than others, as 'Robinson

Crusoe' alone would prove, a book which my uncle remembered had nearly cost him his life on a badly-made raft on the mill-dam, when he was a lad, and which would be read by boys with the real stuff in them, when half these modern books the Woods littered the farm parlour with were lighting the fire. My Uncle Henry had come forward in a very gratifying way. He had mentioned that Benson, an exceedingly intelligent clerk of his, had spoken of me in the highest terms, and seemed to think that there was hardly anything in the way of distinction in an adventurous career which might not be open to me. I was not to be made vain by this, as Benson appeared to be an affectionate fellow, with a respect for the family of his employer very rare in these days. It had been a great comfort to my father, this visit from Uncle Henry. They were both greyheaded now, and Jem and I were all they had to come after them. Blood was thicker than water. As to my poor mother——

For a few minutes the letter danced up and down as if writ in water ; then I dried my eyes, and found that she bore up pretty well in hopes of my return, and that Uncle Henry was communicating by this mail with a man of business in Halifax, N.S., who was instructed to take a passage home for me in a good vessel, and to defray any expenses of a reasonable nature in connection with my affairs. When I was safe home, my father added, he would take the best advice as to sending me to sea in a proper and suitable way. Dr. Brown had some relatives who were large ship-owners, and he seemed to be much interested in my career, out of regard to the family. I was to let nothing hinder me from coming home at once, as I valued the love and blessing of my affectionate father.

My mother's letter was infinitely tender, and it was curiously strong. Not a reproach or a lamentation, but some good counsel, shrewd as well as noble, and plenty of home news. Only at the end did she even speak of her-

self : " You see, my son, I have never had men belonging
to me who earned their livelihood in foreign countries and
by dangerous ways, but you may trust your old mother to
learn to do and bear what other mothers go through with.
She will learn to love the sea because you are a sailor, but,
Jack, you must always give her a woman's bitter-sweet
privilege of saying good-bye, and of packing up your things.
I am getting the time over till you come back with socks.
I am afraid they will blister your feet. Martha does not
like them because they are like what the boys wear in the
coal-pits, but Dr. Brown declares they are just right. He
chose the worsted when we went to see Miss Bennet's
mother at the Berlin shop, and left it himself as he drove
home, with a bottle of red lavender for my palpitations. I
shall never forget his kindness. He sat here for an hour
and a half on Sunday, and spoke of you to your father as
if you had been his own son ; and he said himself he walked
up and down Miss Bennet's, right through the shop and
into the back parlour and out again, talking about you, till
the place was quite full, and Mrs. Simpson could not remember what she had dropped in for, which, as Dr. Brown
said, was not to be wondered at, considering Miss Bennet
completely forgot to take him upstairs to see her mother,
and it never crossed his own mind till he stopped at our
door and found the old lady's sleeping draught with my
red drops. He says he called at your Uncle Henry's office,
and congratulated him on having a nephew of spirit, and it
was market day, so the office was full. Jem says I am to
leave room for him, as he can't think of enough to say to fill
a letter of his own, so I will only say GOD bless you ! my
darling boy, and bring you safe home to your poor mother.

" P.S.—If you love me, come as quick as you can. You
shall go off again."

This was Charlie's letter :

" MY DEAR JACK—I was so glad to get your letter. I
knew you had gone off at last. It did not surprise me, for

I was sure you would go some day. I believe I have a
very mean spirit, for I felt rather hurt at first that you did
not tell me; but Mr. Wood gave me a good scolding, and
said I was not fit to have a friend if I could not trust him
out of sight or out of hearing. And that's quite true.
Besides, I think I knew more about it after Jem had been
down. He has been so jolly to me since you left. It
must be a splendid life on board-ship, and I am glad you
have been in the rigging, and didn't fall off. I wish you
had seen an iceberg or a water-spout, but perhaps you
will. For two days and two nights I was very miserable,
and then Jenny rode down on Shag, and brought me a
book that did me a great deal of good, and I'll tell you
why. It's about a man whose friend is going to travel
round the world, like you, and he has to be left behind,
like me. Well, what does he do but make up his mind to
travel round his own garden, and write a history of his
adventures, just as if he had been abroad. And that's the
book ; and you can't tell what a jolly one it is. I mean to
do the same, only as you are at sea I shall call it a Log.
' Log of a voyage round the Garden, the Croft, and the
Orchard, by the Friend he left behind him.' That's good,
isn't it ? I've been rather bothered about whether I should
have separate books for each, or mix them all up; and
then, besides, I've got to consider how to manage about
the different times of year, for you know, of course, the
plants and the beasts and everything are different at
different times ; but if I have a log of each place for each
month, it would not be done by the time you come home.
I think perhaps I shall have note-books for the four
seasons, and that'll take a good while. Two of the best
chapters in Jenny's book are called ' on my face ' and ' on
my back,' and they are about what he sees lying on his
face and then on his back. I'm going to do the same
and put down everything, just as it comes ; beetles,
chrysalises, flowers, funguses, mosses, earth-nuts, and

land-snails, all just as I find them. If one began with different note-books for the creatures, and the plants, and the shells, it would be quite endless. I think I shall start at that place in the hedge in the croft where we found the humble-bee's nest. I should like to find a mole-cricket, but I don't know if they live about here. Perhaps our soil isn't light enough for them to make their tunnels in, but one ought to find no end of curious burrowing creatures when one is on one's face, besides grubs of moths to hatch afterwards. When I am on my back, I fancy what I shall see most of are spiders. You can't conceive what a lot of spiders there are in the world, all sorts and sizes. They are divided into hunters, wanderers, weavers, and swimmers. I expect you'll see some queer ones, if you go to hot places. And oh, Jack ! talking of burrows, of course you're in Nova Scotia, and that's where Cape Sable is, where the stormy petrels make their houses in the sand. They are what sailors call Mother Carey's Chickens, you know. I'm sure we've read about them in adventure books ; they always come with storms, and sailors think they build their nests on the wave. But they don't, Jack, so *you* mustn't think so. They make burrows in the sand, and all day they are out on the wing, picking up what the storms toss to the top, and what the cooks throw overboard, and then they go home, miles and miles and miles at night, and feed their young. They don't take the trouble to make houses if they can find any old rabbit-burrows near enough to the sea, Mr. Wood says ; like the puffins. Do you know, one evening when old Isaac came to see me, I made him laugh about the puffins till the tears ran down his face. It was with showing him that old stuffed puffin, and telling him how the puffin gets into a rabbit-burrow, and when the rabbit comes back they set to and fight, and the puffin generally gets the best of it with having such a great hooked nose. Isaac *was* so funny. He said he'd seen the rabbits out on the spree many and many a moonlight night when sober folks were in bed ; and then he smacked his knees and said, ' But I'd give owt to see one on 'em just nip home and find a Pooffin upon t' hearthstun.' And, my dear Jack, who else has been to see me, do you think ? Fancy ! Lorraine ! You remember our hearing the poor colonel was dead, and had left Lorraine all that he had ? Well, do you know it is a great deal more than we thought. I mean he's got a regular estate and a big house with old pictures inside, and old trees outside. Quite a swell. Poor Lorraine ! I don't mean poor because of the estate, because he's rich, of course ; but do you know, I think he's sadder than ever. He's very much cut up that the colonel died, of course, but he seems desperate about everything, and talks more about suicide than he did at Snuffy's, Jem says. One thing he is quite changed about ; he's so clean ! and quite a dandy. He looked awfully handsome, and Jenny said he was beautifully dressed. She says his pocket-hankerchief and his tie matched, and that his clothes fitted him so splendidly, though they were rough. Well, he's got a straight back, Jack ; like you ! It's hard he can't be happy. But I'm so sorry for him. He went on dreadfully because you'd gone, and said that was just his luck, and then he wished to Heaven he were with you, and said you were a lucky dog, to be leading a devil-me-care life in the open air, with nothing to bother you. He didn't tell me what he'd got to bother him. Lots of things, he said. And he said life was a wretched affair, all round, and the only comfort was none of his family lived to be old.

" *Wednesday.* I had to stop on Monday, my head and back were so bad, and all yesterday too. Dr. Brown came to see me, and talked a lot about you. I am better to-day. I think I had rather wound up my head with note-books. You know I do like having lists of every-thing, and my sisters have been very good. They got a

lot of ruled paper very cheap, and have made me no end
of books with brown paper backs, and Dr. Brown has
given me a packet of bottle labels. You've only got to
lick them and stick them on, and write the titles. He
gave me some before, you remember, to cut into strips
to fasten the specimens in my fern collection. I've got a
dozen and a half books, but there will not be one too
many. You see eight will go at once, with the four
seasons ' on my face,' and the four ' on my back.' Then
I want two or three for the garden. For one thing I must
have a list of our perennials. I am collecting a good lot.
Old Isaac has brought me no end of new ones out of
different gardens in the village, and now the villagers
know I want them, they bring me plants from all kinds
of out-of-the way places, when they go to see their friends.
I've taken to it a good deal the last few weeks, and I'll
tell you why. It was the week before you ran away that
Bob Furniss came up one evening, and for a long time
I could not think what he was after. He brought me a
Jack-in-the-green polyanthus and a crimson bergamot
from his mother, and he set them and watered them, and
said he ' reckoned flowers was a nice pastime for any one
that was afflicted,' but I felt sure he'd got something
more to say, and at last it came out. He is vexed that
he used to play truant so at school and never learned
anything. He can't read a newspaper, and he can't write
or reckon, and he said he was ' shamed ' to go to school
and learn among little boys, and he knew I was a good
scholar, and he'd come to ask if I would teach him now
and then in the evening, and he would work in the garden
for me in return. I told him I'd teach him without that,
but he said he 'liked things square and fair,' and Mr.
Wood said I was to let him ; so he comes up after work-
hours one night and I teach him, and then he comes up
the next evening and works in the garden. It's very jolly
because now I can plot things out my own way, and do

them without hurting my back. I'm going to clear all
the old rose-bushes out of the shady border. The trees
are so big now, it's so shady that the roses never come
to anything but blight, and I mean to make a fernery
there instead. Bob says there's a little wood belonging
to Lord Beckwith that the trustees have cut down completely, and it's going to be ploughed up. They're stubbing
up the stumps now, and we can have as many as we like
for the carting away. Nothing makes such good ferneries,
you get so many crannies and corners. Bob says it's not
far from the canal and he thinks he could borrow a hand-
cart from the man that keeps the post-office up there, and
get a load or two down to the canal-bank, and then fetch
them down to our place in the 'Adela.' Oh, how I wish
you were here to help! Jem's going to. He's awfully
kind to me now you're gone. Talking of the 'Adela,' if
you are very long away (and some voyages last two or three
years), I think I shall finish the garden, and the croft and
the orchard, or at any rate one journey round them ; and I
think for another of your voyages, I will do the log of the
'Adela' on the canal, for with water-plants, and shells,
and larvæ, and beasts that live in the banks, it would be
splendid. Do you know one might give a whole book up
easily to a list of nothing but willows and osiers, and the
different kinds of birds and insects that live in them? But
the number of kinds there are of some things is quite
wonderful. What do you think of more than a hundred
species of iris, and I've only got five in the garden, but
one of them is white. I don't suppose you'll have much
time to collect things, but I keep hoping that some day,
if I live, you'll command a ship of your own, and take me
with you, as they do take scientific men some voyages.
I hope I shall live. I don't think I get any worse.
Cripples do sometimes live a long time. I asked Dr.
Brown if he believed any cripple had ever lived to be a
hundred, and he said he didn't know of one, nor yet ninety

nor eighty, for I asked him. But he's sure cripples have
lived to be seventy. If I do, I've got fifty-four years yet.
That sounds pretty well, but it soon goes, if one has a lot
to do. Mr. Wood doesn't think it likely you could command a vessel for twenty years at least. That only leaves
thirty-four for scientific research, and all the arranging
at home besides. I've given up one of my books to
plotting this out in the rough, and I see that there's
plenty of English work for twenty years, even if I could
count on all my time, which (that's the worst of having
a bad back and head !) I can't. There's one thing I
should like to find out, if ever you think of going to Japan,
and that's how they dwarf big plants like white lilacs,
and get them to flower in tiny pots. Isaac says he thinks
it must be continual shifting that does it—shifting and
forcing. But I fancy they must have some dodge of
taking very small cuttings from particular growths of the
wood. I mean to try some experiments. I am marking
your journeys on a map, and where anything happens to
you I put A, for adventure, in red ink. I have put A,
where you picked up Dennis O'Moore. He must be very
nice. Tell him I hope I shall see him some day, and
your Scotch friend too ; I hope they won't make you quite
forget your poor friend Charlie.

"P.S. — Since I finished, a parcel came. What do
you think Lorraine has done ? He has paid for me to be
a life member of a great London library and sent me
the catalogue. I can have out fifteen books at a time.
There are hundreds of volumes. I can't write any more,
my back aches so with putting crosses against the books
I want to read. The catalogue is rather heavy. I think
I shall use one of my books to make a list in of what I
want to read during this year. Isn't it good of Lorraine ?
Poor Lorraine ! "

Having devoured **my** own letters, **I** looked up **to see**

how my comrades were enjoying their share of the budget
which the Halifax postmaster had faithfully forwarded.

The expression on Dennis O'Moore's face was so mixed
that it puzzled me, but he did not look satisfied with
his letter, for he kept drawing it out again, and shaking
it, and peeping into the envelope as if he had lost something. At last he put the whole thing into his pocket with
a resigned air, and drove his hands through his black
curls, saying—

" The Squire all over, GOD help him ! "

" What has he done now ? " I asked.

" Sent me twenty pounds, and forgotten to enclose it ! "

———— ◆ ————

CHAPTER XXVII.

" Thus the merry Pau-Puk-Keewis
  Danced his Beggar's Dance to please them,
  And, returning, sat down laughing."
                                        Hiawatha.

" GOD be thanked, the meanest of His creatures
  Boasts two soul-sides ; one to face the world with,
  One to show a woman when he loves her."
                                        Robert Browning.

THE fact that when we got back to the Water-Lily,
Alister found the captain dead drunk in his cabin, sealed
our resolution to have nothing more to do with her when
we were paid off, and our engagement ended (as had been
agreed upon), in the Georgetown harbour.   There was no
fear that we should fail to get berths as common seamen
now, if we wanted them ; and there was not a thing to
regret about the ' Slut,' except perhaps Alfonso, of whom
we were really fond.   As it turned out, we had not even to
mourn for him, for he cut cable from the Water-Lily too,
having plans of his own, about which he made a great deal

of mystery and displayed his wonted importance, but whether they were matrimonial or professional, I doubt if even Dennis knew at the time.

Alister *had* something to lose. It was not a small consideration to give up his mate's berth, but he said the whole conduct of the ship was " against his conscience," and that settled the matter, to him.

When we were our own masters once more, we held another big council about our future. If I went home at once, I must, somehow or other, get back to Halifax before I could profit by Uncle Henry's arrangement. If Dennis went home, he must equally depend on himself, for there was no saying when the Squire would, or would not, find out and rectify his omission. Alister's mother had sent him some stamps for postage, and his paternal relative had sent him a message to the effect that having had neither word nor wittens of him for a considerable period, and having feared the worst, he was thankful to learn of his safe arrival in Halifax, Nova Scotia ; and trusted that the step he had taken, if a thought presumptuous at his years, yet betokened a spirit of self-reliance, and might prove not otherwise than conducive to his welfare in the outcome.

Altogether, we were, practically, as much dependent on ourselves as when we sat under the pine-trees in Nova Scotia.

" We'll look up my cousin, to begin with," said Dennis.

" Are ye pairfectly convinced that he's here ? " asked Alister, warned by his own experience.

" Certainly," said Dennis.

" Have ye corresponded with him of late ? " pursued Alister.

" Not I indeed. The O'Moores are by no means good letter-writers at the best of times, but he'd have let us know if he was dead, anyhow, and if he's alive, we'll be as welcome as the flowers."

Before Alister could reply, he was interrupted by a message from our late captain. The Water-Lily was still in harbour, and the captain wanted the ex-mate to help him on some matters connected with the ship or her cargo. Alister would not refuse, and he was to be paid for the job, so we hastily arranged that he should go, and that Dennis and I should devote the evening to looking up the Irish cousin, and we appointed to meet on the "stelling" or wharf, alongside of which the Water-Lily lay, at eleven o'clock on the following morning.

"I was a fool not to speak to that engineer fellow the other night," said Dennis, as we strolled on the shady side of a wide street, down the middle of which ran a wide water-dyke fringed with oleanders. "He would be certain to know where my cousin's place is."

"Do you know him?" I asked, with some eagerness, for the young officer was no small hero in my eyes.

"Oh, yes, quite well. He's a lieutenant in the Engineers. He has often stayed at my father's for shooting. But he has been abroad the last two or three years, and I suppose I've grown. He didn't know——"

"There he is!" said I.

He was coming out of a garden-gate on the other side of the street. But he crossed the road saying, "Hi, my lads!" and putting his hand into his pocket as he came.

"Here's diversion, Jack!" chuckled Dennis; "he's going to tip us for our assistance in the gunpowder plot. Look at him now! Faith, he's as short of change as myself. How that half-crown's eluding him in the corner of his pocket! It'll be no less, I assure ye. He's a liberal soul. Now for it!"

And as the young lieutenant drew near, Dennis performed an elaborate salute. But his eyes were brimming with roguishness, and in another moment he burst out laughing, and after one rapid glance, and a twist of his moustache that I thought must have torn it up by the roots, the young officer exploded in the same fashion.

"DENNIS!—What in the name of the mother of mischief (and I'm sure she was an O'Moore) are you masquerading in that dress for, out here?" But before Dennis could reply, the lieutenant became quite grave, and turning him round by the arm, said, "but this isn't masquerading, I see. Dennis, my dear fellow, what does it mean?"

"It means that I was a stowaway, and my friend here a castaway—I mean that I was a castaway, and Jack was a stowaway. Willie, do you remember Barney Barton?"

"Old Barney? Of course I do. How did he come to let you out of his sight?"

Dennis did not speak. I saw that he could not, so I took upon me to explain.

"They were out in the hooker, off the Irish coast, and she went to pieces in a gale. Old Barney was lost, and we picked Dennis up."

He nodded to me, and with his hand through Dennis O'Moore's arm, said kindly, "We'll go to my quarters, and talk it all over. Where are you putting up?"

"We're only just paid off," said I.

"Then you'll rough it with me, of course, both of you."

I thanked him, and Dennis said, "Willie, the one thing I've been wanting to ask you is, if you know where that cousin of my father's lives, who is in business out here. Do you know him?"

"Certainly. I'm going there to-night, for a dance, and you shall come with me. I can rig you out."

They went ahead, arm-in-arm, and I followed at just sufficient distance behind to catch the backward looks of amazement which the young officer's passing friends were too polite to indulge when exactly on a level with him. He capped first one and then another with an air of

T

apparent unconsciousness, but the contrast between his
smart appearance and spotless white uniform, and the
patched remains of Dennis's homespun suit (to say nothing
of the big bundle in which he carried his " duds "), justified
a good deal of staring, of which I experienced an humble
share myself.

Very good and pleasant are the comforts of civilisation,
as we felt when we were fairly established in our new
friend's quarters.   Not that the first object of life is to be
comfortable, or that I was moved by a hairsbreadth from
my aims and ambitions, but I certainly enjoyed it ; and,
as Dennis said, " Oh, the luxury of a fresh-water wash ! "
—for salt-water really will not clean one, and the only way
to get a fresh-water wash at sea is to save out of one's
limited allowance.   We had done this, to the extent of
two-thirds of a pailful, as we approached Guiana, and had
been glad enough all to soap in the same bucket (tossing
for turns) and rinse off with clean sea-water, but real
" tubs " were a treat indeed !

I had had mine, and, clothed in a white suit, nearly as
much too big for me as the old miser's funeral gloves, was
reposing in a very easy chair, when Dennis and his friend
began to dress for the dance.   The lieutenant was in his
bedroom, which opened to the left out of the sitting-room
where I sat, and Dennis was tubbing in another room
similarly placed on the right.   Every door 'and window
was open to catch what air was stirring, and they shouted
to each other, over my head, so to speak, while the
lieutenant's body-servant ran backwards and . forwards
from one to the other.   He was, like so many soldiers, an
Irishman, and having been with his master when he
visited the O'Moores, he treated Dennis with the utmost
respect, and me with civility for Dennis' sake.   He was
waiting on his master when the lieutenant shouted,

" Dennis ! what's your length, you lanky fellow ? "

" Six foot two by the last notch on the front door.   I

stood in my socks, and the Squire measured it with his tape."

"Well, there's half an inch between us if he's right; but that tape's been measuring the O'Moores from the days of St. Patrick, and I've a notion it has shrunk with age. I think my clothes will do for you."

"Thank you, thank you, Willie! You're very good."

In a few minutes O'Brien came out with his arms full of clothes, and pursued by his master's voice.

"O'Brien's bringing you the things; can he go in? Be quick and finish off that fresh-water business, old fellow, and get into them. I promised not to be late."

I tried to read a newspaper, but the cross-fire of talk forbade anything like attention.

"Was ye wanting me, sorr?"

"No, no. Never mind me, O'Brien. Attend to Mr. O'Moore. Can he manage with those things?"

"He can, sorr. He looks illigant," replied O'Brien from the right-hand chamber. We all laughed, and Dennis began to sing:

"Oh, once we were illigant people,
    Though we now live in cabins of mud;
And the land that ye see from the steeple,
    Belonged to us all from the flood.
My father was then king of Connaught——"

"And mislaid his crown, I'll be bound!" shouted the lieutenant. "Look here, Dennis, you'll get no good partners if we're late, and if you don't get a dance with your cousin's daughter, you'll miss a treat, I can tell you. But dancing out here isn't trifled with as it is in temperate climates, and cards are made up early."

By-and-by he shouted again,

"O'Brien!"

"Coming, your honour."

"I don't want you. But *is* Mr. O'Moore ready?"

" He is, sorr, barrmg the waistcoat. *Take a fresh tie,
Master Dennis. The master'll not be pleased to take ye
out with one like that. Sure it's haste that's the ruin
of the white ties all along.* Did ye find the young
gentleman a pair of shoes, sorr ? "

" Won't those I threw in fit you ? " asked our host.

" I've got them.   The least bit too large.   A thousand
thanks."

" Can you dance in them ?"

" I'll try," replied Dennis, and judging by the sound, he
did try then and there, singing as he twirled,

> " Bad luck to this marching,
> Pipe-claying and starching,
> How neat one must be to be killed by the French !"

But O'Brien's audible delight and the progress of the
song were checked by the lieutenant, who had dressed
himself, and was now in the sitting-room.

' O'Brien !"

" Sorr !"

" If Mr. O'Moore is not ready, I must go without
him."

" He's ready and waiting, sorr," replied O'Brien. " *Have
ye got a pocket-handkerchief, Master Dennis, dear ?
There's the flower for your coat. Ye'll be apt to give
it away, maybe; let me use a small pin. Did the master
not find ye any gloves ? Now av the squire saw ye, it's
a proud man he'd be !* Will I give the young gentleman
one of your hats, sorr ? "

" Yes, of course. Be quick ! So there you are at
last, you young puppy. Bless me ! how like the squire
you are."

The squire must have been amazingly handsome,
I thought, as I gazed admiringly at my comrade.
Our staring made him shy, and as he blushed and
touched up the stephanotis in his buttonhole, the engineer

changed the subject by saying, " Talking of the squire, is it true, Dennis, what Jack tells me about the twenty pounds? Did he really forget to put it in ? "

" As true as gospel," said Dennis, and taking up the tails of his coat he waltzed round the room to the tune of

> " They say some disaster
> Befell the paymaster,
> On my conscience, I think that the money's not there ! "

I stood out on the verandah to see them off, Dennis singing, and chaffing and chattering to the last. He waved his hat to me as his friend gathered the reins, a groom sprang up behind, and they were whirled away. The only part of the business I envied them was the drive.

It was a glorious night, despite the oppressive heat and the almost intolerable biting of mosquitoes and sand-flies. In the wake of the departing trap flew a solitary beetle, making a noise exactly like a scissor-grinder at work. Soft and silent moths—some as big as small birds—went past my face, I fear to the hanging lamp behind me. Passing footfalls echoed bluntly from the wooden pavement, and in the far-away distance the bullfrogs croaked monotonously. And down below, as I looked upon the trees, I could see fire-flies coming and going, like pulsations of light, amongst the leaves.

O'Brien waited on me with the utmost care and civility ; served me an excellent supper, with plenty of ice and cooling drinks, and taught me the use of the "swizzle stick" for mixing them. I am sure he did not omit a thing he could think of for my comfort. He had been gone for some time, and I had been writing letters, turning over the engineer's books, and finally dozing in his chair, when I was startled by sounds from his bedroom, as if O'Brien were engaged, first in high argument, and then in deadly struggle with some intruder. I rushed to his

assistance. and found him alone, stamping vehemently
on the floor.

"What's the matter?" said I.

"Matther is it?   Murther's the matther," and he gave
another vicious stamp, and then took a stride that nearly
cost him his balance, and gave another.   "I beg yor
pardon, sorr ; but it's the cockroaches. The place swarms
wid 'em.   Av they'd keep peaceably below, now, but
invading the master's bedroom—that's for ye, ye thief!"
and he stamped again.

"The creatures here are a great plague," said I,
slapping a mosquito upon my forehead.

"And that as true a word as your honour ever spoke.
They're murderous no less! Many's the time I'm
wishing myself back in old Ireland, where there's no
venomous beasts at all, at all.   Arrah! Would ye, ye
skulking——"

I left him stamping, and streaming with perspiration,
but labouring loyally on in a temperature where labour
was little short of heroism.

I went back to my chair, and began to think over my
prospects.   It is a disadvantage of idleness that one
wearies oneself with thinking, though one cannot act.
I wondered how the prosperous sugar-planter was receiving Dennis, and whether he would do more for him
than one's rich relations are apt to do.   The stars
began to pale in the dawn without my being any the
wiser for my speculations, and then my friends came
home. The young officer was full of hopes that I had
been comfortable, and Dennis of regrets that I had
not gone with them.   His hair was tossed, his cheeks
were crimson, and he had lost the flower from his
buttonhole.

"How did you get on with your cousin?" I asked.
The reply confounded me.

"Oh, charmingly! Dances like a fairy. I say, Willie,

as a mere matter of natural history, d'ye believe any other
human being ever had such feet ? "

A vague wonder crept into my brain whether the cousin
could possibly have become half a nigger, from the climate,
which really felt capable of anything, and have developed
feet like our friend the pilot ; but I was diverted from this
speculation by seeing that Dennis was clapping his pockets
and hunting for something.

" What have you lost now ? " asked his friend.

" My pocket-handkerchief. Ah, there it is !" and he
drew it from within his waistcoat, and with it came his
gloves, and a third one, and they fell on the floor. As he
picked the odd one up the lieutenant laughed.

" What size does she wear, Dennis—sixes ? "

" Five and three quarters—long fingers ; so she tells
me." He sighed, and then wandered to the window,
whistling ' Robin Adair.'

" Now, Dennis, you promised me to go straight to bed.
Turn in we must, for I have to be on an early parade."

" All right, Willie. Good-night, and a thousand thanks
to you. It's been a great evening—I never was so happy
in my life. Come along, Jack."

And off he went, tossing his head and singing to the air
he had been whistling:

> "Who in the song so sweet ?
> Eileen aroon !
> Who in the dance so fleet !
> Eileen aroon !
> Dear were her charms to me,
> Dearer her laughter free,
> Dearest her constancy,
> Eileen aroon !"

" She'll be married to a sugar-planter before you've cut
your wisdom teeth !" bawled the engineer from his bedroom.

" *Will she ?* " retorted Dennis, and half-laughing, half-sentimentally, he sang on louder than before,

> " Were she no longer true,
>   Eileen aroon !
> What should her lover do ?
>   Eileen aroon !
> Fly with his broken chain,
> Far o'er the bounding main,
> Never to love again,
>   Eileen aroon !"

Willie made no reply. He evidently meant to secure what sleep there was to be had, and as Dennis did not seem in the mood for discussing our prospects as seamen, I turned into my hammock and pulled it well round my ears to keep out bats, night-moths, and the like.

It was thus that I failed at first to hear when Dennis began to talk to somebody out of the window. But when I lifted my head I could hear what he said, and from the context I gathered that the other speaker was no less than Alister, who, having taken his sleep early in the night, was now refreshing himself by a stroll at dawn. That they were squabbling with unusual vehemence was too patent, and I was at once inclined to lay the blame on Dennis, who ought, I felt, to have been brimming over with generous sympathy, considering how comfortable we had been, and poor Alister had not. But I soon discovered that the matter was no personal one, being neither more nor less than an indignant discussion as to whether the air which Dennis was singing was " Scotch " or " Irish." As I only caught the Irish side of the argument, I am not qualified to pronounce any opinion.

" Of course facts are facts, no one denies that. And it's likely enough your grandmother sang ' Robin Adair' to it, and your great-grandmother too, rest her soul ! But it would take an uncommonly *great-grandmother* of mine to have sung it when it was new, for it's one of the oldest of old Irish airs."

*　　*　　*　　*　　*

" Stole it of course! as they did plenty more in those times—cattle and what not. I'd forgive them the theft, if they hadn't spoilt the tune with a nasty jerk or two that murders the tender grace of it intirely."

*　　*　　*　　*　　*

"Alister, me boy! You're not going? Ye're not cross, are ye? Faith, I'd give my life for ye, but I can't give ye Eileen aroon. Come in and have some swizzle! We're in the height of luxury here, and hospitality as well, and ye'll be as welcome as daylight."

*　　*　　*　　*　　*

" Up so late? Up so early, ye mean! Ah, don't put on that air of incorruptible morality. Wait now till I get in on the one side of my hammock and out at the other, and I'll look as early-rising-proud as yourself. Alister! Alister, dear!——"

Through all this the engineer made no sign, and it struck me how wise he was, so I pulled the hammock round me again and fell asleep; not for long, I fancy, for those intolerable sandflies woke me once more before Dennis had turned in.

I looked out and saw him still at the window, his eyes on a waning planet, his cheek resting on the little glove laid in his right hand, and singing more sweetly than any nightingale:

> "Youth must with time decay,
> 　　Eileen aroon !
> Beauty must fade away,
> 　　Eileen aroon !
> Castles are sacked in war,
> Chieftains are scattered far,
> Truth is a fixèd star,
> 　　Eileen aroon !"

CHAPTER XXVIII.

"Which is why I remark,
   And my language is plain,
That for ways that are dark,
   And for tricks that are vain,
The heathen Chinee is peculiar."

Bret Harte.

ALISTER did more than pick pink-pale oleanders by the dyke, side that morning. His business with the captain was soon despatched, and in the course of it he "fore-gathered," as he called it, with the man of business who had spoken to us on the night of the great fire, and whose own warehouse was in ruins. He proved to be a Scotch-man by birth, and a man of energy (not a common quality in the tropics), and he was already busy about retrieving his fortune. The hasty repair of part of the building, in which to secure some salvage, and other similar matters, was his first object ; and he complained bitterly of the difficulty of inducing any of the coloured gentlemen to do a " fair day's work for a fair day's wage," except when immediate need pressed them. They would then work, he said, but they would not go on working till the job was done, only till they had earned enough wages to take another idle " spell " upon.

Several Chinamen were already busy among the ruins of the burnt houses, as we saw, and it was Chinese labour that Alister's friend had resolved to employ ; but he seemed to think that, though industrious, those smiling, smooth-faced individuals, who looked as if they had come to life off one of my mother's old tea-cups, were not to be trusted alone among the salvage.

" Every thief among 'em 's as good as a conjurer," he
declared, " and can conceal just anything up his sleeve."

Thus it came about that when Dennis and I went down
to the stelling to meet Alister, as we had agreed, and
delivered the messages of hospitality with which the young
engineer and Dennis's cousin had charged us, we found
that he had made an engagement to help the burnt-out
store-owner for such time as we should be out of seamen's
work, on terms which were to include his board and
lodging.

" Alister, dear ! I admire ye with all me heart," said
Dennis impetuously. " I never saw such an industrious,
persevering fellow. If all Scotch lads take the tide of
life at the flood as you do, small blame to ye for making
your fortunes ; and well ye deserve it."

" There's not a doubt about it," replied Alister compla-
cently. " And I'll tell ye more. Find me any grand work,
if it's at the other end of the airth, whether it's digging a
dyke in the desert, or bigging a mountain up to the moon,
and I'll find ye an Aberdeenshire man not far from the
head of it."

Dennis's face seemed to twitch with a dozen quick
thoughts and smiles, as Alister turned away to meet his
new employer, who had just appeared on the stelling.

" They have wonderful qualities," he said gently. " I
envy them, I can tell ye, Jack. What's an idle lout like
me good for ? Will I ever be able to make a home for
myself, or for any one else ? *They do !* " He spoke
earnestly, and then suddenly relapsing into an imitation
of Alister's accent, which was his latest joke, he added
with twinkling eyes, " and they save a *wee* in wages to
their *ain* trumpeters—*whiles !* "

And having drawled out the word " whiles " to the utter-
most possible length, he suddenly began to snap his fingers
and dance an Irish jig upon the wooden planks of the
stelling. This performance completely demoralised the

Chinamen who caught sight of it. "Eyah!" they cried, they stopped work, they chuckled, they yelled, they doubled themselves up, some of their pig-tails came down, and one and all they laughed so frankly and immoderately, it was hard to believe that anything like deception could be amongst the faults of these almond-eyed children of the Flowery Land.

Mr. Macdonald (the store-owner) seemed, however, to think that they required pretty close watching, and I do not think he would have been willing to let Alister go back with us to luncheon at Willie's, but for his appreciation of social rank. It was obvious that it did Alister no harm that he had a friend in an officer of her Majesty's Service, and a comrade in the nephew of a sugar-planter of the uppermost level of Demerara society.

We three held a fresh council as we sat with the young engineer. He and Alister got on admirably, and he threw himself into our affairs with wonderful kindness. One point he disposed of at once, and that was *my* fate! There could be no question, he said, that my duty was to get back to Halifax, "report myself" to Uncle Henry's agent there, and then go home.

"You're ruthlessly dismembering the Shamrock, Willie," Dennis objected.

"I don't see that. *You're* not to stay here, for instance."

"You're mighty positive," said Dennis, blushing.

"Of course I am. I wouldn't encourage you to waste sentiment anyhow; and the West Indies is no latitude for boys, to go on with. And you know as well as I do, that it's rather more than time the Squire started you in life. You must go home, Dennis!"

"If I do, I go with Jack. And what about Alister?"

The young officer tugged his moustaches right and left. Then he said, "If I were exactly in your place, Auchterlay——"

" Well, sir ? " said Alister, for he had hesitated.

—" I should—enlist in the Royal Engineers."

" Nothing like gunpowder," whispered Dennis to me. I kicked him in return.

The pros and cons of the matter were not lengthy. If Alister enlisted in any regiment, the two advantages of good behaviour and good education would tell towards his advancement more rapidly and more certainly than perhaps in any other line of life. If he enlisted into a scientific corps, the chance of being almost immediately employed as a clerk was good, very much of the work would be interesting to an educated and practical man ; the " marching, pipe-claying. and starching," of which Dennis sang, was a secondary part of " R.E." duties at any time, and there were special opportunities of employment in foreign countries for superior men. Alister was not at all likely to remain long a private, and it was quite " on the cards " that he might get a commission while he was still young. So much for " peace time." But if—in the event of—and supposing (here the young engineer made a rapid diversion into the politics of the day) there was a chance of " active service "—the Royal Engineers not only offered far more than drill and barrack duties in time of peace, but no branch of the army gave nobler opportunities for distinguished service in time of war. At this point he spoke with such obvious relish, that I saw Dennis was ready to take the Queen's Shilling on the spot. Alister's eyes gave a flash or two, but on the whole he " kept a calm sough," and put the other side of the question.

He said a good deal, but the matter really lay in small compass. The profession of arms is not highly paid. It was true that the pay was poor enough as a seaman, and the life far harder, but then he was only bound for each voyage. At other times he was his own master, and having " gained an insight into " trading from his late captain, he saw indefinite possibilities before him. Alister seemed to have great faith in openings, opportunities, chances, etc., and he said frankly that he looked upon his acquired seamanship simply as a means of paying his passage to any part of the habitable globe where fortunes could be made.

"Then why not stick together?" cried Dennis. "Make your way up to Halifax with us, Alister, dear. Maybe you'll find your cousin at home this time, and if not, at the worst, there's the captain of our old ship promised ye employment. Who knows but we'll all go home in her together? Ah, let's keep the Shamrock whole if we can?"

"But you see, Dennis," said the lieutenant, "Alister would regard a voyage to England as a step backward, as far as his objects are concerned."

Dennis always maintained that you could never contrive to agree with Alister so closely that he would not find room to differ from you.

So he nudged me again (and I kicked him once more) when Alister began to explain that he wouldn't just say *that*, for that during the two or three days when he was idle at Liverpool he had been into a free library to look at the papers, and had had a few words of converse with a decent kind of an old body, who was a care-taker in a museum where they bought birds and beasts and the like from seafaring men that got them in foreign parts. So that it had occurred to him that if he could pick up a few natural curiosities in the tropics, he might do worse, supposing his cousin be still absent from Halifax, than keep himself from idleness, by taking service in our old ship, with the chance of doing a little trading at the Liverpool Museum.

"I wish I hadn't broken that gorgeous lump of coral Alfonso gave me," said Dennis. "But it's as brittle as egg-shell, though I rather fancy the half of it would astonish most museums. You're a wonderful boy, Alister! Ah, we'll all live to see the day when you're a millionaire, laying the foundation-stone of some of these big things the Aberdeen men build, and speechifying away to the rising generation of how ye began life with nothing but a stuffed Demerary parrot in your pocket. Willie, can't ye lend me some kind of a gun, that I may get him a few of these highly painted fowl of the air? If I had but old Barney at my elbow now—GOD rest his soul!—we'd give a good account of ourselves among the cockatoos. Many's the lot of seabirds we've brought home in the hooker to stuff the family pillows. But I'm no hand at preparing a bird for stuffing."

" I'll cure them," said I ; " the schoolmaster taught me."

" Then we're complete entirely, and Alister'll die Provost of Aberdeen. Haven't I got the whole plan in my head? (And it's the first of the O'Moores that ever developed a genius for business !) Swap crimson macaws with green breasts in Liverpool for cheap fizzing drinks, trade them in the thirsty tropics for palm-oil; steer for the north pole, and retail that to the oleaginous Esquimaux for furs ; sell them in Paris in the autumn for what's left of the summer fashions, and bring these back to the ladies of Demerary ; buy——"

" Dennis ! stop that chattering," cried our host ; " there's some one at the door."

We listened. There was a disturbance below stairs, and the young officer opened the door and shouted for his servant, on which O'Brien came up three steps at a time.

"What is it, O'Brien ?"

" A Chinee, your honour. I asked him his business, and not a word but gibberish will he let out of him. But he's brought no papers nor parcels at all, and sorra peep will I let him have of your honour's room. The haythen thafe !"

But even as O'Brien spoke, a Chinaman, in a China-blue dress, passed between him and the door-post, and stood in the room.

" Who are you?" asked the engineer peremptorily.

" Ah-Fo," was the reply, and the Chinaman bowed low.

" You can understand English, if you can't speak it, eh ? "

The Chinaman smiled. His eyes rolled round the room till he caught sight of Alister, then suddenly producing three letters, fanwise, as if he were holding a hand at whist, he jerked up the centre one, like a " forced" card in a trick, and said softly, " For you "—and still looking round with the others in his hand, he added, " For two ; allee same as you," and as Alister distributed them to Dennis and me, his wooden face took a few wrinkles of contempt, and he added, " One nigger bringee. Mister Macdonald, he send me."

After this explanation he stood quite still. Even his face was unmoved, but his eyes went round and into every corner of the room. I was so absorbed in watching him that Dennis was reading his letter aloud before I had opened mine. But they were all alike, with the exception of our names. They were on pink paper, and highly scented. This was Dennis O'Moore's :

" *Hymeneal.* — Mr. Alfonso St. Vincent and Miss Georgiana Juba's compliments are respectfully offered, and will be happy of Mr. Dennis O'Moore's company on the occasion of the celebration of their nuptials. Luncheon at twelve on the auspicious day, Saturday——"

" Oh, botheration ! It's six weeks hence," said Dennis. " Will we be here, I wonder?"

" We'll go if we are." " Poor old Alfonso ! " " Well done, Alfonso !" Such were our sentiments, and we expressed them in three polite notes, which the Chinaman instantaneously absorbed into some part of his person, and having put the hand with which he took them to his head and bowed lowly as before, he went away. And O'Brien, giving one vicious dust with his coat-sleeve of the doorpost, which Ah-Fo had contaminated by a passing touch, followed the " heathen thief" to see him safe off the premises.

" That's a strange race, now——" began Alister, but I ran to the window, for Dennis was on the balcony watching for the Chinaman, and remembering the scene on the stelling, I anticipated fun.

"Hi, there! Fe-fo-fum, or whatever it is that they call ye !"

Ah-Fo looked up with a smile of delighted recognition, which, as Dennis gave a few preliminary stamps, and began to whistle and shuffle, expanded into such hearty laughter, that he was obliged to sit down to it by the roadside.

" Look here, Dennis," said our host ; " we shall have a crowd collecting if you go on with this tomfoolery. Send him off."

" All right, old fellow. Beg your pardon. Good-bye Te-to-tum."

It was not a respectful farewell, but there is a free-masonry of friendliness apart from words. Dennis had a kindly heart toward his fellow-creatures everywhere, and I never knew his fellow-creatures fail to find it out.

" Good-bye," said Ah-Fo, lingeringly.

" Good-bye again. I say, old mandarin," added the incorrigible Dennis, leaning confidentially over the balcony, "got on pretty well below there? Or did O'Brien keep the tail of his eye too tight on ye ? Did ye manage to coax a great-coat or a hall-table, or any other trifle of the kind up those sleeves of yours ? "

This time Ah-Fo looked genuinely bewildered, but he gazed at Dennis as if he would have given anything to understand him.

" Uppee sleevee—you know ! " said Dennis, illustrating his meaning by signs. ("Chinese is a mighty easy language, Willie, I find, when you're used to it.")

A grin of intelligence spread from ear to ear on Ah-Fo's countenance.

U

"Eyah!" said he, and with one jerk he produced our three letters, fan-fashion, in his right hand, and then they vanished as quickly, and he clapped his empty palms and cried, "Ha, ha! Ha, ha!"

"It's clever, there's no denying," said Alister, "but it's an uncanny kind of cleverness."

Something uncannier was to come. Ah-Fo had stood irresolute for a minute or two, then he appeared to make up his mind, and coming close under the balcony he smiled at Dennis and said, "You lookee here." Then feeling rapidly in the inner part of his dress he brought out a common needle, which he held up to us, then pricked his finger to show that it was sharp, and held it up again, crying "You see?"

"I see," said Dennis. "Needle. Allee same as pin, barring that a pin's got a head with no eye in it, and a needle's got an eye with no head to it."

"You no talkee, you lookee," pleaded Ah-Fo.

"One for you, Dennis," laughed the engineer. We looked, and Ah-Fo put the needle into his mouth and swallowed it. He gave himself a pat or two and made some grimaces to show that it felt rather prickly going down, and then he produced a second needle, and tested and then swallowed that. In this way he seemed to swallow twelve needles, nor, with the closest watching, could we detect that they went anywhere but into his mouth.

"Will he make it a baker's dozen, I wonder!" gasped Dennis.

But this time Ah-Fo produced a small ball of thread, and it followed the needles, after which he doubled himself up in uneasy contortions, which set us into fits of laughter. Then he put his fingers into his mouth—we watched closely—and slowly, yard after yard, he drew forth the unwound thread, and all the twelve needles were upon it. And whilst we were clapping and cheering him, both needles and thread disappeared as before.

Ah-Fo was evidently pleased by our approval, and by the shower of coins with which our host rewarded his performance, but when he had disposed of them in his own mysterious fashion, some source of discontent seemed yet to remain. He looked sadly at Dennis and said, "Ah-Fo like to do so, allee same as you." And then began gravely to shuffle his feet about, in vain efforts, as became evident, to dance an Irish jig. We tried to stifle our laughter, but he was mournfully conscious of his own failure, and, when Dennis whistled the tune, seemed to abandon the task in despair, and console himself by an effort to recall the original performance. After standing for a few seconds with his eyes shut and his head thrown back, so that his pigtail nearly touched the ground, the scene appeared fully to return to his memory. " Eyah ! " he chuckled, and turned to go, laughing as he went.

" Don't forget the letters. Uppee sleevee, old Teatray ! " roared Dennis.

Ah-Fo flirted them out once more. " Ha ! Ha ! Ha ! " laughed he, and went finally away.

CHAPTER XXIX.

" Das Haar trennt."

German Proverb.

WE three were not able to be present at Alfonso's wedding, for the very good reason that we were no longer in British Guiana. But the day we sailed for Halifax, Alfonso and his Georgiana came down to see us on the stelling. " Georgiana " was as black as a coal, but Alfonso had not boasted without reason of the cut of her clothes. She had an upright pretty figure, and her dress fitted it to perfection. It was a white dress, and she had a very

U 2

gorgeous parasol, deeply fringed, and she wore a kerchief
of many colours round her shoulders, and an equally
bright silk one cleverly twisted into a little cap on her
woolly head.   Her costume was, in short, very gay indeed.

"Out of all the bounds of nature and feminine modesty,"
said Aliste .

"Of your grandmother's nature and modesty, maybe,"
retorted Dennis.   "But she's no gayer than the birds of
the neighbourhood, anyway, and she's as neat, which is
more than ye can say for many a young lady that's not so
black in the face."

In short, Dennis approved of Alfonso's bride, and I
think the lady was conscious of it.   She had a soft voice,
and very gentle manners, and to Dennis she chatted away
so briskly that I wondered what she could have found to
talk about, till I discovered from what Dennis said to
Alister afterwards, that the subject of her conversation was
Alfonso's professional prospects.

"Look here, Alister dear," said Dennis; "don't be
bothering yourself whether she employs your aunt's dress-
maker or no, but when you're about halfway up that ladder
of success, that I'll never be climbing (or I'd do it myself),
say a good word for Alfonso to some of these Scotch
captains with big ships, that want a steward and
stewardess.   That's what she's got her eye on for Alfonso,
and Alfonso has been a good friend to us."

"I'll mind," said Alister.   And he did.   For (to use his
own expression) our Scotch comrade was "aye better than
his word."

Dennis O'Moore's cousin behaved very kindly to us.
He was not only willing to find Dennis the money which
the Squire had failed to send, but he would have advanced
my passage-money to Halifax.   I declined the offer for
two reasons.   In the first place, Uncle Henry had only
spoken of paying my passage from Halifax to England,
and I did not feel that I was entitled to spend any money

that I could avoid spending ; and, secondly, as Alister had
to go north before the mast, I chose to stick by my
comrade, and rough it with him. This decided Dennis.
If Alister and I were going as seamen, he would not
" snea'r home as a passenger."

The elderly cousin did not quite approve of this, but the
engineer officer warmly supported Dennis, and he was also
upheld in a quarter where praise was still dearer to him,
as I knew, for he took me into his confidence, when his
feelings became more than he could comfortably keep to
himself.

"Perhaps she won't like your being a common sailor,
Dennis," I had said, "and you know Alister and I shall
quite understand about it. We know well enough what a
true mate you've been to us, and Alister was talking to me
about it last night. He said he didn't like to say anything
to you, as he wouldn't take the liberty of alluding to the
young lady, but he's quite sure she won't like it, and I
think so too."

I said more than I might otherwise have done, because
I was very much impressed by Alister's unusual vehemence
on the subject. He seldom indeed said a word that was
less than a boast of Scotland in general, and Aberdeenshire in particular, but on this occasion it had burst forth
that though he had been little "in society" in his native
country, he had "seen enough to know that a man would
easier live down a breach of a' the ten commandments
than of any three of its customs." And when I remembered, for my own part, how fatal in my own neighbourhood were any proceedings of an unusual nature, and
how all his innocence, and his ten years of martyrdom,
had not sufficed with many of Mr. Wood's neighbours to
condone the "fact" that he had been a convict, I agreed
with Alister that Dennis ought not to risk the possible ill
effects of what, as he said, had a "ne'er-do-weel, out-at-
elbows, or, at last and least, an uncommon look about it ;"

and that having resumed his proper social position, our Irish comrade would be wise to keep it in the eyes he cared most to please.

" Alister has a fine heart," said Dennis, " but you may tell him I told her," and he paused.

" What did she say ? " I asked anxiously.

" She said," answered Dennis slowly, " that she'd small belief that a girl could tell if a man were true or no by what he seemed as a lover, but there was something to be done in the way of judging of his heart by seeing if he was kind with his kith and faithful to his friends."

It took me two or three revolutions of my brain to perceive how this answer bore upon the question, and when I repeated it to Alister, his comment was almost as enigmatical.

" A man," he said sententiously, " that has been blessed with a guid mother, and that gives the love of his heart to a guid woman, may aye gang through the ills o' this life, like the children of Israel through the Red Sea, with a wall on 's right hand and a wall on 's left."

But it was plain to be seen that the young lady approved of Dennis O'Moore's resolve, when she made us three scarlet night-caps for deck-wear, with a tiny shamrock embroidered on the front of each.

Indeed, as to clothes and comforts of all sorts, we began our homeward voyage in a greatly renovated condition, thanks to our friends. The many kindnesses of the engineer officer were only matched by his brusque annoyance if we " made a fuss about nothing," and between these, and what the sugar-planter thought due to his relative, and what the sugar-planter's daughter did for the sake of Dennis, the only difficulty was to get our kits stowed within reasonable seaman's limits. The sugar-planter's influence was of course invaluable to us in the choice of a ship, and we were very fortunate. The evening we went on board I accompanied Dennis to his cousin's house to bid good-bye, and when we left, Miss Eileen came with us through the garden to let us out by a short cut and a wicket-gate. She looked prettier even than usual, in some sort of pale greenish-grey muslin, with knots of pink ribbon about it, and I felt very much for Dennis's deplorable condition, and did my best in the way of friendship by going well ahead among the oleanders and evergreens, with a bundle which contained the final gifts of our friends. Indeed I waited at the wicket-gate not only till I was thoroughly tired of waiting, but till I knew that we dare wait no longer, and then I went back to look for Dennis.

About twenty yards back I saw him, as I thought, mixed up in some way with an oleander-bush in pink blossom, but, coming nearer, I found that it was Eileen's grey-green dress with the pink bows, which, like a slackened sail, was flapping against him in the evening breeze, as he knelt in front of her.

" Dennis," said I, not too loud ; not loud enough in fact, for they did not hear me ; and all that Dennis said was, " Take plenty, Darlin' ! "

He was kneeling up, and holding back some of the muslin and ribbons with one hand, whilst with the other he held out a forelock of his black curls, and she cut it off with the scissors out of the sailor's housewife which she had made for him. I turned my back and called louder.

" I know, Jack. I'm coming this instant," said Dennis.

The night was noisy with the croaking of frogs, the whirring and whizzing of insects, the cheeping of bats, and the distant cries of birds, but Dennis and Eileen were silent. Then she called out, " Good-bye, Jack, GOD bless you."

" Good-bye, Miss Eileen, and GOD bless you," said I, feeling nearly as miserable as if I were in love myself. And then we ran all the rest of the way to the stelling.

Alister was already on board, and the young officer was

there to bid us GOD speed, and Dennis was cheerful almost to noisiness.

But when the shores of British Guiana had become a muddy-looking horizon line, I found him, with his cropped forehead pressed to the open housewife, shedding bitter tears among the new needles and buttons.

----◆----

CHAPTER XXX.

"Zur tiefen Ruh, wie er sich auch gefunden.
　　*　　　*　　　*　　　*　　　*
Sein Geist ist's, der mich ruft."

Wallenstein's Tod.

NOT the least troublesome part of our enlarged kit was the collection of gay-plumaged birds. Their preservation was by no means complete, and I continued it at sea. But between climate and creatures, the destructiveness of the tropics is distracting to the collector, and one or two of my finest specimens fell into heaps of mangled feathers, dust, and hideous larvæ under my eyes. It was Dennis O'Moore's collection. He and his engineer friend were both good shots, and they had made an expedition on purpose to get these birds for Alister. There were some most splendid specimens, and the grandest of all, to my thinking, was a Roseate Spoonbill, a wading, fish-catching bird of all shades of rose, from pale pink to crimson. Even his long horny legs were red. But he was not a pleasant subject for my part of the work. He smelt like · the Water-Lily at her worst, before we got rid of the fish cargo.

Knowing that he had got them for Alister, I was rather surprised one day when Dennis began picking out some of the rares* birds and put them aside. It was so unlike him to keep things for himself. But as he turned over the specimens, he began to ask me about Cripple Charlie, whose letter he had read. Meanwhile he kept selecting specimens, and then returning them to the main body again, saying, " Ah, we mustn't be robbing Alister, or he'll never die Provost of Aberdeen." In the end he had gathered a very choice and gorgeous little lot, and then I discovered their destination. " We'll get them set up when we get home," he said ; " I hope Charlie'll like 'em. They'll put the old puffin's nose out of joint anyway, for as big as it is ! "

Our ship was a steamship, a well-found vessel, and we made a good passage. The first mate was an educated man, and fond of science. He kept a meteorological log, and the pleasantest work we ever did was in helping him to take observations. We became very much bitten with the subject, and I bought three pickle-bottles from the cook, and filled them with gulf-weed and other curiosities for Charlie, and stowed these away with the birds.

Dennis found another letter from his father awaiting him at the Halifax post-office. The Squire had dis-covered his blunder, and sent the money, and the way in which Dennis immediately began to plan purchases of all sorts, from a birch-bark canoe to a bearskin rug, gave me a clue to the fortunes of the O'Moores. I do not think he would have had enough left to pay his passage if we had been delayed for long. But our old ship was expected any hour, and when she came in we made our way to her at once, and the upshot of it all was, that Dennis and I shipped in her for the return voyage as passengers, and Alister as a seaman.

Nothing can make the North Atlantic a pleasant sea. Of the beauty and variety of warmer waters we had nothing, but we had the excitement of some rough weather, and a good deal of sociability and singing when it was fair, and we were very glad to be with our old mates again, and yet more glad that every knot on our course was a step nearer home. Dennis and I were not idle because we were independent, and we enjoyed ourselves thoroughly. As to Alister, there was no difficulty in seeing how well he stood with the red-bearded captain, and how good a friend his own energy and perseverance (with perhaps some touch of clannishness to boot) had gained for him. Dennis and I always shared his watches, and they were generally devoted to the discussing and rediscussing of our prospects, interspersed with fragmentary French lessons.

From the day that Alister had heard Dennis chatter to the squaw, through all our ups and downs, at sea and ashore, he had never flagged in his persistent profiting by Dennis's offer to teach him to speak French. It was not, perhaps, a very scholarly method which they pursued, but we had no time for study, so Dennis started Alister every day with a new word or sentence, and Alister hammered this into his head as he went about his work, and recapitulated what he had learned before. By the time we were on our homeward voyage, the sentences had become very complex, and it seemed probable that Alister's ambition to take part in a " two-handed crack " in French with his teacher, before the shamrock fell to pieces, would be realized.

" What he has learnt is wonderful, I can tell ye," said Dennis to me, " but his accent's horrid ! And we'd get on faster than we do if he didn't argue every step we go, though he doesn't know a word that I've not taught him."

But far funnier than Alister's corrections of his teacher, was a curious jealousy which the boatswain had of the Scotch lad's new accomplishment. We could not quite make out the grounds of it, except that the boatswain himself had learned one or two words of what he called *parly voo* when he was in service at the boys' school,

WE AND THE WORLD.

and he was jealously careful of the importance which his shreds and scraps of education gave him in the eyes of the ordinary uneducated seaman. With Dennis and me he was uniformly friendly, and he was a most entertaining companion.

Owing to head winds, our passage was longer than the average. A strange thing happened towards the end of it. We had turned in for sleep one night, when I woke to the consciousness that Dennis had got out of his berth, and was climbing past mine, but I was so sleepy that I did not speak, and was only sure that it was not a dream, when Alister and I went on deck for the next watch, and found Dennis walking up and down in the morning mist.

" Have you had no sleep ? " I asked, for his face looked haggard.

" I couldn't. For dreaming," he said, awkwardly.

I laughed at him.

" What have you been dreaming about ? "

" Don't laugh, Jack. I dreamt of Barney."

" Well, that's natural enough, Dennis. This end of the oyage must recall the poor fellow."

" I wouldn't mind if it was a kindly dream. But I dreamed he'd an old woman's bonnet on and a handker-thief tied over it. It haunts me."

" Go back to bed," I advised. " Perhaps you'll dream of him again looking like himself, and that will put this out of your head."

Dennis took my advice, and I stood Alister's watch with him, and by-and-by Dennis appeared on deck again looking more at ease.

" Did you dream of him again ? " I asked. He nodded.

" I did—just his own dear self. But he was sitting alone on the edge of some wharf gazing down into the water, and not a look could I get out of him till I woke."

The following morning Dennis was still sound asleep

when I rose and went on deck. The coast of Ireland was just coming into sight through the haze when he joined me, but before pointing it out to him, I felt curious to know whether he had dreamed a third time of old Barney.

" Not I," said he ; " all I dreamed of was a big rock standing up out of the sea, and two children sitting on it had hold of each other's hands."

" Children you know ? "

" Oh dear, no ! Just a little barefoot brother and sister."

He seemed to wish to drop the subject, and at this moment a gleam of sunshine lit up the distant coast line with such ethereal tints, that I did not wonder to see him spring upon the bulwarks and catching a ratlin with one hand, wave his cap above his head with the other, crying, " GOD bless the Emerald Isle ! "

We reached Liverpool about four o'clock in the afternoon, and as we drew up alongside of the old wharf, my first thought was to look for Biddy Macartney. Alister had to remain on board for a time, but Dennis came willingly with me in search of the old woman and her coffee-barrow. At last we betook ourselves to the Dock-gatekeeper, to make inquiries, and from him we heard a sad story. The old woman had " failed a deal of late," he said. He " *had* heard she wasn't right in her mind, but whether they'd shifted her to a 'sylum or not, he couldn't say." If she was at home, she was at an address which he gave us.

" Will you go, Dennis ? I must. At once."

" Of course."

Biddy was at home, and never whilst I live can I forget the " home." Four blocks of high houses enclosed a small court into which there was one entrance, an archway through one of the buildings. All the houses opened into the court. There were no back-doors, and no back premises whatever. All the dirt and (as to washing) all the cleanliness of a crowded community living in rooms in flats, the quarrelling and the love-making, the old people's resting, and the children's playing ;—from emptying a slop-pail to getting a breath of evening air—this court was all there was for it. I have since been told that if we had been dressed like gentlemen, we should not have been safe in it, but I do not think we should have met with any worse welcome if we had come on the same errand—"to see old Biddy Macartney."

Roughly enough, it is true, we were directed to one of the houses, the almost intolerable stench of which increased as we went up the stairs. By the help of one inmate and another, we made our way to Biddy's door, and then we found it locked.

" The missis 'll be out," said a deformed girl who was pulling herself along by the balustrades. She was decent-looking and spoke civilly, so I ventured to ask, " Do you mean that old Biddy is out ? "

" Nay, not Biddy. The woman that sees to her. When she's got to go out she locks t'old lass up to be safe," and volunteering no further help, the girl rested for a minute against the wall with her hand to her side, and then dragged herself in to one of the rooms and shut the door in our faces.

The court without and the houses within already resounded so to the squalling of children, that I paid no attention to the fact that more of this particular noise was coming up the stairs ; but in another moment a woman, shaking a screaming baby in her arms and dragging two crying children at her skirts, clenched her disengaged fist (it had a key in it) close to our faces and said, " And which of you vagabones is t'old lass's son ? "

" Neither of us," said I, " but we want to see her, if we may. Are you the woman who takes care of her ? "

" I've plenty to do minding my own, I can tell ye," she

grumbled, "but I couldn't abear to see t'ould lass taken to
a 'sylum. They're queer places some on 'em, as I know.
And as to t'House ! There's a many folks says, 'Well
if t'guardians won't give her no relief, let her go in.' But
she got hold on me one day, and she says, 'Sally,
darling' (that's t'ould lass's way, is calling ye Darling. It
sounds soft, but she is but an old Irish woman, as one
may say) 'if ever,' she says, 'you hear tell of their coming
to fetch me, GOD bless ye,' she says, 'just give me a
look out of your eye, and I'm gone. I'll be no more
trouble to any one,' she says, 'and maybe I'll make it
worth your while too.'"

At this point in her narrative the woman looked
mysterious, nodded her head, craned over the banisters
to see that no one was near, slapped the children and
shook up the baby as a sort of mechanical protest against
the noise they were making (as to effects they only
howled the louder), and drawing nearer to us, spoke in
lower tones :

" T'old lass has money, it's my belief, though she gives
me nowt for her lodging, and she spends nowt on herself.
She's many a time fair clemmed, I'll assure ye, till I can't
abear to see it, and I give her the bit and sup I might
have had myself, for I'm not going to rob t'children
neither for her nor nobody. Ye see it's her son that's
preying on her mind. He wrote her a letter awhile ago,
saying times was bad out yonder, and he was fair heart-
broke to be so far away from her, and she's been queer
ever since. She's wanted for everything herself, slaving
and saving to get enough to fetch him home. Where she
hides it I know no more nor you, but she wears a sight of
old rags, one atop of another, and pockets in all of 'em for
aught I know—hold your din, ye unrewly children !—
there's folks coming. I'll let ye in. I lock t'old lass up
when I go out, for she might be wandering, and there's
them hereabouts that would reckon nought of putting her

out of t'way and taking what she's got, if they heard tell on't."

At last the door was unlocked and we went in. And sitting on a low box, dressed as before, even to the old coat and the spotted kerchief over her bonnet, sat Biddy Macartney.

When she lifted her face, I saw that it was much wasted, and that her fine eyes had got a restless uneasy look in them. Suddenly this ceased, and they lit up with the old intelligence. For half an instant I thought it was at the sight of me, but she did not even see me. It was on Dennis O'Moore that her eyes were bent, and they never moved as she struggled to her feet, and gazed anxiously at his face, his cap, and his seafaring clothes, whilst, for his part, Dennis gazed almost as wildly at her. At last she spoke :

" GOD save ye, Squire ! Has the old counthry come to this ? Is the O'Moore an alien, and all ? "

" No, no. I'm the Squire's son," said Dennis. " But tell me quick, woman, what are you to Barney Barton ? "

" Barney is it ? Sure he was brother to me, as who knows better than your honour ? "

" Did *you* live with us, too ? "

" I did, acushla. In the heighth of ease and comfort, and done nothin' for it. Wasn't I the big fool to be marryin' so early, not knowin' when I was well off ! "

" I know. Barney has told me. A Cork man, your husband, wasn't he ? A lazy, drunken, ill-natured rascal of a fellow."

" That's him, your honour ! "

" Well, you're quit of him long since. And, as your son's in New York, and all I have left of Barney is you——"

" She doesn't hear you, Dennis."

I interrupted him, because in his impetuosity he had not noticed that the wandering look had come back over the old woman's face, and that she sat down on the box, and fumbled among her pockets for Mickey's letter, and then crouched weeping over it.

We stayed a long time with her, but she did not really revive. With infinite patience and tenderness, Dennis knelt beside her, and listened to her ramblings about Mickey, and Mickey's hardships, and Mickey's longings for home. Once or twice, I think, she was on the point of telling about her savings, but she glanced uneasily round the room and forbore. Dennis gave the other woman some money, and told her to give Biddy a good meal—to have given money to her would have been useless—and he tried hard to convince the old woman that Mickey was quite able to leave America if he wished. At last she seemed to take this in, and it gave her, I fear, undue comfort, from the conviction that, if this were so, he would soon be home.

After we left Biddy, we went to seek decent lodgings for the night. For Dennis was anxious to see her again in the morning, and of course I stayed with him.

"Had you ever seen her before?" I asked, as we walked.

"Not to remember her. But Jack, it wasn't Barney I saw in that first dream. It was Bridget."

Dennis was full of plans for getting her home with him to Ireland ; but when we went back next day, we found a crowd round the archway that led into the court. Prominent in the group was the woman who "cared for" Biddy. Her baby was crying, her children were crying, and she was crying too. And with every moment that passed the crowd grew larger and larger, as few things but bad news can make a crowd grow.

We learnt it very quickly. Biddy had been so much cheered up by our visit, that when the woman went out to buy supper for them, she did not lock the door. When she came back, Biddy was gone. To do her neighbours justice, we could not doubt—considering how they talked then—that they had made inquiries in all the streets and courts around.

" And wherever t'owld lass *can* ha' gone ! " sobbed the woman who had been her neighbour, in the noblest sense of neighbourhood.

I was beginning to comfort her when Dennis gripped me by the arm :

" I know," said he. " Come along ! "

His face was white, his eyes shone, and he tossed his head so wildly he looked madder than Biddy had looked ; but when he began to run, and roughs in the streets began to pursue him, I ran too, as a matter of safety. We drew breath at the dock-gates.

The gatekeeper told us that old Biddy, "looking quite herself, only a bit thinner like," had gone through the evening before, to meet some one who was coming off one of the vessels, as he understood, but he had not noticed her on her return. He had heard her ask some man about a ship from New York.

I wanted to hear more, but Dennis clutched me again and dragged me on.

" I'll know the wharf when I see it," said he.

Suddenly he stopped, and pointed. A wharf, but no vessel, only the water sobbing against the stones.

That's the wharf," he gasped. " That's where he sat and looked down. *She's there !* "

*   *   *   *   *

He was right. We found her there at ebb of tide, with no sign of turmoil or trouble about her, except the grip that never could be loosened with which she held Mickey's one letter fast in her hand.

CHAPTER XXXI.

"Oh ! dream of joy ! is this indeed
The lighthouse-top I see ?
Is this the hill ? Is this the Kirk
Is this mine own countree ?

" We drifted o'er the harbour bar,
And I with sobs did pray—
O let me be awake, my GOD !
Or let me sleep alway."

The Ancient Mariner.

WHEN Alister joined us the first evening after we came
back from poor Biddy, he was so deeply interested in
hearing about her, that he would have gone with us the
next morning, if he had not had business on hand. He
had a funny sort of remorse for having misjudged her
the day she befooled the sentry to get me off. Business
connected with Biddy's death detained Dennis in Liverpool
for a day or two, and as I had not given any warning of
the date of my return to my people, I willingly stayed
with him. My comrades had promised to go home with
me before proceeding on their respective ways, but (in
answer to the letter which announced his safe arrival in
Liverpool) Alister got a message from his mother sum-
moning him to Scotland at once on important family
matters, and the shamrock fell to pieces sooner than we
had intended. In the course of a few days, Dennis and
I heard from our old comrade.

" The Braes of Buie.

" MY DEAR JACK AND DENNIS : I am home safe and
sound, though not in time for the funeral, which (as partly

consequent on the breaking of a tube in one engine, and
a trifling damage to the wheels of a second that was
attached, if ye understand me, with the purpose of rectify-
ing the deficiencies of the first, the Company being, in my
humble judgment, unwisely thrifty in the matter of second-
hand boilers) may be regarded as a Dispensation of
Providence, and was in no degree looked upon by any
member of the family as a wanting of respect towards the
memory of the deceased. With the sole and single exception of Miss Margaret MacCantywhapple, a far-away
cousin by marriage, who, though in good circumstances,
and a very virtuous woman, may be said to have seen her
best days, and is not what she was in her intellectual
judgment, being afflicted with deafness and a species of
palsy, besides other infirmities in her faculties. I misdoubt
if I was wise in using my endeavours to make the poor
body understand that I was at the other side of the world
when my cousin was taken sick, all her response being,
'*they aye say so.*' However, at long and last, she was
brought to admit that the best of us may misjudge, and
as we all have our faults, and hers are for the most part
her misfortunes, I tholed her imputations on my veracity
in the consideration of her bodily infirmities.

" My dear mother, thank GOD, is in her usual, and over-
joyed to see my face once more. She desires me to present
her respects to both of you, with an old woman's blessing.
I'm aware that it will be a matter of kindly satisfaction
to you to learn that her old age is secured in carnal
comforts through my father's cousin having left all his
worldly gear for her support ; that is, he left it to me, which
is the same thing. Not without a testimony of respect
for my father's memory, that all the gear of Scotland would
be cheap to me by the side of ; and a few words as to
industry, energy, and the like, which, though far from
being deserved on my part, sound—like voices out of the
mist upon the mountain side—sweeter and weightier, it

may be, than they deserve, when a body hears them, as ye may say, out of the grave.

" It's an ill wind that blows nobody good, and it's not for me to complain of the downbreak in the engines, seeing that in place of rushing past the coast, we just crawled along the top of these grand cliffs in the bonny sunshine, which hardly wakes a smile upon the stern faces of them, while the white foam breaks at no allowance about their feet. Many's the hour, Jack, I've lain on the moss, and looked down into a dark cove to watch the tide come in, and turn blue, and green, and tawny purple over the weeds and rocks, and fall back again to where the black crags set in creamy surf with sea-birds on their shoulders. Eh ! man, it's sweet to come home and see it all again ; the folk standing at their doors, and bairns sitting on the dykes with flowers in their hands, and the waving barley-fields on the cliff tops shining against the sea and sky, as lights and shades change their places over a woman's hair. There were some decent bodies in the train beside me, that thought I was daft, with my head out of the window, in an awful draught, at the serious risk of brow-ague, not to speak of coal-smuts, which are horrid if ye get them in your eye. And not without reason did they think so, for I'll assure ye I would have been loth to swear whether it was spray or tears that made my cheeks so salt when I saw the bit herring-boats stealing away out into the blue mist, for all the world as if they were laddies leaving home to seek their fortunes, as it might be ourselves.

" But I'm taking up your time with havers about my own country, and I ask your pardon ; though I'm not ashamed to say that, for what I've seen of the world— tropics and all—give me the north-east coast of Scotland !

" I am hoping, at your leisure, to hear that ye both reached home, and found all belonging to ye as ye could wish ; and I'm thinking that if Dennis wrote in French, I might make it out, for I've come by an old French

Dictionary that was my father's. GOD save the shamrock ! Your affectionate friend,

"ALISTER AUCHTERLAY.

" I am ill at saying all that I feel, but I'll never forget."

Dennis and I tramped from Liverpool. Partly for the walk, and partly because we were nearly penniless. His system, as I told him, seemed to be to empty his pockets first, and to think about how he was to get along afterwards. However, it must be confessed that the number and the needs of the poor Irish we came across in connection with Biddy's death and its attendant ceremonies, were enough to be " the ruination " of a far less tenderhearted Paddy than Dennis O'Moore.

And so—a real sailor with a real bundle under my arm —I tramped Home.

Dennis had been a good comrade out in the world ; but that was a trifle to the tact and sympathy he displayed when my mother and father and I were making fools of ourselves in each other's arms.

He saw everything, and he pretended he saw nothing. He picked up my father's spectacles, and waltzed with the dogs whilst the old gentleman was blowing his nose. When Martha broke down in hysterics (for which, it was not difficult to see, she would punish herself and us later on, with sulking and sandpaper), Dennis " brought her to " by an affectionate hugging, which, as she afterwards explained, seemed " that natteral " that she never realised its impropriety till it was twenty-four hours too late to remonstrate.

When my dear mother was calmer, and very anxious about our supper and beds, I ascertained from my father that the Woods were from home, and that Jem had gone down to the farm to sit for an hour or so with Charlie ; so, pending the preparation of our fatted calf, Dennis and I went to bring both Jem and Charlie back for the night.

It was a dark, moonless night, only tempered by the reflections of furnace fires among the hills. Dennis thought they were northern lights. The lane was cool, and fresh and damp, and full of autumn scents of fading leaves, and toadstools, and Herb Robert and late Meadow Sweet. And as we crossed the grass under the walnut-trees, I saw that the old schoolroom-window was open to the evening air, and lighted from within.

I signalled silence to Dennis, and we crept up, as Jem and I had crept years ago to see the pale-faced relation hunting for the miser's will in the tea-caddy.

In the old arm-chair sat Charlie, propped with cushions. On one side of him Jem leant with elbows on the table, and on the other side sat Master Isaac, spectacles on nose.

The whole table was covered by a Map of the World, and Charlie's high, eager voice came clearly out into the night.

" Isaac and I have marked every step they've gone, Jem, but we don't think it would be lucky to make the back-mark over the Atlantic till they are quite safe Home."

Dennis says, in his teasing way, he never believed in my "athletics" till he saw me leap in through that window. He was not far behind.

" Jem ! "

" Jack ! "

When Jem released me and I looked round, Charlie was resting in Dennis O'Moore's arms and gazing up in his own odd, abrupt, searching way into the Irish boy's face.

" Isaac ! " he half laughed, half sobbed : " Dennis is afraid of hurting this poor rickety body of mine. Come here, will you, and pinch me or pull my hair, that I may be sure it isn't all a dream ! "

THE END.

www.ingramcontent.com/pod-product-compliance
Lightning Source LLC
Chambersburg PA
CBHW031727280326
41926CB00098B/632